W9-AOJ-425

McGraw-Hill's
BIG RED
BOOK of
RESUMES

McGraw-Hill

Chicago   New York   San Francisco   Lisbon   London   Madrid   Mexico City
Milan   New Delhi   San Juan   Seoul   Singapore   Sydney   Toronto

Library of Congress Cataloging-in-Publication Data

McGraw-Hill's big red book of resumes / the editors of VGM Career Books.
    p.   cm.
  ISBN 0-07-140195-4
    1. Résumés (Employment)   I. Title: Big red book of resumes.   II. VGM
Career Books (Firm)

HF5383.M337   2002

                          2002025523

McGraw-Hill

*A Division of The **McGraw·Hill** Companies*

We wish to thank Luisa Gerasimo for compiling this volume.

1 2 3 4 5 6 7 8 9 0 CUS/CUS 1 0 9 8 7 6 5 4 3 2

ISBN 0-07-140195-4

This book was set in Minion by Ellen Kollmon
Printed and bound by Von Hoffman Graphics, Inc.

Cover design by Amy Yu Ng

McGraw-Hill books are available at special quantity discounts to use as premiums and sales
promotions, or for use in corporate training programs. For more information, please write to
the Director of Special Sales, Professional Publishing, McGraw-Hill, Two Penn Plaza, New
York, NY 10121-2298. Or contact your local bookstore.

This book is printed on acid-free paper.

Contents

Introduction

Your resume is a piece of paper (or an electronic document) that serves to introduce you to the people who will eventually hire you. To write a thoughtful resume, you must thoroughly assess your personality, your accomplishments, and the skills you have acquired. The act of composing and submitting a resume also requires you to carefully consider the company or individual that might hire you. What are they looking for, and how can you meet their needs? This book shows you how to organize your personal information and experience into a concise and well-written resume, so that your qualifications and potential as an employee will be understood easily and quickly by a complete stranger.

Writing the resume is just one step in what can be a daunting job-search process, but it is an important element in the chain of events that will lead you to your new position. While you are probably a talented, bright, and charming person, your resume may not reflect these qualities. A poorly written resume can get you nowhere; a well-written resume can land you an interview and potentially a job. A good resume can even lead the interviewer to ask you questions that will allow you to talk about your strengths and highlight the skills you can bring to a prospective employer. Even a person with very little experience can find a good job if he or she is assisted by a thoughtful and polished resume.

Lengthy, typewritten resumes are a thing of the past. Today, employers do not have the time or the patience for verbose documents; they look for tightly composed, straightforward, action-based resumes. Although a one-page resume is the norm, a two-page resume may be warranted if you have had extensive job experience or have changed careers and truly need the space to properly position yourself. If, after careful editing, you still need more than one page to present yourself, it's acceptable to use a second page. A crowded resume that's hard to read would be the worst of your choices.

Distilling your work experience, education, and interests into such a small space requires preparation and thought. This book takes you step-by-step through the process of crafting an effective resume that will stand out in today's competitive marketplace. It serves as a workbook and a place to write down your experiences, while also including the techniques you'll need to pull all the necessary elements together. In the following pages, you'll find many examples of resumes that are specific to your area of interest. Study them for inspiration and find what appeals to you. There are a variety of ways to organize and present your information; inside, you'll find several that will be suitable to your needs. Good luck landing the job of your dreams!

PART I
CRAFTING A
WINNING RESUME

Sitting down to write your resume may seem like a daunting task, but our clear guidelines and easy-to-use worksheets will help you organize what you want to say, choose the most effective way to say it, and design an appealing resume. Whether you have years of experience or are just out of school, you will find all of the pointers you need to craft a winning resume!

The Elements of an Effective Resume

An effective resume is composed of information that employers are most interested in knowing about a prospective job applicant. This information is conveyed by a few essential elements. The following is a list of elements that are found in most resumes—some essential, some optional. Later in this chapter, we will further examine the role of each of these elements in the makeup of your resume.

- Heading

- Objective and/or Keyword Section

- Work Experience

- Education

- Honors

- Activities

- Certificates and Licenses

- Publications

- Professional Memberships

- Special Skills

- Personal Information

- References

The first step in preparing your resume is to gather information about yourself and your past accomplishments. Later you will refine this information, rewrite it using effective language, and organize it into an attractive layout. But first, let's take a look at each of these important elements individually so you can judge their appropriateness for your resume.

Heading

Although the heading may seem to be the simplest section of your resume, be careful not to take it lightly. It is the first section your prospective employer will see and it contains the information she or he will need to contact you. At the very least, the heading must contain your name, your home address, and a phone number where you can be reached easily.

In today's high-tech world, many of us have multiple ways that we can be contacted. You may list your E-mail address if you are reasonably sure the employer makes use of this form of communication. Keep in mind, however, that others may have access to your E-mail messages if you send them from an account provided by your current company. If this is a concern, do not list your work E-mail address on your resume. If you are able to take calls at your current place of business, you should include your work number, because most employers will attempt to contact you during typical business hours.

If you have voice mail or a reliable answering machine at home or at work, list its number in the heading and make sure your greeting is professional and clear. Always include at least one phone number in your heading, even if it is a temporary number, where a prospective employer can leave a message.

You might have a dozen different ways to be contacted, but you do not need to list all of them. Confine your numbers or addresses to those that are the easiest for the prospective employer to use and the simplest for you to retrieve.

Objective

When seeking a specific career path, it is important to list a job or career objective on your resume. This statement helps employers know the direction you see yourself taking, so they can determine whether your goals are in line with those of their organization and the position available. Normally, an objective is one to two sentences long. Its contents will vary depending on your career field, goals, and personality. The objective can be specific or general, but it should always be to the point. See the sample resumes in this book for examples.

If you are planning to use this resume online, or you suspect your potential employer is likely to scan your resume, you will want to include a "keyword" in the objective. This allows a prospective employer, searching hundreds of resumes for a specific skill or position objective, to locate the keyword and find your resume. In essence, a keyword is what's "hot" in your particular field at a given time. It's a buzzword, a shorthand way of getting a particular message across at a glance. For example, if you are a lawyer, your objective might state your desire to work in the area of corporate litigation. In this case, someone searching for the keyword "corporate litigation" will pull up your resume and know that you want to plan, research, and present cases at trial on behalf of the corporation. If your objective states that you "desire a challenging position in systems design," the keyword is "systems design," an industry-specific, shorthand way of saying that you want to be involved in assessing the need for, acquiring, and implementing high-technology systems. These are keywords and every industry has them, so it's becoming more and more important to include a few in your resume. (You may need to conduct additional research to make sure you know what keywords are most likely to be used in your desired industry, profession, or situation.)

There are many resume and job-search sites online. Like most things in the online world, they vary a great deal in quality. Use your discretion. If you plan to apply for jobs online or advertise your availability this way, you will want to design a scannable resume. This type of resume uses a format that can be easily scanned into a computer and added to a database. Scanning allows a prospective employer to use keywords to quickly review each applicant's experience and skills, and (in the event that there are many candidates for the job) to keep your resume for future reference.

Many people find that it is worthwhile to create two or more versions of their basic resume. You may want an intricately designed resume on high-quality paper to mail or hand out *and* a resume that is designed to be scanned into a computer and saved on a database or an online job site. You can even create a resume in ASCII text to E-mail to prospective employers. To get you started, in Chapter 3 we have included a list of things to keep in mind when creating electronic resumes. For further information, you may wish to refer to the *Guide to Internet Job Searching*, by Frances Roehm and Margaret Dikel, updated and published every other year by VGM Career Books, a division of the McGraw-Hill Companies. This excellent book contains helpful and detailed information about formatting a resume for Internet use.

Although it is usually a good idea to include an objective, in some cases this element is not necessary. The goal of the objective statement is to provide the employer with an idea of where you see yourself going in the field. However, if you are uncertain of the exact nature of the job you seek, including an objective that is too specific could result in your not being considered for a host of perfectly acceptable positions. If you decide not to use an objective heading in your resume, you should definitely incorporate the information that would be conveyed in the objective into your cover letter.

Work Experience

Work experience is arguably the most important element of them all. Unless you are a recent graduate with little or no relevant work experience, your current and former positions will provide the central focus of the resume. You will want this section to be as complete and carefully constructed as possible. By thoroughly examining your work experience, you can get to the heart of your accomplishments and present them in a way that demonstrates and highlights your qualifications.

If you are just out of school, your resume will probably focus on your education, but you should also include information on your work or volunteer experiences. Although you will have less information about work experience than a person who has held multiple positions or is advanced in his or her career, the amount of information is not what is most important in this section. How the information is presented and what it says about you as a worker and a person is what really counts.

As you create this section of your resume, remember the need for accuracy. Include all the necessary information about each of your jobs, including your job title, dates of employment, name of your employer, city, state, responsibilities, special projects you handled, and accomplishments. Be sure to list only accomplishments for which you were directly responsible. And don't be alarmed if you haven't participated in or worked on special projects, because this section may not be relevant to certain jobs.

The most common way to list your work experience is in *reverse chronological order*. In other words, start with your most recent job and work your way backward. This way, your prospective employer sees your current (and often most important) position before considering your past employment. Your most recent position, if it's the most important in terms of responsibilities and relevance to the job for which you are applying, should also be the one that includes the most information as compared to your previous positions.

If you are just out of school, highlight your summer employment, internships, and part-time work. As a recent graduate, however, you will probably begin your resume with your education section. The experience you gain with "starter jobs" in the workplace and your ability to juggle school and employment are important to most employers, even if the work itself seems unrelated to your proposed career path. If you were promoted or given greater responsibilities or commendations, be sure to mention that fact.

The following worksheet is provided to help you organize your experiences in the working world. It will also serve as an excellent resource to refer to when updating your resume in the future.

WORK EXPERIENCE

Job One:

Job Title _____

Dates _____

Employer _____

City, State _____

Major Duties _____

_____

_____

_____

_____

_____

_____

_____

_____

Special Projects _____

_____

_____

_____

Accomplishments _____

_____

_____

_____

_____

_____

_____

_____

_____

Job Two:

Job Title _____

Dates _____

Employer _____

City, State _____

Major Duties _____

_____

_____

_____

_____

_____

_____

Special Projects _____

_____

_____

_____

Accomplishments _____

_____

_____

_____

_____

_____

_____

Job Three:

Job Title _____

Dates _____

Employer _____

City, State _____

Major Duties _____

_____

_____

_____

_____

_____

_____

_____

Special Projects _____

_____

_____

_____

Accomplishments _____

_____

_____

_____

_____

_____

_____

_____

_____

Job Four:

Job Title _____

Dates _____

Employer _____

City, State _____

Major Duties _____

_____

_____

_____

_____

_____

_____

Special Projects _____

_____

_____

_____

Accomplishments _____

_____

_____

_____

_____

_____

_____

Education

Education is usually the second most important element of a resume. Your educational background is often a deciding factor in an employer's decision to interview you. Highlight your accomplishments in school as much as you did those accomplishments at work. If you are looking for your first professional job, your education will be your greatest asset because your related work experience will probably be minimal. In this case, the education section becomes the most important means of selling yourself.

Include in this section all the degrees or certificates you have received; your major or area of concentration; all of the honors you earned; and any relevant activities you participated in, organized, or chaired. Again, list your most recent schooling first. If you have completed graduate-level work, begin with that and work your way back through your undergraduate education. If you have completed college, you generally should not list your high school experience; do so only if you earned special honors, you had a grade point average that was much better than the norm, or this was your highest level of education.

If you have completed a large number of credit hours in a subject that may be relevant to the position you are seeking, but did not obtain a degree, you may wish to list the hours or classes you completed. Keep in mind, however, that you may be asked to explain why you did not finish the program. If you are currently in school, list the degree, certificate, or license you expect to obtain and the projected date of completion.

The following worksheet will help you gather the information you need for this section of your resume.

EDUCATION

School One _____

Major or Area of Concentration _____

Degree _____

Dates _____

School Two _____

Major or Area of Concentration _____

Degree _____

Dates _____

Honors

If you include an honors section in your resume, you should highlight any awards, honors, or memberships in honorary societies that you have received. (You may also incorporate this information into your education section.) Often, the honors are academic in nature, but this section also may be used for special achievements in sports, clubs, or other school activities. Always include the name of the organization awarding the honor and the date(s) received. Use the following worksheet to help you gather your information.

HONORS

Honor One _____

Awarding Organization _____

Date(s) _____

Honor Two _____

Awarding Organization _____

Date(s) _____

Honor Three _____

Awarding Organization _____

Date(s) _____

Honor Four _____

Awarding Organization _____

Date(s) _____

Honor Five _____

Awarding Organization _____

Date(s) _____

Activities

Perhaps you were active in different organizations or clubs during your years at school; often an employer will look at such involvement as evidence of initiative, dedication, and good social skills. Examples of your ability to take a leading role in a group should be included on a resume, if you can provide them. (Information about your activities also may be incorporated into your education section.) If you have been out of school for some time, the activities section of your resume can present neighborhood and community activities, volunteer positions, and so forth. In general, you may want to avoid listing any organization whose name indicates the race, creed, sex, age, marital status, sexual orientation, or nation of origin of its members because this could expose you to discrimination. Use the following worksheet to list the specifics of your activities.

ACTIVITIES

Organization/Activity _____

Accomplishments _____

_____

_____

Organization/Activity _____

Accomplishments _____

_____

_____

Organization/Activity _____

Accomplishments _____

_____

_____

As your work experience grows through the years, your school activities and honors will carry less weight and be emphasized less in your resume. Eventually, you will probably list only your degree and any major honors received. As time goes by, your job performance and the experience you've gained become the most important elements in your resume, which should change to reflect this.

Certificates and Licenses

If your chosen career path requires specialized training, you may already have certificates or licenses. You should list these if the job you are seeking requires them and you, of course, have acquired them. If you have applied for a license but have not yet received it, use the phrase "application pending."

License requirements vary by state. If you have moved or are planning to relocate to another state, check with that state's board or licensing agency for all licensing requirements.

Always make sure that all of the information you list is completely accurate. Locate copies of your certificates and licenses, and check the exact date and name of the accrediting agency. Use the following worksheet to organize the necessary information.

CERTIFICATES AND LICENSES

Name of License _____

Licensing Agency _____

Date Issued _____

Name of License _____

Licensing Agency _____

Date Issued _____

Name of License _____

Licensing Agency _____

Date Issued _____

Publications

Some professions strongly encourage or even require that you publish. If you have written, coauthored, or edited any books, articles, professional papers, or works of a similar nature that pertain to your field, you will definitely want to include this element. Remember to list the date of publication and the publisher's name, and specify whether you were the sole author or a coauthor. Book, magazine, or journal titles are generally italicized, while the titles of articles within a larger publication appear in quotes. (Check with your reference librarian for more about the appropriate way to present this information.) For scientific or research papers, you will need to give the date, place, and audience to whom the paper was presented.

Use the following worksheet to help you gather the necessary information about your publications.

PUBLICATIONS

Title and Type (Note, Article, etc.) _____

Title of Publication (Journal, Book, etc.) _____

Publisher _____

Date Published _____

Title and Type (Note, Article, etc.) _____

Title of Publication (Journal, Book, etc.) _____

Publisher _____

Date Published _____

Title and Type (Note, Article, etc.) _____

Title of Publication (Journal, Book, etc.) _____

Publisher _____

Date Published _____

Professional Memberships

Another potential element in your resume is a section listing professional memberships. Use this section to describe your involvement in professional associations, unions, and similar organizations. It is to your advantage to list any professional memberships that pertain to the job you are seeking. Many employers see your membership as representative of your desire to stay up-to-date and connected in your field. Include the dates of your involvement and whether you took part in any special activities or held any offices within the organization. Use the following worksheet to organize your information.

PROFESSIONAL MEMBERSHIPS

Name of Organization _____

Office(s) Held_____

Activities _____

Dates _____

Name of Organization _____

Office(s) Held_____

Activities _____

Dates _____

Name of Organization _____

Office(s) Held_____

Activities _____

Dates _____

Name of Organization _____

Office(s) Held_____

Activities _____

Dates _____

Special Skills

The special skills section of your resume is the place to mention any special abilities you have that relate to the job you are seeking. You can use this element to present certain talents or experiences that are not necessarily a part of your education or work experience. Common examples include fluency in a foreign language, extensive travel abroad, or knowledge of a particular computer application. "Special skills" can encompass a wide range of talents, and this section can be used creatively. However, for each skill you list, you should be able to describe how it would be a direct asset in the type of work you're seeking because employers may ask just that in an interview. If you can't think of a way to do this, it may be extraneous information.

Personal Information

Some people include personal information on their resumes. This is generally not recommended, but you might wish to include it if you think that something in your personal life, such as a hobby or talent, has some bearing on the position you are seeking. This type of information is often referred to at the beginning of an interview, when it may be used as an "icebreaker." Of course, personal information regarding your age, marital status, race, religion, or sexual orientation should never appear on your resume as *personal information*. It should be given only in the context of memberships and activities, and only when doing so would not expose you to discrimination.

References

References are not usually given on the resume itself, but a prospective employer needs to know that you have references who may be contacted if necessary. All you need to include is a single sentence at the end of the resume: "References are available upon request," or even simply, "References available." Have a reference list ready—your interviewer may ask to see it! Contact each person on the list ahead of time to see whether it is all right for you to use him or her as a reference. This way, the person has a chance to think about what to say *before* the call occurs. This helps ensure that you will obtain the best reference possible.

Chapter 2

Writing Your Resume

Now that you have gathered the information for each section of your resume, it's time to write it out in a way that will get the attention of the reviewer—hopefully, your future employer! The language you use in your resume will affect its success, so you must be careful and conscientious. Translate the facts you have gathered into the active, precise language of resume writing. You will be aiming for a resume that keeps the reader's interest and highlights your accomplishments in a concise and effective way.

Resume writing is unlike any other form of writing. Although your seventh-grade composition teacher would not approve, the rules of punctuation and sentence building are often completely ignored. Instead, you should try for a functional, direct writing style that focuses on the use of verbs and other words that imply action on your part. Writing with action words and strong verbs characterizes you to potential employers as an energetic, active person, someone who completes tasks and achieves results from his or her work. Resumes that do not make use of action words can sound passive and stale. These resumes are not effective and do not get the attention of any employer, no matter how qualified the applicant. Choose words that display your strengths and demonstrate your initiative. The following list of commonly used verbs will help you create a strong resume:

administered	assembled
advised	assumed responsibility
analyzed	billed
arranged	built

carried out

channeled

collected

communicated

compiled

completed

conducted

contacted

contracted

coordinated

counseled

created

cut

designed

determined

developed

directed

dispatched

distributed

documented

edited

established

expanded

functioned as

gathered

handled

hired

implemented

improved

inspected

interviewed

introduced

invented

maintained

managed

met with

motivated

negotiated

operated

orchestrated

ordered

organized

oversaw

performed

planned

prepared

presented

produced

programmed

published

purchased

recommended

recorded

reduced

referred

represented

researched

reviewed

saved	supervised
screened	taught
served as	tested
served on	trained
sold	typed
suggested	wrote

Let's look at two examples that differ only in their writing style. The first resume section is ineffective because it does not use action words to accent the applicant's work experiences:

WORK EXPERIENCE
Regional Sales Manager

Manager of sales representatives from seven states. Manager of twelve food chain accounts in the East. In charge of the sales force's planned selling toward specific goals. Supervisor and trainer of new sales representatives. Consulting for customers in the areas of inventory management and quality control.

Special Projects: Coordinator and sponsor of annual food industry sales seminar.

Accomplishments: Monthly regional volume went up 25 percent during my tenure while, at the same time, a proper sales/cost ratio was maintained. Customer-company relations were improved.

In the following paragraph, we have rewritten the same section using action words. Notice how the tone has changed. It now sounds stronger and more active. This person accomplished goals and really *did* things.

WORK EXPERIENCE
Regional Sales Manager

Managed sales representatives from seven states. Oversaw twelve food chain accounts in the eastern United States. Directed the sales force in planned selling toward specific goals. Supervised and trained new sales representatives. Counseled customers in the areas of inventory management and quality control. Coordinated and sponsored the annual Food Industry Seminar. Increased monthly regional volume 25 percent and helped to improve customer-company relations during my tenure.

One helpful way to construct the work experience section is to make use of your actual job descriptions—the written duties and expectations your employers had for a person in your current or former position. Job descriptions are rarely written in proper resume language, so you will have to rework them, but they do include much of the information necessary to create this section of your resume. If you have access to job descriptions for your former positions, you can use the details to construct an action-oriented paragraph. Often, your human resources department can provide a job description for your current position.

The following is an example of a typical human resources job description, followed by a rewritten version of the same description employing action words and specific details about the job. Again, pay attention to the style of writing instead of the content, as the details of your own experience will be unique.

WORK EXPERIENCE
Public Administrator I

Responsibilities: Coordinate and direct public services to meet the needs of the nation, state, or community. Analyze problems; work with special committees and public agencies; recommend solutions to governing bodies.

Aptitudes and Skills: Ability to relate to and communicate with people; solve complex problems through analysis; plan, organize, and implement policies and programs. Knowledge of political systems, financial management, personnel administration, program evaluation, and organizational theory.

WORK EXPERIENCE
Public Administrator I

Wrote pamphlets and conducted discussion groups to inform citizens of legislative processes and consumer issues. Organized and supervised 25 interviewers. Trained interviewers in effective communication skills.

After you have written your resume, you are ready to begin the next important step: assembly and layout.

Chapter 3

Assembly and Layout

A t this point, you've gathered all the necessary information for your resume and rewritten it in language that will impress your potential employers. Your next step is to assemble the sections in a logical order and lay them out on the page neatly and attractively to achieve the desired effect: getting the interview.

Assembly

The order of the elements in a resume makes a difference in its overall effect. Clearly, you would not want to bury your name and address somewhere in the middle of the resume. Nor would you want to lead with a less important section, such as special skills. Put the elements in an order that stresses your most important accomplishments and the things that will be most appealing to your potential employer. For example, if you recently graduated from school and have no full-time work experience, you will want the reviewer to read about your education before any part-time jobs you may have held during vacations. On the other hand, if you have been gainfully employed for several years and currently hold an important position in your company, you should list your work accomplishments ahead of your educational information, which has become less pertinent with time.

Certain things should always be included in your resume, but others are optional. The following list shows you which are which. You might want to use it as a checklist to be certain that you have included all of the necessary information.

Essential	Optional
Name	Cellular Phone Number
Address	Pager Number
Phone Number	E-Mail Address or Website Address
Work Experience	Voice Mail Number
Education	Job Objective
References Phrase	Honors
	Special Skills
	Publications
	Professional Memberships
	Activities
	Certificates and Licenses
	Personal Information
	Graphics
	Photograph

Your choice of optional sections depends on your own background and employment needs. Always use information that will put you in a favorable light—unless it's absolutely essential, avoid anything that will prompt the interviewer to ask questions about your weaknesses or something else that could be unflattering. Make sure your information is accurate and truthful. If your honors are impressive, include them in the resume. If your activities in school demonstrate talents that are necessary for the job you are seeking, allow space for a section on activities. If you are applying for a position that requires ornamental illustration, you may want to include border illustrations or graphics that demonstrate your talents in this area. If you are answering an advertisement for a job that requires certain physical traits, a photo of yourself might be appropriate. A person applying for a job as a computer programmer would *not* include a photo as part of his or her resume. Each resume is unique, just as each person is unique.

Types of Resumes

So far we have focused on the most common type of resume—the *reverse chronological* resume—in which your most recent job is listed first. This is the type of resume usually preferred by those who have to read a large number of resumes, and it is by far the most popular and widely circulated. However, this style of presentation may not be the most effective way to highlight *your* skills and accomplishments.

For example, if you are reentering the workforce after many years or are trying to change career fields, the *functional* resume may work best. This type of resume puts the focus on your achievements instead of the sequence of your work history. In the functional resume, your experience is presented through your general accomplishments and the skills you have developed in your working life.

A functional resume is assembled from the same information you gathered in Chapter 1. The main difference lies in how you organize the information. Essentially, the work experience section is divided in two, with your job duties and accomplishments constituting one section and your employers' names, cities, and states; your positions; and the dates employed making up the other. Place the first section near the top of your resume, just below your job objective (if used), and call it *Accomplishments* or *Achievements*. The second section, containing the bare essentials of your work history, should come after the accomplishments section and can be called *Employment History*, since it is a chronological overview of your former jobs.

The other sections of your resume remain the same. The work experience section is the only one affected in the functional format. By placing the section that focuses on your achievements at the beginning, you draw attention to these achievements. This puts less emphasis on whom you worked for and when, and more on what you did and what you are capable of doing.

If you are changing careers, the emphasis on skills and achievements is important. The identities of previous employers (who aren't part of your new career field) need to be downplayed. A functional resume can help accomplish this task. If you are reentering the workforce after a long absence, a functional resume is the obvious choice. And if you lack full-time work experience, you will need to draw attention away from this fact and put the focus on your skills and abilities. You may need to highlight your volunteer activities and part-time work. Education may also play a more important role in your resume.

The type of resume that is right for you will depend on your personal circumstances. It may be helpful to create both types and then compare them. Which one presents you in the best light? Examples of both types of resumes are included in this book. Use the sample resumes in Chapter 5 to help you decide on the content, presentation, and look of your own resume.

Special Tips for Electronic Resumes

Because there are many details to consider in writing a resume that will be posted or transmitted on the Internet, or one that will be scanned into a computer when it is received, we suggest that you refer to the *Guide to Internet Job Searching*, by Frances Roehm and Margaret Dikel, as previously mentioned. However, here are some brief, general guidelines to follow if you expect your resume to be scanned into a computer.

- Use standard fonts in which none of the letters touch.

- Keep in mind that underlining, italics, and fancy scripts may not scan well.

- Use boldface and capitalization to set off elements. Again, make sure letters don't touch. Leave at least a quarter inch between lines of type.

- Keep information and elements at the left margin. Centering, columns, and even indenting may change when the resume is optically scanned.

- Do not use any lines, boxes, or graphics.

- Place the most important information at the top of the first page. If you use two pages, put "Page 1 of 2" at the bottom of the first page and put your name and "Page 2 of 2" at the top of the second page.

- List each telephone number on its own line in the header.

- Use multiple keywords or synonyms for what you do to make sure your qualifications will be picked up if a prospective employer is searching for them. Use nouns that are keywords for your profession.

- Be descriptive in your titles. For example, don't just use "assistant"; use "legal office assistant."

- Make sure the contrast between print and paper is good. Use a high-quality laser printer and white or very light-colored 8½-by-11-inch paper.

- Mail a high-quality laser print or an excellent copy. Do not fold or use staples, as this might interfere with scanning. You may, however, use paper clips.

In addition to creating a resume that works well for scanning, you may want to have a resume that can be E-mailed to reviewers. Because you may not know what word processing application the recipient uses, the best format to use is ASCII text. (ASCII stands for "American Standard Code for Information Exchange.") It allows people with very different software platforms to exchange and understand information. (E-mail operates on this principle.) ASCII is a simple, text-only language, which means you can include only simple text. There can be no use of boldface, italics, or even paragraph indentations.

To create an ASCII resume, just use your normal word processing program; when finished, save it as a "text only" document. You will find this option under the "save" or "save as" command. Here is a list of things to *avoid* when crafting your electronic resume:

- Tabs. Use your space bar. Tabs will not work.

- Any special characters, such as mathematical symbols.

- Word wrap. Use hard returns (the return key) to make line breaks.

- Centering or other formatting. Align everything at the left margin.

- Bold or italic fonts. Everything will be converted to plain text when you save the file as a "text only" document.

Check carefully for any mistakes before you save the document as a text file. Spellcheck and proofread it several times, then ask someone with a keen eye to go over it again for you. Remember: the key is to keep it simple. Any attempt to make this resume pretty or decorative may result in a resume that is confusing and hard to read. After you have saved the document, you can cut and paste it into an E-mail or onto a website.

Layout for a Paper Resume

A great deal of care—and much more formatting—is necessary to achieve an attractive layout for your paper resume. There is no single appropriate layout that applies to every resume, but there are a few basic rules to follow in putting your resume on paper:

- Leave a comfortable margin on the sides, top, and bottom of the page (usually one to one and a half inches).

- Use appropriate spacing between the sections (two to three line spaces are usually adequate).

- Be consistent in the *type* of headings you use for different sections of your resume. For example, if you capitalize the heading EMPLOYMENT HISTORY, don't use initial capitals and underlining for a section of equal importance, such as <u>Education</u>.

- Do not use more than one font in your resume. Stay consistent by choosing a font that is fairly standard and easy to read, and don't change it for different sections. Beware of the tendency to try to make your resume original by choosing fancy type styles; your resume may end up looking unprofessional instead of creative. Unless you are in a very creative and artistic field, you should almost always stick with tried-and-true type styles like Times New Roman and Palatino, which are often used in business writing. In the area of resume styles, conservative is usually the best way to go.

- Always try to fit your resume on one page. If you are having trouble with this, you may be trying to say too much. Edit out any repetitive or unnecessary information, and shorten descriptions of earlier jobs where possible. Ask a friend you trust for feedback on what seems unnecessary or unimportant. For example, you may have included too many optional sections. Also consider using a smaller font size, within reason, or fewer blank lines between sections to condense your resume to a single page. Today, with the prevalence of the personal computer as a tool, there is no excuse for a poorly laid-out resume. Experiment with variations until you are pleased with the result.

CHRONOLOGICAL RESUME

Lucas Jackson
2399 S. Division • Grand Rapids, MI 49503
(616) 555-9354
Cell: (616) 555-2819
lucasjackson@xxx.com

Objective

Apply my skills as a content expert to a new challenge with a company focused on quality, dedication, and ingenuity.

Work

1998 to present

Content Strategist, Sonic Consulting, Grand Rapids, MI

> Provide digital solutions for clients interested in establishing their presence online. Make recommendations on content assets, third-party content partnerships, and content management systems. Direct copywriters and design teams to fulfill the clients' objectives and create brand strategies.

1996 to 1998

Website Manager, *Crash! Magazine*, Detroit, MI

> Directed the online version of *Crash! Magazine* and ensured design and content guidelines of the site followed those of the print version. Coordinated special events to drive traffic to the site resulting in a 75 percent increase in hits over four months. Created and edited content specifically for the site to establish its own identity.

1994 to 1996

Writer, *Digital City Magazine*, Detroit, MI

> Researched and wrote articles covering the emerging Internet business and issues that relate to that unique business sector. Interviewed people involved in cutting-edge development on the Web and analyzed the business implications of this unique medium.

Skills

- Intimate familiarity with standard style guides including *AP*, *Chicago Manual*, *MLA*, and *Wired*.
- Very knowledgeable in the use and merits of content management systems such as Vignette, ePrise, and BroadVision.
- Uncanny ability to merge creative vision with business objectives to create distinctive and engaging content.

References available upon request

FUNCTIONAL RESUME

Katrina Parker
1402 Greenbriar Road
Charleston, WV 25304
(304) 555-1704

Applications & Systems Programmer

Credentials

- B.S. in Computer Science—March 1995—University of Michigan; minor in Accounting
- Knowledge of COBOL, FORTRAN, Pascal, C, C Plus, BASIC, CAD/CAM, RPG II, ASSEMBLY language #68000, 8086 & 6502, and dbase
- High level of self-motivation and attention to detail

Job Duties

- Code, test, debug, and maintain programs
- Create program documentation
- Integrate new hardware into existing systems
- Diagnose and correct systems failures
- Maintain monitors, database packages, compilers, assemblers, and utility programs
- Select and modify new hardware and software to company specifications

Achievements

- Designed programs in C Plus for Heritage Bank to coordinate functions of ATM machines
- Purchased new hardware and software for Advantage Publishers, modified equipment to suit company's needs, and resolved interoperability issues

Employers

Heritage Bank   6/99 to Present
Advantage Publishers   4/96 to 6/99

References

Marta Dalton   Renu Das
Vice President of Finance   Director of Human Resources
Heritage Bank   Advantage Publishers
411 Watkins Street   694 Dale Street
Charleston, WV 25304   Deer Park, NY 11729
(304) 555-2225, Ext. 203   (516) 555-7937

Remember that a resume is not an autobiography. Too much information will only get in the way. The more compact your resume, the easier it will be to review. If a person who is swamped with resumes looks at yours, catches the main points, and then calls you for an interview to fill in some of the details, your resume has already accomplished its task. A clear and concise resume makes for a happy reader and a good impression.

There are times when, despite extensive editing, the resume simply cannot fit on one page. In this case, the resume should be laid out on two pages in such a way that neither clarity nor appearance is compromised. Each page of a two-page resume should be marked clearly: the first should indicate "Page 1 of 2," and the second should include your name and the page number, for example, "Julia Ramirez—Page 2 of 2." The pages should then be stapled together. You may use a smaller font (in the same font as the body of your resume) for the page numbers. Place them at the bottom of page one and at the top of page two. Again, spend the time now to experiment with the layout until you find one that looks good to you.

Always show your final layout to other people and ask them what they like or dislike about it, and what impresses them most when they read your resume. Make sure that their responses are the same as what you want to elicit from your prospective employer. If they aren't the same, you should continue to make changes until the necessary information is emphasized.

Proofreading

After you have finished typing the master copy of your resume and before you have it copied or printed, thoroughly check it for typing and spelling errors. Do not place all your trust in your computer's spellcheck function. Use an old editing trick and read the whole resume backward—start at the end and read it right to left and bottom to top. This can help you see the small errors or inconsistencies that are easy to overlook. Take time to do it right because a single error on a document this important can cause the reader to judge your attention to detail in a harsh light.

Have several people look at the finished resume just in case you've missed an error. Don't try to take a shortcut; not having an unbiased set of eyes examine your resume now could mean embarrassment later. Even experienced editors can easily overlook their own errors. Be thorough and conscientious with your proofreading so your first impression is a perfect one.

We have included the following rules of capitalization and punctuation to assist you in the final stage of creating your resume. Remember that resumes often require use of a shorthand style of writing that may include sentences without periods and other stylistic choices that break the standard rules of grammar. Be consistent in each section, and throughout the whole resume, with your choices.

RULES OF CAPITALIZATION

- Capitalize proper nouns, such as names of schools, colleges, and universities; names of companies; and brand names of products.

- Capitalize major words in the names and titles of books, tests, and articles that appear in the body of your resume.

- Capitalize words in major section headings of your resume.

- Do not capitalize words just because they seem important.

- When in doubt, consult a manual of style such as *Words into Type* (Prentice-Hall) or *The Chicago Manual of Style* (The University of Chicago Press). Your local library can help you locate these and other reference books. Many computer programs also have grammar help sections.

RULES OF PUNCTUATION

- Use commas to separate words in a series.

- Use a semicolon to separate series of words that already include commas within the series. (For an example, see the first rule of capitalization.)

- Use a semicolon to separate independent clauses that are not joined by a conjunction.

- Use a period to end a sentence.

- Use a colon to show that examples or details follow that will expand or amplify the preceding phrase.

- Avoid the use of dashes.

- Avoid the use of brackets.

- If you use any punctuation in an unusual way in your resume, be consistent in its use.

- Whenever you are uncertain, consult a style manual.

Putting Your Resume in Print

You will need to buy high-quality paper for your printer before you print your finished resume. Regular office paper is not good enough for resumes; the reviewer will probably think it looks flimsy and cheap. Go to an office supply store or copy shop and select a high-quality bond paper that will make a good first impression. Select colors like white, off-white, or possibly a light gray. In some industries, a pastel may be acceptable, but be sure the color and feel of the paper makes a subtle, positive statement about you. Nothing in the choice of paper should be loud or unprofessional.

If your computer printer does not reproduce your resume properly and produces smudged or stuttered type, either ask to borrow a friend's or take your disk (or a clean original) to a printer or copy shop for high-quality copying. If you anticipate needing a large number of copies, taking your resume to a copy shop or a printer is probably the best choice.

Hold a sheet of your unprinted bond paper up to the light. If it has a watermark, you will want to point this out to the person helping you with copies; the printing should be done so that the reader can read the print and see the watermark the right way up. Check each copy for smudges or streaks. This is the time to be a perfectionist—the results of your careful preparation will be well worth it.

The Cover Letter

Once your resume has been assembled, laid out, and printed to your satisfaction, the next and final step before distribution is to write your cover letter. Though there may be instances where you deliver your resume in person, you will usually send it through the mail or online. Resumes sent through the mail always need an accompanying letter that briefly introduces you and your resume. The purpose of the cover letter is to get a potential employer to read your resume, just as the purpose of the resume is to get that same potential employer to call you for an interview.

Like your resume, your cover letter should be clean, neat, and direct. A cover letter usually includes the following information:

1. Your name and address (unless it already appears on your personal letterhead) and your phone number(s); see item 7.

2. The date.

3. The name and address of the person and company to whom you are sending your resume.

4. The salutation ("Dear Mr." or "Dear Ms." followed by the person's last name, or "To Whom It May Concern" if you are answering a blind ad).

5. An opening paragraph explaining why you are writing (for example, in response to an ad, as a follow-up to a previous meeting, at the suggestion of someone you both know) and indicating that you are interested in whatever job is being offered.

6. One or more paragraphs that tell why you want to work for the company and what qualifications and experiences you can bring to the position. This is a good place to mention some detail about

that particular company that makes you want to work for them; this shows that you have done some research before applying.

7. A final paragraph that closes the letter and invites the reviewer to contact you for an interview. This can be a good place to tell the potential employer which method would be best to use when contacting you. Be sure to give the correct phone number and a good time to reach you, if that is important. You may mention here that your references are available upon request.

8. The closing ("Sincerely" or "Yours truly") followed by your signature in a dark ink, with your name typed under it.

Your cover letter should include all of this information and be no longer than one page in length. The language used should be polite, businesslike, and to the point. Don't attempt to tell your life story in the cover letter; a long and cluttered letter will serve only to annoy the reader. Remember that you need to mention only a few of your accomplishments and skills in the cover letter. The rest of your information is available in your resume. If your cover letter is a success, your resume will be read and all pertinent information reviewed by your prospective employer.

Producing the Cover Letter

Cover letters should always be individualized because they are always written to specific individuals and companies. Never use a form letter for your cover letter or copy it as you would a resume. Each cover letter should be unique, and as personal and lively as possible. (Of course, once you have written and rewritten your first cover letter until you are satisfied with it, you can certainly use similar wording in subsequent letters. You may want to save a template on your computer for future reference.) Keep a hard copy of each cover letter so you know exactly what you wrote in each one.

After you have written your cover letter, proofread it as thoroughly as you did your resume. Again, spelling or punctuation errors are a sure sign of carelessness, and you don't want that to be a part of your first impression on a prospective employer. This is no time to trust your spellcheck function. Even after going through a spelling and grammar check, your cover letter should be carefully proofread by at least one other person.

Print the cover letter on the same quality bond paper you used for your resume. Remember to sign it, using a good, dark-ink pen. Handle the letter and resume carefully to avoid smudging or wrinkling, and mail them together in an appropriately sized envelope. Many stores sell matching envelopes to coordinate with your choice of bond paper.

Keep an accurate record of all resumes you send out and the results of each mailing. This record can be kept on your computer, in a calendar or notebook, or on file cards. Knowing when a resume is likely to have been received will keep you on track as you make follow-up phone calls.

About a week after mailing resumes and cover letters to potential employers, contact them by telephone. Confirm that your resume arrived and ask whether an interview might be possible. Be sure to record the name of the person you spoke to and any other information you gleaned from the conversation. It is wise to treat the person answering the phone with a great deal of respect; sometimes the assistant or receptionist has the ear of the person doing the hiring.

You should make a great impression with the strong, straightforward resume and personalized cover letter you have just created. We wish you every success in securing the career of your dreams!

PART II
SAMPLE RESUMES

These chapters contain dozens of sample resumes for people pursuing a wide variety of jobs and careers.

There are many different styles of resumes in terms of layout and presentation of information. These samples also represent people with varying amounts of education and work experience. Model your resume after these samples. Choose one resume or borrow elements from several different resumes to help you construct your own.

Resumes for Re-entering the Job Market or Changing Careers

DONALD E. PFEIFER

3188 Bradshaw Road
Manchester, CT 06040
(203) 555-1286 home office
(203) 555-8787 cellular

EMPLOYMENT OBJECTIVE

To obtain a position in graphic design or related area requiring advanced design and illustration skills

RELATED SKILLS AND EXPERIENCE

- Highly experienced in graphic design and illustration
- Experienced in various techniques for developing illustrations for posters, graphs, charts, training aids, brochures, books, and other publications
- Accomplished in using a variety of media including pencil, pen and ink, water color, art markers, and other media
- Skilled in producing both realistic and cartoon-style drawings and other illustrations
- Experienced in using a wide range of equipment including copy cameras, orthographic equipment, and other graphics arts and audiovisual presentation equipment
- Highly flexible in completing different types of assignments, working with others, and using creativity in practical applications

WORK BACKGROUND

1994–2002 Chief Illustrator Draftsman (E-7), United States Navy.
Honorably discharged after nine years of service; decided against re-enlistment in favor of civilian life. Received several promotions and recognitions; complete military record available on request. Portfolio also available.

REFERENCES WILL BE PROVIDED ON REQUEST

John Weaver

14 Roger Road
Macon, Georgia 31207
(478) 555-6868

Education

Mercer University, Walter F. George School of Law, Macon, Georgia
J.D., June 1998
Academic Record: Top 20

Emory University, Atlanta, Georgia
B.A., Religion, June 1996
Academic Record: 3.20/4.00

Work Experience

Summer 1997
Burns, Brooks & Ferry
Macon, Georgia

Summer 1996
Red Lobster
Macon, Georgia

Honors & Activities

Law School
- Chairman, Moot Court Board
- Law Review
- Honor Committee
- Student Bar Association
- Orientation Committee
- Teaching Assistant, Freshman Legal Research Course
- Publication: Note - "Summer School Tuition Does Not Violate State Constitutional Duty to Provide Free and Adequate Education," 31 *Mercer Law Review* 116 (1997)
- Dean's List
- First Year Oralist Finalist Award in Moot Court Competition
- Student Government

References available upon request.

ANNA GUPTA
3892 Barbary Road
Sacramento, CA 95813
(916) 555-9283

OBJECTIVE

Buyer/Manager for an independent bookstore

EDUCATION

1980 M.L.S.   University of Washington, Seattle
1975 B.A.   Comparative Literature, University of California, Berkeley

PROFESSIONAL EXPERIENCE

1990 - present   *Director, Media Services*
West Sacramento School District

Direct the library services of 20 elementary, middle, and high schools in district. Supervise ten professionals. Designed the high school library media center of 50,000 print and nonprint items.

1985 - 1989   *Head Librarian*
Berryman School Library, Sacramento, California

Directed the acquisitions and functioning of this school library serving 1,200 students and 95 professionals. Supervised five para-professionals.

1980 - 1985   *Acquisitions Librarian*
Timberland Regional Library, Olympia, Washington

Served as acquisitions librarian for this regional branch of libraries.

1975 - 1980   *Teacher, Literature and Writing*
St. Mary's Girls Academy, Olympia, Washington

Taught literature and writing courses to high school students at this private high school.

REFERENCES AVAILABLE ON REQUEST

JENNIE LYNN BLOOM

132 Palm Court • San Pedro, CA • Work: 310/555-1267 • Pager: 310/555-8772

OBJECTIVE

To seek a position as a sales representative for a fitness/exercise company.

SUMMARY OF QUALIFICATIONS

- Aspire to successful achievements in my chosen field as a sales representative.
- Extremely fitness minded and health conscious.
- Possess a bodybuilding physique that defines muscularity and femininity.
- Enjoy competing on the dais as well as in career-oriented situations.
- Relate to people personally regardless of whether or not their philosophy coincides with mine.

AWARDS & ACHIEVEMENTS

- First runner-up for Ms. Southern California bodybuilding contest, Los Angeles, 2001.
- Second runner-up for Ms. Laguna Beach Bunny competition, Laguna Beach, 2000.
- Semifinalist contestant in the "American Gladiators" television series competition, Hollywood, 1999.
- Received second-place trophy for mixed-pairs posing-routine competition held in Atlanta, 1998.
- Awarded first-place crown for Ms. San Diego Natural Physique contest, San Diego, 1997.

EMPLOYMENT

Gold's Gym/Santa Monica, California
Personal Trainer, part-time, 1996 - 2000. Worked closely with a variety of clients. Researched and applied fitness regiments specialized for each client.

Vic Tanny's Vitamin World, Inc./Los Angeles, California
Sales Clerk, 1995 - 1998. Assisted customers in vitamin and health food selections.

Dunham's Sport World/Santa Monica, California
Sales Clerk, 1993 - 1995. Helped customers in purchasing weight training equipment, workout attire, and sports clothes. Assisted in setting up new store locations in Southern California. Helped train new sales staff clerks.

EDUCATION

UCLA/Riverside campus
B.S. in Physical Education, Degree awarded 1993.

International Sports Sciences Association/Santa Barbara
Fitness Trainer Certification, 1997.

References available upon request.

CHARLES H. INGRAM
Route 4, Box 112
Isleboro, Maine 04848
(207) 555-1219

SUMMARY OF QUALIFICATIONS

Energetic, highly motivated team player experienced in working with others to achieve common goals. Physically fit and mentally vigorous. Available to take on new challenges following successful period of military service.

EXPERIENCE

1997 - 2003 United States Navy
Rating: Mineman First Class (E-6)

- Maintained, installed, and inspected underwater explosive devices
- Instructed junior personnel in handling explosives and detonation agents
- Supervised handling, assembling, disassembling, testing, and storage of mines
- Prepared mine cases and other components for assembly
- Used a wide variety of tools and testing devices
- Performed other related duties requiring diligence, concentration, and adherence to safety

1996 - 1997 Stocker, Cook's Grocery, 21 Main Street, Isleboro, Maine. Performed general store duties while employed on part-time basis.

EDUCATION

Diploma, Isleboro High School, Isleboro, Maine, 1997
Graduate, Fleet and Mine Warfare Training Center, Charleston, South Carolina, 1998

REFERENCES

Available on request

Amelia Nelson
1545 Arboretum Drive, Apt. 34
Rutland, Vermont 05701
(802) 555-3828

OBJECTIVE   A corporate position in sales that involves extensive customer contact.

WORK
EXPERIENCE   *Public Relations Assistant*
Applebury Inc., Burlington, Vermont, 1995 - present.
- Direct interface with clients and the public, assessing needs and providing solutions. Assist in product inquiries and setting up discounting programs for qualified customers. Represent company in trade shows. Exhibit strong product knowledge in handling customer complaints through analysis and evaluation of complaint report. Support for sales force and on-site technicians.

Management/Marketing Assistant
Divan Management, Rutland, Vermont, 1985 - 1995.
- Assisted marketing research projects and conducted a general management survey for mini-warehouse industry. Coordinated promotional campaigns, utilizing database analysis to focus on target market.

Special Promotion Assistant, Sideline Sales
University Bookstore, Burlington, Vermont, 1982 - 1985.
- Responsible for selecting, ordering, and promoting the sales of sportswear to organizations and a student body of 40,000 students, averaging more than $75,000 in sales. Demonstrated skills in leadership, organization, and group motivation.

Entrepreneur
Nelson Promotions, Burlington, Vermont, 1980 - 1982.
- Sold custom-made sportswear to Greek system and dormitories. Examined and evaluated on- and off-campus markets through on-site observations and informal interviews. Supervised two employees.

EDUCATION   B.A., 1980, Business and Marketing
University of Vermont, Burlington

REFERENCES AVAILABLE ON REQUEST

CARMELLA MADEROS

4008 Puget Sound Drive • Seattle, WA 98789
206/555-3116 • cm71@xxx.com

CAREER OBJECTIVE

To obtain a position as a court reporter and to utilize my past experience in the legal and administrative field.

EDUCATION

Stenographic Technical Business School, Seattle
Court Reporting, Certification received in September 2000
Two-year curriculum included Court Reporting Procedures and Technology, English Grammar, Legal Terminology, Anatomy and Medical Terminology.

Olympia School of Secretarial Studies, Olympia
Diploma, May 1990
Courses included Word Processing, Speed-Typing, Shorthand, Transcription, Office Procedures, Bookkeeping, Communication Skills, and Basic Computer Course.

WORK EXPERIENCE

Payne and DelaRosa, Attorneys at Law, Bellevue   Secretary/Receptionist, 1994 - 1998
Typed correspondence, coordinated appointments for clients, recorded accounts receivable and payable entries.

Department of Motor Vehicles, Seattle   Clerk, 1990 - 1994
Reissued vehicle registration forms, processed car dealership registrations, issued driver's licenses, and conducted written driver's license tests to Spanish-speaking applicants.

SPECIAL SKILLS

Fluent Spanish
Computer experience -- Lotus and Microsoft Office Suite

MEMBERSHIPS

National Court Reporters Association, NCRA, 2000
Spanish Society of Seattle since 1988
Offices held:
Secretary -- 1985
Vice President -- 1993 & 1994.

REFERENCES
Furnished upon request.

SUSAN A. LOMBARDO

PERMANENT ADDRESS:
21 Lake Avenue Circle
Palos Heights, Illinois 60463
(312) 555-4376 (voice)
(312) 555-6062 (fax)

SUMMARY OF QUALIFICATIONS

• Experienced military police officer.

• Highly trained and experienced in performing basic law enforcement duties.

• Dependable, levelheaded, and energetic.

• Adept at using good judgment in a wide range of settings and situations.

WORK EXPERIENCE

United States Army, 1995–2003

Role: Military Police Officer

Duties: Performed a wide range of duties. Experience included base security, routine and special patrols, traffic management, and assisting in criminal investigations.

EDUCATION

Graduate of Military Police School, Fort McClellan, Alabama.

Completed additional courses in criminal investigation methods, Fort Gordon, Georgia.

High school graduate with six college credits through dual enrollment program (English Composition and American History).

TECHNICAL SKILLS

Highly skilled in a wide range of law enforcement skills including crowd control, appropriate weapons use, and arrest procedures.

REFERENCES

Personal and professional references available on request.

Myrna J. Myers

1786 Starlight Drive
Newton, MA 05342
Home: 617/555-8932
Pager: 617/555-3112

OBJECTIVE
To obtain an entry-level position in public relations.

EDUCATION
Bachelor of Science in Business Administration, 1990
Holister State University
Holister, Massachusetts
Major: Public Relations
GPA 3.2

WORK EXPERIENCE
The Meteor Weekly, Langdon, Massachusetts
Advertising Sales Representative 1992 - 1996
　　Responsible for a sales territory consisting of more than 200,000 people.
　　Conducted sales canvassing with local merchants, and once sale was made,
　　followed the development of the ad until publication.

The Suntel Communications Co., Langdon, Massachusetts
Receptionist and Advertising Media Assistant 1990 - 1992
　　Greeted and received clients; scheduled appointments for advertising
　　account representatives on sales leads.

CAREER RELATED ACTIVITIES
Cochairperson for the annual Early American Cultural Festival for the past six
years in Holister, Massachusetts. Integrated advertising and local cultural information into a yearly program book, from which all profits are contributed to a
local charity.

Advertising Editor for the Holister State University newspaper:
1988 - 1990

SEMINARS & WORKSHOPS
Dale Carnegie course in Public Speaking
Newton, Massachusetts 1992

Creative Writing
Newton, Massachusetts 1993

REFERENCES
Available upon request.

FRANCINE P. SMITH

786 Quartz Street
Bangor, ME 04401
(207) 555-8692

Occupational Goal: I would like to become a dietician. Presently, I am seeking a part-time job that will allow me to attend school in order to prepare for my chosen field.

Education: High School: Bangor High School
Degree: High school diploma, 2000
Grade average: A-/B+

Special Skills: I learn rapidly and work well with other people.
I am skilled in word processing and using the Internet.

Hobbies: Exercising
Skiing
Playing the guitar

Activities: Member of the Bangor High School Key Club and American Field Service during my junior year.
Member of the Bangor High School Concert and Marching Band during my freshman and sophomore years.

Work Experience:

6/00 - 9/00 Child-care provider for fifteen hours a week.

9/99 - 5/00 Housecleaner for three to four hours a week.

6/98 - 8/99 Baby-sitter for four to five hours a week.

References: Available upon request.

Sandra B. Walters
334 Northwest Vineland Ave., Concord, NH 03321 (603) 555-2214

Career Interest: Outward Bound Instructor in Mountain Climbing Division

Important Skills & Experience:

- First American woman to climb Tengeboche Himal in Nepal.
- Completed solo 1,000 mile trek in Chilean Andes.
- Made ascent to 21,000-foot elevation on Everest before weather ended expedition.
- Climbed seven major peaks in the Cascade Mountain Range in Oregon and Washington.
- Organized and led climbs to four major peaks in Rocky Mountains in Colorado and Wyoming.
- Organized and led treks on the Pacific Crest Trail from Canada to Mexico.
- Wrote book (as yet unpublished) on experience trekking in Third World countries.

Related Work Experience:

- Taught high school history in public schools for 12 years.
- Provided counseling assistance in program for drug-dependent youth.
- Taught short courses in backpacking and mountain climbing for local sporting goods store.
- Taught courses and led trips for university student outdoor recreation center.

Employment History:

History Teacher, South Concord High School, 1990 to 1998
History Teacher, Washington Lee High School, Boston, 1986 to 1990

Additional Work Experience:

Real Estate Sales, Central Home Realty, Boston, 1980 to 1986
Secretary, Central Home Realty, Boston, 1976 to 1980

Education:

Coursework in Counseling, University of New Hampshire, 1996 to 1998
B.A., History, Boston University, 1986

References available on request

ELAINE REYNOLDS

2324 Wainwright Drive
Marionville, NJ 08229
609/555-8965

CAREER OBJECTIVE
A position as a TV sales host for a cable television shopping network.

EXPERIENCE
WKBC Cable Entertainment Network, Philadelphia, PA
Advertising Sales Representative, 1996 - 1999
Sold TV advertising spots within six counties to merchants, businesses, and services. Consistently achieved annual sales goal quota of $300,000.

Cherry Hill Herald Daily News, **Cherry Hill, NJ**
Sales Representative, 1992 - 1996
Processed classified advertising sales orders over the telephone and conducted direct sales calls.

Bergen Bulletin Weekly, **Bergen, NJ**
Receptionist/Clerk, 1990 - 1992
Greeted clients, transferred incoming calls, managed all correspondence, and created ad copy.

EDUCATION
Philadelphia School of Visual Arts, Philadelphia, PA
Major: TV and Radio Broadcasting and Advertising
Diploma awarded 1989

RELATED ACTIVITIES
- WKBC TV sales host fill-in for the New Product Department segment when regular hosts were on vacation.

- Assistant TV sales auctioneer for annual children's summer camp benefit program sponsored by WKBC.

HONORS
- Recipient of the Philadelphia School of Visual Arts annual award for the most accomplished student in the School of Broadcasting, 1989.

- Dean's List, five semesters.

REFERENCES
Furnished upon request.

Ramon C. Cortez
3856 N. Harvard Avenue • Washington, D.C. 20023 • Home: 202/555-3355

Career Objective

To become a Medical Transcriptionist and utilize my past medical experience as a foundation.

Summary of Qualifications

- Self-starter and perfectionist
- Self-disciplined and committed to learning
- Strong interest in medicine
- Able to concentrate for long periods
- Willing to assist others
- Able to work with minimal supervision
- Dedicated to professional development and achievement

Education

Bethesda Medical Training Institute, Bethesda, Maryland
Medical Transcriptionist: Two-year program; Diploma, 1997
Curriculum included the following courses: Stenotype, Medical/Legal Dictation, Word Processing, Medical Terminology, Anatomy and Physiology, Pharmacology, Human Diseases, and Surgical Problems.

Capitol Community College, Washington, D.C.
Administrative Technical Training: Certification, 1995
Course study and application of computer training in the following programs: Lotus, Microsoft Word, Excel, and Access.

Employment

Wolfert Pharmaceutical Supply, Washington, D.C.
Supply Clerk, part-time, 1994 - 2000
Filled orders and packed pharmaceutical supplies for shipping to medical offices and facilities.

Drug Castle Chemists, Washington, D.C.
Sales Clerk, 1989 - 1994
Conducted cash and credit card sales transactions. Stocked merchandise, delivered prescription drugs, assisted in training new personnel.

References

Available upon request.

ALLISON GOSNEY

206 Jeffries Drive
Riverdale, NY 10471
(212) 555-2013

EMPLOYMENT OBJECTIVE

To obtain a challenging position in the airline industry

RELATED SKILLS AND EXPERIENCE

- Experienced in various aspects of providing service for air passengers
- Skilled in all steps required for processing passenger reservations
- Thoroughly familiar with automated data processing functions for passenger reservations
- Experienced in developing positive relations with customers and maintaining good customer relations
- Highly motivated self-starter interested in taking on new challenges

WORK BACKGROUND

1996–2003. Air Passenger Specialist, United States Air Force.

Completed special job-related training by correspondence through Air Force Extension Course Institute, Gunter Air Force Base, AL. Received excellent evaluations of job performance. Complete military record available on request.

REFERENCES

Complete reference information will be provided on request.

ROBERTO I. MARTINEZ

1690 Sandy Lane • Marianna, FL 34619 • (813) 555-7758

JOB OBJECTIVE

Technician/Assistant Engineer
Industrial/Production Electronics

A position offering upward mobility in a quiet, professional environment. I am confident I can adapt successfully to the industrial/production environment and as a self-starter, I will learn whatever additional skills the position requires.

PART-TIME WORK EXPERIENCE

Summer occupation 1997 to 1999 - Marianna Radio/TV, Marianna, FL
TV, VCR, and Stereo Technician.

Summer occupation 1996 - Allen TV Service, Marianna, FL
TV/Stereo Technician.

Summer occupation 1995 - McDonald's restaurant, Marianna, FL
Food Server and Maintenance Worker.

PERSONAL EVALUATION

I am an electronics technician with a strong background in repairing consumer electronic products. I have designed and breadboarded many electronic devices such as TTL circuits up to 14 ICs, audio special-effects projects, laser and power supply projects, security systems, infrared and ultrasonic measuring tools, and surface mount technology projects.

EDUCATION

2000 Graduate of Chipola Junior College, Marianna, FL

A.A. Equivalence Certificates in Electronics, AC/DC, Semiconductors, Circuits, Digital Electronics, and Microprocessors.

1998 Graduate of Marianna High School, Marianna, FL
General education.

REFERENCES ON REQUEST

ELIZABETH R. CAMPBELL

622 Byrn Avenue
Houston, TX 77504
Cellular Phone: 713/555-7878
lizcampbell@xxx.com

OBJECTIVE

A position as a job recruiter in a personnel office or agency where my experience can be utilized.

EDUCATION

Kent State University/Kent, OH, 1974 - 1978
B.S. in Human Resources; Dean's List 1978

PROFESSIONAL EXPERIENCE

Jobcorp Employment Agency/Pittsburgh, PA
Placement Officer: 1983 - 1990
Interviewed candidates for full- and part-time employment opportunities. Conducted testing in clerical and aptitude requirements designated by employer. Interviewed college seniors on local college campuses.

Snelling and Snelling Agency, Inc./Kent, OH
Receptionist/Secretary: 1979 - 1983
Coordinated appointments for clients. Typed correspondence and maintained filing system. Periodically interviewed clients for part-time manual labor positions.

SUMMARY OF QUALIFICATIONS

- Project oriented and motivated to complete challenging tasks.
- Work well under stressful conditions.
- Conduct and maintain well-organized interviews.

MEMBERSHIPS

- Toastmasters Organization, 1999 - present
  Office held: Recording Secretary, 2001
- Sigma Sigma Sigma Social Sorority, Active: 1975 - 1978
  Office held: Vice President, 1977

HONORS

- Toastmaster of the Year Award, 2001
- Article entitled "Getting That First Job," published in the *Job Market* magazine, April 1989

REFERENCES

Available upon request.

JONATHAN B. OWENS
2245 RIVER ROAD
NEWPORT, OR 97366
(503) 555-2435

OBJECTIVE

After twenty years of active duty in the Coast Guard, I am seeking a management position in Program Development and Implementation that will utilize my extensive background in these areas.

EXPERIENCE

1995 - present: Branch Chief for Emergency Medical Central Training Center, U.S. Coast Guard, Newport, OR

Responsibilities

Developed, designed, and implemented the curriculum for training Coast Guard personnel. Responsible for selecting and evaluating staff of 30. Managed an annual budget of $200,000 for staff training and operations.

Contributions

Established new computer system to improve communications utilizing electronic mail. Developed and implemented new internal and external valuation programs to test new performance-based curricula. Designed and implemented new instructor development plans, which included continuing educational programs for personnel.

1993 - 1995: Operations Officer, U.S. Coast Guard, Ilwaco, WA

Responsibilities

Scheduled all ship movement activities. Supervised program for conducting boardings at sea to ensure compliance of commercial and recreational vessels to federal law. Supervised 20 personnel, including training and evaluation.

Contributions

Developed new unit training program by fostering a supportive educational environment.

1991 - 1993: Operations Officer, U.S. Coast Guard, Bethel, AK

Responsibilities

In charge of vessel traffic control for the safe passage of large crude oil carriers traveling in and out of Prince William Sound. Managed work schedules for both vessel traffic and communications watch standing personnel. Responsible for training, development, and performance evaluations for 15 personnel. Managed the maintenance of a remote microwave communications and vessel traffic radar system for all of Prince William Sound.

Page 1 of 2

JONATHAN B. OWENS

Page 2 of 2

EXPERIENCE (cont.)

Contributions

Installed new radar tracking system, which included upgrading remote power supply unit for one radar site. Improved personnel watch rotations to maximize time spent on the job as well as improve flexibility of time off. Implemented the hiring of civilian employees to replace Coast Guard personnel as permanent watch standers in the Vessel Traffic Center. Improved relations between Coast Guard and Maritime Industries.

1987 - 1991: Administration Officer, U.S. Coast Guard Marine Safety Office, Ilwaco, WA

Responsibilities

In charge of personnel and supply administration for a 50-person unit. Direct supervisor for seven personnel, including training and performance evaluations. Managed an annual budget of $350,000 for the maintenance and upkeep of an office building and a 29-unit housing complex.

Contributions

Centralized administrative personnel to take a team approach to handle all unit administrative matters. Eliminated unnecessary reports. Expedited the process of all administrative work by purchasing new computer hardware and software to increase efficiency.

1984 - 1987: Instructor, Leadership School, U.S. Coast Guard, San Diego, CA

Responsibilities

Involved with developing, designing, and implementing curriculum for newly established leadership and management program for Coast Guard personnel.

Contributions

Developed two-week curriculum for the school from the latest leadership and management practices. Participated in design, development, and testing of the new performance evaluation system currently used by the Coast Guard.

EDUCATION

Master of Arts in Educational Administration, University of Oregon, Eugene, OR
Bachelor of Science in Human Relations and Organizational Behavior, University of
   Oregon, Eugene, OR

REFERENCES AVAILABLE UPON REQUEST

Horoko Kimura

111 Southwest Blvd.
East Providence, RI 02777
401/555-4871
Kimura@xxx.com

CAREER OBJECTIVE

Seeking a staff accountant position enabling me to utilize my diverse skills, knowledge, and experience, that simultaneously offers an opportunity for growth and advancement.

SKILLS & ACHIEVEMENTS

- Designed a user-friendly Lotus template for project development staff providing an instrument of measurement to track investment contract expenditures.
- Streamlined time spent processing payroll and improved accuracy by implementing automated time clock system to replace punch clock format.
- Improved efficiency and growth of project direction by taking an active role in communicating daily with the departments involved in investment contracts.

EMPLOYMENT HISTORY

Rankin, Smith and Hightower Investment Group, Inc. - Providence, RI
Senior Staff Accountant, 1993 - 2000
Prepared and reviewed financial statements for management, assisted in annual budgeting, audited disbursements for accuracy and validity, and maintained commission programs.

Margate & Paynter Financial Brokers, Inc. - Providence, RI
Accounting Clerk, 1990 - 1993
Prepared weekly physical inventory report and reconciliation, monthly accounts receivable aging report, sales and purchase ledger reconciliation, invoice coding, and product sales pricing. Developed and installed new coding program, assisted in reprogramming of invoice and collection data system.

EDUCATION

University of Providence - Providence, RI
B.S. in Accounting, GPA 3.6
Degree awarded: 2001
A.S. in Accounting, GPA 3.4
Associate degree awarded: 1992

SUMMARY OF QUALIFICATIONS

- Eagerly accept challenges and new opportunities.
- Strong analytical and problem-solving abilities.
- Project and goal oriented.
- Easily adapt to new systems and programs.

COMPUTER SKILLS

Microsoft Applications including: Word, Excel, PowerPoint, and Publisher.
Lotus 1-2-3, Professional Write, and PageMaker.

REFERENCES

Furnished upon request.

Marcia Penas Smith

55 Alexandria Street, Apt. 25   Washington, D.C., 20013   (202) 555-0988

OBJECTIVE

A position as translator for a federal or state agency

LANGUAGES

Fluent in written and spoken Spanish, Portuguese, and French

EDUCATION

M.A. in Spanish and Portuguese, 1998, Middlebury College, Middlebury, VT
B.A. in French and Psychology, 1978, Arizona Sate University, Tempe, AZ
Foreign Study Program in Oaxaca, Mexico, 1975 - 1976

WORK EXPERIENCE

English Teacher, English Department, Madrid University, Spain, 1994 - 1996

Taught reading and conversation to undergraduates and teachers of non-English majors. Developed curriculum for and taught elective reading course on North American short stories. Taught beginning conversation to small group of primary school students. Informally advised Spanish students on living and studying in the U.S.

Assistant to Director, Office of International Education, Arizona State System of Higher Education, Arizona State University, 1986 - 1994

Developed and administered Latin American summer exchange program for high school students. Assisted with foreign student and foreign study orientation programs. Coordinated visits of international guests. Assisted in administration of foreign study programs.

Office Assistant, Office of International Programs and Summer Session, Arizona State University, 1978 - 1986

Assisted in administration of overseas programs. Assisted with information meetings and predeparture orientations. Gave general advising to students interested in study and work abroad. Handled summer session and special programs registrations. Responsible for general secretarial-receptionist duties.

ROLANDA MARIE PAGANINI

3212 Loganberry Avenue
Cedar Rapids, Iowa 52447
319/555-8877
Paganini@xxx.com

OBJECTIVE

A challenging position as a graphic artist in which my computer and educational background can be utilized.

QUALIFICATIONS

- Highly motivated and dependable in achieving goals.
- Strong organizational skills, attention to detail.
- Ability to analyze and solve problems in a constantly changing work environment.
- Self-motivated and confident in making independent decisions.
- Competitive, efficient, hard working, and enthusiastic.

EDUCATION

Cedar Rapids School of Visual Arts, Cedar Rapids, Iowa
A.S. Degree in Graphic Design, 1995

CTC Computer Training College, Cedar Rapids, Iowa
Certificate received, 1993
Curriculum: PC training including computerized Accounting and Microsoft Suite including Word, PowerPoint, Access, and Excel

EMPLOYMENT

NATIONWIDE COMPUTER OUTLET STORE, IOWA CITY, IOWA
ADVERTISING DEPARTMENT, 1996 - 2000
Assisted Art Director in creating graphic art for weekly newspaper advertising. Researched competitive ads in the central Midwest and maintained files in order to prevent duplication.

ABC ARTS, INC., CEDAR RAPIDS, IOWA
ASSISTANT MANAGER, 1993 - 1996
Responsible for three part-time employees, trained new personnel, ordered stock for two stores, evaluated employee performance.

INTERESTS

Oil painting, photography, stained-glass art.

REFERENCES

Furnished upon request.

Linda Diaz Davis
708 Carson Road
Morganton, North Carolina 28655
(704) 555-3795 Home
(704) 555-0990 Cellular/Voice Mail

OBJECTIVE: A position in industrial security, hospital security, or a related area.

RELEVANT SKILLS AND EXPERIENCE

- Experienced in various aspects of protecting property and personnel.
- Skilled in performing physical security inspections.
- Familiar with effective procedures for reducing threats, anticipating security problems, and dealing with contemporary security issues.
- Skilled in using fire equipment, weapons, locks, alarms, and other devices and equipment related to security.
- Adept at various self-defense measures.
- Highly reliable in following orders, implementing procedures, and acting independently when needed.

WORK HISTORY

1994–2003 United States Marine Corps

- Completed basic training at Paris Island, South Carolina.
- Served as security guard at military installations including assignment at United States Embassy in Cairo, Egypt.
- Received several commendations for outstanding service.
- Decided not to reenlist after two tours of duty in favor of a civilian career in security.

EDUCATION

- Graduate, Security Guard School, Quantico, Virginia, 1996.
- Completed more than 100 hours of language training, specializing in Arabic.
- Fluent in Spanish.
- Completed several correspondence courses and seminars related to security practices and procedures.

REFERENCES ON REQUEST

JEAN K. SCHUMANN

389 SW 13th AVENUE   OLYMPIA, WA 97301   (206) 555-3982

CAREER OBJECTIVE

To obtain a position as Scientific Technician for the Washington Department of Fisheries or the U.S. Department of National Resources.

SUMMARY OF EXPERIENCE

- Collected biological data as Biological Aide at Washington Coastal Aquarium.
- Participated in field study emphasizing terrestrial vegetation, geological features, and marine organisms, and maintained field journal of activities, including plot studies.
- Participated in compiling environmental report for county sub-area plan, producing vegetation map, writing and editing sections of report, and presenting group results to planning committee.
- Maintained records of shipments, collected and prepared ore samples for chemical analysis, and assisted in surveying for Taber Shipments, Inc.
- Developed and implemented Marine Biology (Intertidal Organisms and Rocky and Cobbled Shore Habitat) and Cedar and Salmon Natural and Cultural History Programs for use at girl scout camps.
- Assisted in supervising and training staff, planning programs, and evaluating performance and programs.
- Taught and led nature activities for children and adults in marine and terrestrial biology, intertidal habitats and organisms, forest ecosystems and habitats, botany, zoology, and meteorology.

WORK HISTORY

Community Resources Staff, Campus Recreation Center, Deschutes University, Olympia, WA, 1995 - present

Assistant Director, Program Planner, Rainier Girl Scout Council, Tacoma, WA, 1990 - 1995

Program Development Intern, Rainier Girl Scout Council, Tacoma, WA, 1989

Biological Aide, Washington Coast Aquarium, Long Beach, WA, summers 1985 - 1989

Biological Assistant, Taber Shipments, Inc., Spokane, WA, 1984

EDUCATION

B.A. in Biology, Deschutes University, Olympia, WA, 1989

JILL REISMAN

•••

80 Crescent Circle
Hinsdale, IL 60870
j_reisman@xxx.com
708/555-2568

••• OBJECTIVE
To obtain a position as a hostess/party counselor for a restaurant or party center.

••• SUMMARY OF QUALIFICATIONS
- Organizational and problem-solving capabilities.
- Excellent motivational skills.
- Eager to accept challenging tasks.
- Ready to assist where help is needed.
- Outstanding work performance.
- Congenial professional attitude.

••• RELATED ACTIVITIES
- Organized and coordinated banquet dinner parties, dinner dances, class reunions, holiday event parties, and wedding receptions.
- Assisted in planning daily menus for elementary schools, convalescent homes, and day care centers.
- Consultant to various companies and businesses planning awards and retirement functions.

••• EMPLOYMENT
The Cranston Country Club/Hinsdale, IL
Hostess and Manager, 1996 - 2000
Managed main dining room and coffee bar. Seated customers, supervised eight waiters and four lunch counter personnel. Responsible for all table and counter set-ups. Hired and trained staff, planned work schedules, and took table reservations.

The Biltmore Hotel/Chicago, IL
Dining Room Hostess, 1992 - 1995
Seated dinner guests. Filled in as assistant dining room manager during assistant manager's vacation. Recorded hotel guests' dinner charges for front desk accounting records. Conducted biyearly inventory of table linens, dinnerware, and silverware. Assisted in recruitment of personnel.

••• EDUCATION
University of Illinois/Chicago, IL
Major: Bachelor of Fine Arts; Degree, 1991
Awards: *Cum laude,* Dean's List, 1990 - 1991

Memberships: Beta Sigma Omicron Social Sorority; offices held:
Recording Secretary, 1983 - 1984,
Vice President, 1984 - 1985
Students for the Appreciation of Fine Arts Association, 1982 - 1985

••• SEMINARS
- Hotel Dining Room Management, Carbondale, IL -- June 1993.
- Dining Table Art, Chicago School of Design, Chicago, IL -- September 1994.
- European Hotel Cuisine, International Cooking School, Chicago, IL -- November 1994.
- Wines Worldwide, Midwest Wine Conference, Chicago, IL -- October 1995.
- Introduction to Computerized Inventories for Food Services, New York, NY -- May 1996.

••• REFERENCES
Available upon request.

marlena comninel

22 South Avon Street
Charleston, South Carolina 29411
Home: (435) 555-2238
Pager: (435) 555-7773

objective
To return to the field of audiology in a major medical center

education
Stanford University, Palo Alto, California -- M.A. Audiology, 1970
Duke University, Durham, North Carolina -- B.A. Psychology, 1968

activities
Lived in Nauplia, Greece; 1991 - 2001
Attended the Center for Social Planning; studied Anthropology and Psychology.
Volunteered at the local church to counsel adults with hearing loss.
Led hiking groups through the Pindus Mountains of Northern Greece.

employment
1970 - 1991
Durham Eye and Ear Hospital, Durham, North Carolina; Audiologist
Provided direct clinical services to patients with communication disorders.
This included testing, evaluation, and treatment.

accomplishments
- Developed and conducted community-based hearing-protection programs.
- Administered community outreach activities.
- Supervised three audiologists and five administrative assistants.
- Counseled individuals and families about hearing disorders.
- Taught behavioral techniques to improve communication.
- Consulted with Fortune 500 companies regarding the development of hearing conservation programs.
- Served as assistant editor of *Hear*, a publication of the Southern California Hearing Council.

associations
American Speech and Hearing Association
American Academy of Audiologists

certification
Certificate of Clinical Competence

references
Available upon request

J. Doyle Baines
200 N. Elm St.
Bedford, MA 01730

Objective:

A position in club management, restaurant management, hotel management, or a related area

Experience:

1999 - 2000 *Club Manager*, U.S. Army.
Rank: Warrant Officer.
Assignment: Officers' Club, Fort Lee, Petersburg, VA

Duties:
Performed a wide range of duties providing day-to-day management of officers' club. Coordinated purchasing and inventory of supplies. Coordinated food and beverage services. Supervised personnel. Achieved high performance ratings.

1996 - 99 *Assistant Club Manager*, Officers' Club, Fort Picket, Blackstone, VA

Duties:
Assisted club manager in all aspects of club management.

1994 - 96 *Waiter*, Twin Oaks Restaurant, 21 Ross Avenue, Bedford, MA 01730

Education:

Associate of Arts Degree, J. S. Reynolds Community College, Richmond, VA.

Additional training through Army courses including communication skills, food and beverage management, cost control systems, and personnel management.

References on request

CARLOS RAMIREZ
529 Venetian Way, Augusta, ME 04330   (207) 555-6053

OBJECTIVE: *To obtain a position in management or finance.*

EDUCATION: *Harvard Graduate School of Business Administration,
                   M.B.A., 2000
                   Columbia University, B.A. Economics, 1995*

COMPUTER
EXPERIENCE: *Programs and Software: WordPerfect and Microsoft Word,
                   Computer-Assisted Design and Drafting, and
                   Statistical Analysis System
                   Hardware: IBM, HP, Dell, Gateway, and Macintosh*

PROFESSIONAL
EXPERIENCE:
1999 - Present   *PITTMAN EQUITIES CORPORATION, Augusta, ME
                   Investment Processor*

*Responsible for operation of personal computer systems, design and preparation of
company sales reports and financial reports, and design of the company's databases using
Personal Decision Series software.*

1995 - 1998   *McCORMICK COMPANY, New York, NY
                   Manager and Director of Investment Services*

*Managed all aspects of a 40-node 3Com 3Plus local-area network, including software
configuration and installation, user maintenance, file maintenance, backup procedures, and
all day-to-day operations. Responsibilities included portfolio analysis and account
management in Investment Services Department.*

AWARDS: *• Harvard University - Baker Scholar
                   • Phi Beta Kappa - 1995*

INTERESTS: *Traveling, waterskiing, and reading.*

REFERENCES: *Available upon request.*

IDA LOPEZ
1740 PALMETTO DRIVE
ORLANDO, FL 32816
(305) 555-1173

OBJECTIVE
To utilize my problem-solving and communication skills in a credit agency that offers management potential.

EDUCATION
University of Central Florida, Orlando, FL
M.B.A. program. 9/00 - present
University of Florida, Gainesville, FL
Major: Accounting 1973

VOLUNTEER EXPERIENCE
10/97 - 7/00
Psychiatric Institute, Orlando, FL
Member of a team that included psychologists and psychiatrists.
• Implemented treatment plans.
• Observed patients and reported meaningful symptomatic behavior to professional staff.
• Engaged in therapeutic activities with patients.
• Influenced patients' treatment by offering emotional support.

EMPLOYMENT EXPERIENCE
Macys, Orlando, FL
Assistant Credit Manager, 11/78 - 2/82
• Assisted in the development and implementation of a credit policy for the store.
• Managed all aspects of store accounts.
• Engaged in collection activities and increased earnings by 48 percent.
• Prepared reports making specific recommendations to management.

Paul Harper Men's Wear, Inc., Orlando, FL
Credit Counselor, 7/73 - 11/78
• Interviewed and counseled customers applying for credit.
• Evaluated income information and made decisions regarding credit lines.
• Investigated credit histories for any discrepancies.

ATTRIBUTES
Willingness to work nights and weekends.
Ability to influence others and achieve desired outcome.

REFERENCES
Furnished upon request.

ALETHA BESSEY
4893 ARLINGTON AVENUE
INDIANAPOLIS, INDIANA 46201
(317) 555-9889
bessey@xxx.com

OBJECTIVE
A position in marketing with a strongly customer-oriented, multinational corporation.

PROFESSIONAL EXPERIENCE

Research Scientist, International Feminine Care, Beverly Jones Corporation, Indianapolis, IN, 1997 - present

- Evaluate, recommend, and develop product changes to meet performance expectation of a new feminine care product for three international regions of this Fortune 500 multinational, consumer products company manufacturing such brand products as Bouncies and Comforts.

- Establish quantitative measures for subjective functional performance evaluations and product comparisons.

- Work closely with international marketing research department in suggesting and implementing improvements to consumer market research questionnaires.

- Design product development plans for market research efforts.

- Obtain medical clearances, coordinate materials, prepare product samples, and schedule equipment and testing.

- Work with U.S. product development group to integrate United States and international program support.

- Provide engineering with product information for equipment designs.

- Participate in regional project update meetings in the United States, Asia, Latin America, and Europe.

- Provide support to process trials in Mexico and Taiwan.

- Prepare reports on product functional tests.

- Participate on Product Development Seminar Committee to define format for company-wide seminar.

Scientist II, Scientist I, Senior Research Technician, Beverly Jones Corporation, Indianapolis, IN, 1987 - 1997

- Accountable for all aspects of product development for industrial wipers and washroom towels.

- Successfully developed new washroom hand towel product that out-performed market leader and returned twice the initial sales projections.

(PROFESSIONAL EXPERIENCE cont.)

Scientist II, Scientist I, Senior Research Technician, Beverly Jones Corporation Indianapolis, IN (Cont.)

- Developed new market research techniques to define consumer language in describing products; translated and interpreted terminology for quantitative measures.
- Developed and validated mathematical model for determining user preference from physical test data.
- Developed several line extension products and implemented cost-saving technologies for existing products.
- Member of multifunctional business team; assisted in defining market needs, designing products to meet cost requirements, verifying advertising claims, providing technical sales support, and implementing product roll-outs.
- Managed project budgets and established project objectives.
- Analyzed and resolved customer complaints regarding product performance; conducted one-on-one customer interviews and site visits.
- Provided process and product support for start-up of a new converting mill.
- Advised manufacturing personnel in conversion operations to ensure product quality and specifications; assisted in trouble-shooting efforts.
- Wrote product specifications for manufacturing guidelines and worked with Quality Assurance for test methods and quality procedures.
- Consulted with packaging specialists to define packaging specifications.

Quality Assurance Superintendent, Techmill, Inc., Youngstown, OH, 1981 - 1987

- Organized and managed fifteen-person quality department for a new nonwoven cloth manufacturing plant.
- Implemented corporate quality programs.
- Trained personnel and implemented statistical process control systems throughout the plant.
- Wrote and implemented a GMP manual for Class III medical device.

EDUCATION
M.B.A., Kennesaw State College, Kennesaw, GA, 1981
B.S., Mathematics/Engineering, University of Minnesota, Crookston, MN, 1979

REFERENCES AVAILABLE UPON REQUEST

Nancy Mantello

6 Horizon Road
Whindham, Ohio 44288
216-555-9361

Related Experience

<u>Treasurer, Board of Directors, Horizon House, Whindham, Ohio</u>
1994 - present
- Conserved $80,000 on air-conditioning cooling towers
- Arranged a 15-year warranty on building's roof
- Brought about the reduction of $2,000,000 escrow mortgage currency
- Reviewed and changed the specifications of the contract award for fire-doors
- Produced substantial savings in the employees' health insurance package
- Promoted positive action on the lighting in Riverbank Park, as a consequence of an excellent relationship with the mayor and town council members

Work History

<u>Office Manager, Land O' Lakes, Inc., Kent, Ohio</u>
1978 - 1993
- Supervised a clerical staff of 17
- Prepared quarterly and annual reports, tax returns, payroll, and warehouse stock replenishment statistics
- Directed computerized stock reconciliation and rotation processes
- Conducted cash flow, securities analysis, and project feasibility studies
- Prepared and directed yearly management seminars
- Received several promotions after starting at the company as a clerk

<u>Clerk, Giant Eagle, Inc., Warren, Ohio</u>
1969 - 1978
- Supervised and controlled large amounts of cash flow
- Maintained weekly ledgers
- Computed figures with speed and accuracy
- Maintained activity in customer accounts

Education

Youngstown State University, Youngstown, Ohio
Courses included Accounting, Business, Typing, and Dictation

References on request

MOHAMED BEHARI
11805 Boxwood Drive
Costa Mesa, California 92626
(714) 555-4160 (Phone)
(714) 555-4808 (Fax)
(714) 555-8764 (Cellular/Voice Mail)

CAREER GOAL

A rewarding position in dental technology

PROFESSIONAL BACKGROUND

Dental Laboratory Technologist, United States Navy.
Date of Service: September 1997 - January 2003

Duties: Performed comprehensive duties related to dental fabrication including
the following:

- Fabricated basic dental prosthetic devices
- Made complete dentures, removable partial dentures, and fixed partial dentures
- Assisted in dental laboratory management
- Maintained inventory of equipment and supplies
- Completed administrative reports
- Implemented and coordinated quality control measures

EDUCATION/ TRAINING

- Graduate, U.S. Navy School of Dental Assisting and Technology, San Diego,
  California, 1998.
- Additional U.S. Navy courses completed in personnel management.
- Secondary School Diploma, The Carson School, Los Angeles, California, June 1997.

REFERENCES

Provided on request

MARGARET HALVORSEN
154 Shoreline Drive
Chicago, IL 60611
(312) 555-1707 home or (312) 555-3602 office

OBJECTIVE

TECHNICAL WRITING AND EDITORIAL MANAGEMENT

HIGHLIGHTS OF QUALIFICATIONS

- Researched and wrote science biographies for technical reference books.

- Developed and wrote employee training manuals, catalogs, and brochures, advertising copy, and press materials for retail businesses.

- Wrote and edited a broad range of grant proposals for technical and lay audiences.

- Developed, wrote, and designed public relations and fundraising materials.

- Strong background in word processing, desktop publishing, and graphics software on Macintosh and IBM computer platforms.

WORK EXPERIENCE

Director, Corporate & Foundation Relations, University of Chicago Office of Development, Chicago, IL, 1995 - present

Grant Writer, Fundraising & Development Office, University of Chicago Press, Chicago, IL, 1990 - 1995

Promotions Manager and Events Coordinator, Pattersen's Books, Chicago, IL, 1980 - 1985

EDUCATION

Columbia University, B.A. with Distinction, Phi Beta Kappa, English with Creative Writing Emphasis, 1980.

Additional coursework included microbiology, chemistry, calculus, geology, statistics, and computer science.

WRITING PORTFOLIO AND REFERENCES AVAILABLE

Guideon Sol

Present address	**Permanent address**
56 Emek Refaim	*2192 Beverly Rd.*
2192 Jerusalem, Israel	*Springfield, MA 01109*
0019722 555-823	*413-555-9974*

Objective

To work for the United Nations as a translator

Education

Fulbright scholarship to study Hebrew literature and religion 1998 - 2000,
University of Jerusalem
M.A. Hebrew and Theology, 2000, Exchange Program, Boston University,
Division of Religious and Theological Studies, Boston, MA
B.A. French, 1993, Universite Laval, Sainte-Foy, Quebec, Canada,
Summa Cum Laude

Languages

French, Hebrew, Patois, Spanish, Portuguese

Employment History

1995 - 1998 University of Quebec at Montreal, ESL Instructor
1993 - 1995 Lycee A. Petion, Port-Au-Prince, Haiti, ESL Instructor

Created ESL Program. Designed and developed a challenging curricula that included grammar, vocabulary, and reading. Taught advanced courses in American Literature. Instructed beginning, intermediate, and advanced conversational English courses. Designed survey instruments to ascertain student's experiences, expectations, and difficulties with English. Counseled students about scholarships and study in America. Coordinated student activities. Facilitated a cross-cultural group that met weekly. Sponsored several cross-cultural programs.

Achievements

Offered full-time tenure position at the Universite Laval
Recipient of Fulbright Scholarship

Strengths

Ability to work with diverse populations.
Excellent language and communication skills.
Significant teaching ability with various student groups.
Ability and strong interest in assisting others.

Eugene Louie

1254 N. 11th Street
Beaumont, Texas 77702
Cellular: (409) 555-8345

OBJECTIVE

To offer my expertise in business matters on a consulting basis

1994 - present
Business consultant -- VOLUNTEER RETIRED EXECUTIVES
Beaumont, Texas

SELECTED ACCOMPLISHMENTS

- Cofounded Global Plastics Corporation 1950
- Traded in raw materials and machinery
- Instrumental in expanding operations into Central and South America
- Formed affiliates in 1960
- Induced Board of Directors to expand into Australia and Canada
- Sold Company in 1970 for $30 million
- Acquired Inter-Ocean Plastics 1971
- Increased stock buyback to 12.5 million shares
- Focused on core strengths and took an $86 million charge against earnings for costs relating to downsizing
- Restructured and sold off certain manufacturing operations producing an annual savings of $7 million
- Founded and chaired Plastics Association of America (a Washington trade group)

MEMBERSHIPS

National Businessmen's Association

REFERENCES

Available on request

Michael Bleznakov
509 King Street
Evansdale, IN 47713
(812) 555-3618

Education

Bachelor of Arts, University of Kentucky, 1982.
Major: English Literature
Minor: Russian

Professional Experience

Intelligence Analyst for United States Army, 1992–2003.
Interrogator, United States Army, 1983–1992.
Rank: Major

• Performed a wide range of duties requiring strong organizational skills, analytical thinking, and persistence.

• Assembled, integrated, analyzed, and disseminated intelligence information.

• Handled and analyzed information collected from technical, strategic, and tactical sources.

• Supervised receipt, analysis, and storage of intelligence information.

• Compiled, edited, and disseminated intelligence reports.

• Assisted in providing general intelligence training programs.

• Supervised various personnel including interrogators.

Special Interests

Fluent in Russian language.
Highly interested in Eastern European affairs.
Willing to travel.

References and military record available on request.

STUART DAVID MARKS

66-B West 45th Street, Wilmington, Delaware 19835   (302) 555-8223

PROFESSIONAL OBJECTIVE

To bring my extensive experience as a certified accountant into the administration of a large metropolitan art museum.

EDUCATION

University of Chicago   M.B.A., 1983
Emphasis: Finance/Accounting
Illinois State University   B.S., 1978
Emphasis: Accounting

WORK EXPERIENCE

Corporate Accounting Manager, Bowles and Sharp, C.P.A., 1987 to present

- Direct staff of 27 certified public accountants and 15 support staff.
- Responsible for all corporate accounts, valued at more than $7.5 billion.
- Serve as liaison between accounting department and corporate CEOs.
- Reduced losses through implementation of cost accounting controls for two major corporate clients.
- Supervise corporate audits and hold final responsibility for federal and state reporting.
- Develop and maintain strategic corporate plans and accounting division budgets.

Certified Public Accountant, Truant Michaels & Associates, Inc., 1983 to 1987

- Handled ongoing accounting and reporting for 27 corporate clients.
- Prepared corporate and individual federal income tax reports.
- Audited corporate and public organization finances.
- Prepared financial statements for credit reporting and bank financing.

MEMBERSHIPS

Certified Public Accountants of Delaware
National Association of Certified Public Accountants

REFERENCES

Available upon request

NINA MAZZOLA

2017 Menaul N.E.
Albuquerque, New Mexico
(505) 555-9804
Mazzola@xxx.com

OBJECTIVE   A position in International Relations in a Western European Agency

EDUCATION   University of Oregon, Eugene, Oregon
B.A. International Relations, *cum laude*, 1982

SKILLS/ACCOMPLISHMENTS
- Fluent in Spanish and Italian
- Service-oriented, tactful, benevolent
- Work independently, under pressure, flexible hours
- Certified in CPR
- Negotiated innovative work rules with airline executives
- Secured the release of innocent prisoners in New Mexico
- Received four Superior Service awards
- Worked in Spain, assisting foreigners in emergency situations and obtaining legal counsel for them
- Resolved complex cases of consular policy
- Settled disputes with special interest groups
- Developed a public relations campaign and achieved unprecedented working relationships with government employees
- Won support for U.S. foreign policy initiatives

WORK HISTORY
1994 - present
VOLUNTEER, Centurion Ministries, Albuquerque, New Mexico
This prison advocacy group investigates claims of innocence and works for the release of prisoners it finds credible.

1983 - 1994
FOREIGN SERVICE OFFICER, Department of State
Consular officer, 1983 - 1992
Political officer, 1992 - 1994

1982 - 1983
STUDENT, Foreign Service Institute

1975 - 1978
FLIGHT ATTENDANT, Delta Airlines

REFERENCES AVAILABLE UPON REQUEST

Yetta Lewin

3122 High Road
Warwick, Rhode Island 0288
(401) 555-7766
Yetta_Lewin@xxx.com

Education

J.D., Harvard Law School, 1998
Graduated top 10%

B.A. History, Harvard University, 1995
G.P.A. 3.8

Skills

Raised four children.
- Developed tolerance, patience, and negotiating skills.
- Learned to develop strategies to achieve goals.
- Exercised sound judgment in all areas of child rearing.
- Developed useful time-management skills.

As wife to the city comptroller, I accomplished the following:
- Created a foundation that funded three arts centers for the handicapped.
- Established a volunteer theater program in Warwick General Hospital.
- Gained financial assistance for breast cancer support organization.
- Founded the Warwick, RI division of The Breast Cancer Coalition.
- Organized funding activities for the Coalition.
- Instituted a yearly walk-a-thon for the Susan G. Komen Breast Cancer Foundation.

Registration

Member of the Bar Association. Licensed to practice in Rhode Island and Massachusetts.

References are enclosed

William K. Brown
615 Cardinal Drive, Fergus Falls, MN 56537
(218) 555-0464 (voice)
(218) 555-1855 (fax)

Career Objective

A position in surveying or topographic engineering.

Related Skills and Experience

- Highly skilled topographic surveyor with fifteen years' experience in the United States Army.
- Achieved advanced skill level through extensive field experience and Army training courses.
- Thoroughly familiar with the most effective contemporary surveying methods, including use of various types of surveying equipment.

Work Background

As Army topographic surveyor, performed tasks such as the following:

- Recorded topographic survey data
- Operated a variety of survey instruments
- Performed topographic and geodetic computations
- Interpreted maps and aerial photographs
- Performed a wide range of computations including horizontal differences, angular closures, and triangulations
- Supervised other workers including topographic instrument repair specialists
- Supervised programming of electronic calculators
- Prepared technical and personnel reports

Training/Education

Completed military training in mathematics, surveying, engineering computations, technical writing, optics, data processing, and related areas.

References Available on Request

Sarah Louise Hill
865 Woodside Drive
Chattanooga, TN 37403
(615) 555-0469

PROFESSIONAL OBJECTIVE:

To gain a position as a marketing representative with possibility of advancement into management position.

EDUCATION:

UNIVERSITY OF TENNESSEE
Chattanooga, TN
B.S., Business Administration, anticipated May 2002

EXPERIENCE:

Summers 2000, 2001

UNION PLANTERS CORPORATION OF AMERICA
Nashville, TN
Sales Representative: Responsible for service and sales in the Nashville area. Increased sales by 5 percent each summer. Awarded the 1999 Murphy's Trophy for achieving sales expectancy in every product line.

Summer 1999

HEALTHTRUST
Nashville, TN
Sales Representative: Achieved 150 percent expected quota for June to August calling on business and industrial accounts in Tennessee. Ranked #1 out of 12 salespeople.

Summer 1998

A & P SUPERMARKET
Nashville, TN
Cashier

COMPUTER EXPERIENCE:

Word, Access, Excel

HOBBIES AND INTERESTS:

Golf, softball, family activities, travel, volunteer work

REFERENCES:

References will be provided upon request.

Willing to relocate.

YOSHIDO UMEKI   9783 Ridgeway Drive, Evanston, IL 60204   (847) 555-2983

OBJECTIVE

A position as Publicist for a Midwest corporation

SUMMARY OF QUALIFICATIONS

- Excellent public relations skills
- Experienced and published writer
- Accustomed to working on deadline
- Flexible and hardworking
- Knowledgeable about local government, business, and community

HISTORY OF EMPLOYMENT

News Reporter, *Chicago Tribune*, 1995 - present

Specialize in local news. Complete assignments and research leads for newsworthy stories. Interview local government officials, corporate officers, community activists, and business owners. Developed the series "On Your Block" for the weekend edition, featuring various local communities. Developed a five-part story exploring community relations of Illinois corporate businesses.

Education Reporter, *Honolulu Star Bulletin*, 1989 - 1995

Started as a proofreader, within a year had written several feature stories, and within two years obtained responsibility for reporting and researching all education news.

SELECTED LIST OF PUBLICATIONS

- *Hadley and Hadley's Scramble for Community Support*
- *Community Coalition: A Homegrown Response to Woes*
- *Volunteerism: A Way of Life at Wright Brothers*
- *Hawaii's Schools: Rebuilding Promises*
- *Amelia Hunani: A New Breed of Administrator*
- *Tea and Crumpets in the Southeast District*
- *Evanston's Four-story Community: A Look at North Broadway*
- *WESTAR's Model Community Enrichment Program*

EDUCATION

Bachelor of Arts, Journalism and Government, University of Hawaii at Manoa, Honolulu

REFERENCES AND PUBLICATION PORTFOLIO ON REQUEST

HAROLD OVERBAND

1009 Buck Drive
Huntsville, Alabama 35804

Home: (205) 555-3928
Cellular: (205) 555-0091

GOAL
To return to a challenging career in sales and marketing.

EDUCATION
M.B.A. Columbia University, New York, NY, 1972
B.A. Business Administration, University of Alabama at Birmingham, 1970

VOLUNTEER EXPERIENCE
1991 - 1998
Dean Ornish Program, New York, NY
*After retiring due to illness, I successfully completed Dr. Ornish's program
and trained to help others. I taught classes in meditation, nutrition, and food
preparation.*
- Ameliorated the need for surgery for most people attending the course.
- Introduced new concepts that became part of the coursework and were presented
  in Dr. Ornish's new book.
- Reversed my condition to one of perfect health.

WORK EXPERIENCE
1988 - 1991
BRUER ENVELOPE CO., Huntsville, Alabama, Sales and Marketing Manager
- Initiated an aggressive sales campaign and new marketing strategies.
- Contracted 35 new corporate accounts.
- Increased sales from $195,000 to $275,000 over a five-year period.
- Introduced an innovative customer service unit.
- Altered company image by stressing quality products.

1972 - 1988
SAMSONITE LUGGAGE, Birmingham, Alabama, Sales Manager
- Supervised 20 regional salesmen and women.
- Established a novel training program that stimulated sales personnel to generate
  55 percent increase in business after the first year of its inception.
- Increased new accounts with dealers and distributors to more than 100.
- Surveyed needs of customers and developed successful pricing strategies.

MEMBER of the International Sales and Marketing Executive Committee

References available on request

Jay Vasquez

290 Hollywood Boulevard
Los Angeles, California 90063
(213) 555-1226

Career Objective

A position in security in a company that will profit from my extensive experience in law enforcement.

Career History

Twenty-five years experience in police work. Moved up the ranks to detective after only four years on the force.

Skills and Accomplishments

- Conflict resolution skills.
- Worked with disadvantaged youth in South Central High Schools.
- Excellent social and communication skills that enabled me to ease tensions and promote verbal interchange.
- Ability to supervise and educate.
- Received several mayoral, community, and distinguished service awards.
- Sharpshooter.

Experience

1986 - 1999:   Youth Officer, George Washington High School, Los Angeles, CA
               Martin Luther King High School, Los Angeles, CA
1981 - 1986:   Special Agent, U.S. Drug Enforcement Administration
1978 - 1981:   Homicide Detective, 12th precinct, Los Angeles, CA
1974 - 1978:   Patrolman, 12th precinct, Los Angeles, CA

Education

FBI Academy, Quantico, VA. Specialized training in drug enforcement
B.A. Psychology, University of Los Angeles, Los Angeles, CA, 1976

References available on request

LANE TYLER
1892 Red River Road   **Toledo, Ohio 43601**   **(419) 555-2078**

Objective   A position as Instructor of Business and Marketing

Education

M.B.A., 1997, Ohio University, Athens
B.A., 1974, State University of New York at Buffalo

Experience

1993 - present   *Director of Marketing, Business Unit Leader, Foodservice, Pillar Paper Company, Toledo, Ohio*

Responsibilities: Strategic and marketing leadership with profit and loss accountability for a $310 million commercial foodservice business. Develop a competitively advantaged business by providing distinctive marketing, products, and services that support customer and operator needs. Direct development of environmental strategies for paper products. Provide manufacturing with objectives and standards for raw material, sourcing, quality improvement, and cost reduction. Lead business planning process.

Accomplishments: Increased division earnings by 17 percent in 1994. Initiated a new products development program. Introduced operator-focused marketing programs to pull product through distribution.

1991 - 1993   *Senior Marketing Manager, Commercial Products Division, Pillar Paper Company, Toledo, Ohio*

Responsibilities: Led development and marketing of new high performance products and systems for towels and soaps. Developed and led a foodservice venture for the Commercial Products Division. Managed integration efforts with the Foodservice Corporation. With sales management, developed target market strategies.

Accomplishments: Led development and marketing of a new towel brand which contributed over $1 million in new earnings within eighteen months. The foodservice venture generated $2 million incremental earnings in 1993. Awarded one of three Business Excellence awards for my contributions in 1992 - 1993.

1989 - 1991   *Senior Marketing Manager, Foodservice Division, Pillar Paper Company, Toledo, Ohio*

Responsibilities: Directed marketing and development for 650 foodservice products. Developed foodservice strategies that aligned with commercial towel and tissue business objectives. Directed Marketing Communications programs.

Experience (cont.)

Accomplishments: Improved Specialty Products earnings by 10 percent in 1989 and 1990 with a balance of marketing programs and price guideline development.

1986 - 1989   ***Director of Marketing and Sales, American Convenience, Inc., Toledo, Ohio***

Responsibilities: Reported to the president and directed all sales and marketing functions, with accountability for continuous earnings and improvement. Responsible for product and program development, advertising, customer service, and a twenty-five person sales staff.

Accomplishments: Initiated a national accounts program. Introduced American's first sales incentive program which helped drive a 12 percent increase in sales and profits in the first year.

1981 - 1986   ***Group Products Manager, American Convenience, Inc., Toledo, Ohio***

Responsibilities: Accountable for management of all product lines toward profitable growth. Managed promotion, product design, advertising, forecasting, and pricing. Planned all national and regional trade show representation.

Accomplishments: Led development of Spectrum Colors promotional program, which significantly altered the way the industry markets color napkins.

1975 - 1981   ***Branch Sales Manager, Time-Life Books, Pittsburgh, Pennsylvania***

Responsibilities: Staffed, organized, and managed the first branch sales office in the Eastern U.S. Developed and managed testing for retail distribution of our products.

Accomplishments: Developed sales training manual for all branches. Initiated WATS line concept of national selling and reduction of sales costs.

References Provided on Request

Mia Merriweather

20 Cedar Pines Lane
Logan, Utah 84322
(801) 555-2956

• OBJECTIVE

To return to a challenging position as a music therapist.

• EDUCATION

Utah State, Logan, Utah
Bachelor of Science Degree in Recreation Therapy 1987

• VOLUNTEER EXPERIENCE

1996 - present
- Assisted in the affairs of the *Navajo Economic Opportunity Bureau.*
- Established a local community development program.
- Designed projects to improve housing conditions and availability.
- Developed strategies and campaigned to increase funding for medical care and educational facilities.
- Lobbied and achieved funding for a community-based alcoholism treatment program.
- Worked directly with Navajo youth, enrolling them in counseling and job training programs.
- Promoted a successful food drive for the Navajo community.

• PROFESSIONAL EXPERIENCE

Salt Lake Rehabilitation Center, Salt Lake City, Utah
Recreational Therapist, 1987 - 1996
- Sought to reverse the negative effects of disabilities by building self-esteem through various activities
- Developed individual treatment plans.
- Organized and coordinated a yearly arts fair in which all clients participated.
- Presented four plays a year in the community theater. Acting and backstage activities conducted solely by our clients.
- Supervised three recreational therapists in charge of scheduling board game and sports events.
- Supervised two therapists who managed the leisure activities program.
- Encouraged family members to participate in treatment.
- Received Mayor's Award for Achievement in the area of Community Service, 1990 and 1991.

References available on request

YOLANDA WILLIAMS

152 Alexandria Street, Apt. 3W
Washington, DC 20013
Home: (202) 555-9897
Pager: (202) 555-3363

OBJECTIVE
A part-time nursing position to assist a physician in private practice

EDUCATION
BSN, University of Richmond, Richmond, Virginia 1952
Post-RN training program for nurse midwives, District of Columbia
General Hospital, Washington, DC 1974

SUMMARY OF QUALIFICATIONS
Forty years experience in nursing care.
Duties included:
- Assessment and development of treatment plans.
- Participation in the patients' convalescence and rehabilitation.
- Provision of health maintenance, nutritional information, and care for pregnant women.
- Evaluation of the progress of labor.
- Routine labor and deliveries.
- Teaching courses in Lamaze.
- Provision of continuous post-operative pain-management procedures.

ACCOMPLISHMENTS
- Established Lamaze classes at District of Columbia General Hospital.
- Supervised a staff of 7 RNs, 4 LANs, and 10 nursing aids.
- Developed, implemented, and managed convalescence and rehabilitation programs in Richmond Community Hospital that resulted in a 35 percent increase in government and private funding.

EMPLOYMENT
District of Columbia General Hospital, Washington, DC 2/74 - 7/93
Retired in 1993 and traveled extensively throughout Europe
Richmond Community Hospital, Richmond, Virginia, 8/52 - 2/74

References are enclosed

LINDA T. COMBS

Public Relations Specialist
1906 First Street
Coast Mesa Beach, California 92626
(714) 555-3408

SUMMARY OF QUALIFICATIONS

- Energetic, articulate pubic relations professional.
- Skilled in all aspects of writing, designing, editing, and producing publications. Experienced in writing news releases, print ads, newsletters, and other material.

ACHIEVEMENTS

- Developed award-winning series of publications on career opportunities offered by U.S. Coast Guard (Gold Medal Award, California Public Relations Society).
- Completed writing, design, and layout for more than 100 Coast Guard publications.
- Initiated expanded community relations program designed to foster good relations with area businesses and civilian population.
- Designed and wrote newsletter for district personnel and their families.
- Received "Outstanding Communicator Award" from Long Beach Chamber of Commerce.

WORK HISTORY

1997–2002   **Public Affairs Officer**, United States Coast Guard,
            Fifth Coast Guard District, Long Beach, California

- Performed a wide range of duties related to pubic information/public relations. Wrote and designed brochures and other publications.
- Wrote news releases, ads, scripts, and other informational materials.
- Assisted in planning and implementing public relations/public information campaigns.

1995–1997   **Advertising Representative,** K & B Media,
            Long Beach, California

L. T. Combs—page 1 of 2

EDUCATION

B.S., California State University–Long Beach, 1999
Major: Public Relations
Minor: Journalism
GPA: 4.0 in major; 3.83 overall

A.S., Compton Community College, Compton, California, 1995

MEMBERSHIPS

Public Relations Society of America
California Public Relations Society

ELLEN WHITTMAN

145 W. BROAD STREET • CONCORD, NEW HAMPSHIRE 03301 • CELLULAR: (603) 555-7683

OBJECTIVE

Senior position in financial management and analysis

ACCOMPLISHMENTS

American Cancer Society, volunteer
- Counseled women with breast cancer on treatment options, clinical trials, and cancer-related services in local areas
- Organized fund-raising activities that resulted in an increase of 2.3 million dollars for breast cancer research
- Lobbied to expand political action on women's health issues
- Facilitated a group for cancer survivors to support adjusting to life following cancer treatment
- Presented workshops on financial planning

PROFESSIONAL FINANCIAL MANAGEMENT EXPERIENCE

- Developed information systems to assess the present and future financial requirements of the firm
- Supervised 50 professional accountants and support personnel
- Expanded financial and economic policies that increased profits by 30 percent
- Established procedures to implement those policies
- Monitored and controlled the flow of cash receipts, disbursements, and financial instruments

EMPLOYMENT SUMMARY

Taylor Financial Group -- Concord, NH (1985 - 1998)
Amco Corporation -- Concord, NH (1978 - 1985)

EDUCATION

University of New Hampshire
M.A., Accounting, 1977
B.A., Accounting, 1976

REFERENCES

Available upon request

IRA SCHWARTZ

212 West 13th Street
New York, NY 10011
(212) 555-9998

OBJECTIVE

To obtain a position in construction engineering.

EDUCATION

New York University, New York, NY
M.S., Civil Engineering, 1990

Hunter College, City University of NY
B.S., Civil Engineering, 1989

SPECIAL SKILLS

International Chess Master
• Won major chess tournaments
• New York Open -- 1993, 1994
• World Open -- 1991, 1993, 1994
• Albany Open -- 1991

Taught chess classes in three NYC elementary schools.
Sponsored by the PTA (1993-1994).
Captain - Hunter College Chess Team
• Coached team members
• Organized tournaments including travel
• Promoted the team via simultaneous exhibitions throughout the city

ENGINEERING EXPERIENCE

6/90 - 6/91   New York Department of Transportation, Albany, NY
Assistant Engineer
• Inspected the construction of reinforced concrete bridges and roadways
• Provided recommendations to contractors that were implemented
• Assisted in the design of roadways and associated structures
• Responsible for hydrologic aspects of highway design

REGISTRATION

Certified Engineer in Training, 1991

AFFILIATIONS

American Society of Civil Engineers
U.S. Chess Federation

References available on request.

KEVIN FOXWORTH
2114 Renton Street   Kirkland, Washington 98005   (206) 555-3497

CAREER OBJECTIVE   Engineering position with industrial manufacturing company.

CAPABILITIES

- Manage continuous fire furnaces that produce flat pressed glass and glass for machine and hand blowing.
- Plan and supervise all aspects of furnace operation and maintenance, including personnel scheduling and staffing.
- Evaluate alternative production methods and materials to reduce costs and improve product quality.
- Control raw materials inventory, ordering, and inspection.
- Train employees in use and maintenance of equipment.
- Review product availability and equipment developments to keep systems up-to-date for both production and safety concerns.
- Plan, coordinate, and supervise all aspects of glassware production.

ACHIEVEMENTS

- Initiated improved method for raw materials handling that resulted in $250,000 in actual savings.
- Worked with production engineers to develop new heating procedures that made furnaces 20 percent more efficient in start-up time.
- Developed operating procedures that improved worker safety.
- Designed alternative casting that reduced external temperatures dramatically, thus decreasing fire and burn hazard.
- Given Award of Merit for developing material composition that produced greater clarity in present glass products.

WORK HISTORY

1985 - present	Pihuck GlassWorks Factory, Kirkland, Washington
	Furnace/Production Manager
1974 - 1985	Boeing, Renton, Washington
	Senior Technician, Instrumentation Casing Section

EDUCATION

1998	B.S., Engineering, University of Washington
1973	A.A., Technology and Industry Production, Everett Community College, Everett, Washington

REFERENCES   Available when requested

KELLY JOHNSON
546 Balstrode Way
Des Moines, IA 50312
(515) 555-2376

OBJECTIVE:

To obtain a position working in either a restaurant or a drugstore.

EDUCATION:

St. John's High School, 2002
GPA 4.00/4.00
My future educational plans are to attend a four-year state college.

COURSE WORK:

Calculus, Keyboarding, Introduction to Business, and Spanish.

AFFILIATIONS:

Girls High School Swim Team
Interact – A community service club
    Area Representative - Senior
    Vice President - Junior
    Community Commissioner - Sophomore
    Secretary - Freshman

WORK EXPERIENCE:

4/01 - present	**Round Table Pizza.** Cook and Waitress. Assembling pizzas, serving customers and taking their orders, answering phones, and cleaning the restaurant.
6/00 - 8/00	**Prairie Landscapes.** Receptionist. Responsible for answering phones and typing memos.
Weekends	**Baby-sitting**

OTHER EXPERIENCE: Studied Spanish for five years.

OUTSIDE INTERESTS: Reading, playing the piano, and swimming.

REFERENCES: Available upon request.

MARK NUSSBAUM

153 Main Street   Home: (718) 555-5411
Flushing, NY 11367   Pager: (718) 555-7990

CAREER OBJECTIVE: *To secure employment as a travel consultant in an agency*
                          that offers advancement opportunities.

ACTIVITIES: Homemaker
                          Dec. 1994 - present
                          Five years experience raising triplets.
                          • Organized and managed daily routines.
                          • Scheduled educational and play activities.
                          • Prepared meals.
                          • Studied numerous psychology books.
                          • Developed patience, insight, and understanding.

EMPLOYMENT HISTORY: Travel Consultant
                          Aug. 1992 - Dec. 1994
                          F.L.Y. Travel Agency, New York, NY
                          • Arranged conventions for major corporations.
                          • Organized entertainment and recreational activities.
                          • Planned sightseeing trips.
                          • Negotiated with hotels for group room and meal rates.
                          • Prepared efficient and economical business travel
                            plans.

                          Reservation Specialist
                          July 1985 - Aug. 1992
                          TWA Airlines, Peoria, IL
                          • Handled customer requests using World Span
                            computer system.
                          • Arranged hotel and car rental accommodations.
                          • Computed fares.
                          • Resolved disputes.

EDUCATION: B.A. Psychology, Rockford College, 1985

FOREIGN LANGUAGES: Hebrew, French

REFERENCES: *Available on request.*

KATHLEEN McCORNICK

124 Bay Drive • Chicago, IL 60641

(312) 555-7622 • K_McCornick@xxx.com

OBJECTIVE

To obtain a position as a Public Relations Specialist in order to apply my knowledge of promotional and fundraising activities.

RELEVANT EXPERIENCE

Volunteer
The Church of Saint Anthony, 1992 - 1999
Prepared and promoted annual church functions.
Organized recruitment program.
Trained and directed volunteers.
Evaluated annual reports and income statements.
Directed fundraising activities that increased income by 40 percent.

Public Relations Executive
Ruder Finn and Rotman, Inc., Chicago, IL, 1987 - 1992
Drafted budgets and projects for numerous corporations.
Publicized major events.
Developed promotional strategies to support specific marketing objectives.

EDUCATION

B.A., Journalism, 1986
Graduate courses in Public Relations
University of Illinois at Urbana/Champaign

ASSOCIATIONS

The Public Relations Society of America

References available on request.

Edward Hanover

396 Colorado Avenue • Idaho Falls, Idaho 83402 • Cellular: (208) 555-6744

OBJECTIVE

To offer my expertise in advertising to a large agency on the West Coast

VOLUNTEER EXPERIENCE

EARTHWATCH, 2000 - 2001
EASTERN CARPATHIANS BIOSPHERE, POLAND

- Accompanied Drs. Karlsen, Vasquez, and Phillips
- Hiked up to 10 kilometers/day
- Observed and tracked large mammals with radio telemetry
- Captured deer and large predators
- Analyzed brown-bear habitat
- Collected vegetation data

BELIZE'S BARRIER REEF
TOBACCO CAVE, BELIZE

- Accompanied Dr. Y. Schwartz
- Studied how reef communities function and maintain species diversity
- Analyzed habitats and conducted visual fish surveys
- Used scuba equipment to lay down transects to census certain fish and quantify plants
- Monitored coral recruitment and growth rates

EXPERIENCE IN ADVERTISING

MCINTIRE, JAMISON ADVERTISING AGENCY, 1986 - 1998
BOISE, IDAHO
EXECUTIVE CREATIVE DIRECTOR

- Enlivened and energized the creative culture of the agency
- Created a distinct identity to overhaul all aspects of operations
- Revamped strategic planning
- Increased revenue from $710 million to $960 million
- Supervised work on accounts of blue-chip clients that included Black and Decker, Nabisco, Ivory soap, Campbell's, and 7-Eleven
- Tutored executive ranks on using new state-of-the-art computer programming technology

EDUCATION

YALE UNIVERSITY, NEW HAVEN, CT -- MBA 1986
UNIVERSITY OF CALIFORNIA, BERKELEY -- BA BUSINESS 1984
Graduated *cum laude*

KENDRA MACON
444 WEST DIVISION STREET
LAKE MARY, FL 32746
305-555-9032 (HOME)
305-555-6743 (CELLULAR)
kendra2@xxx.com

Objective

Position with local printing press as assistant to warehouse manager, or similar position where I can be a productive liaison between the warehouse and management.

Summary

- 4 years' experience in military press warehouse
- Hardworking, loyal, ambitious, eager to learn
- Able to view problems in a positive way and propose solutions
- Interested in streamlining operations and improving conditions
- Excellent working relations with warehouse staff
- Experienced liaison between workers and management
- Established uniform quantity of books per box at Hilltop, allowing for efficient stacking and shipping, more accurate inventory, and less damage to books
- Installed computer terminal at warehouse for immediate update of inventory

Education

B.A., Liberal Arts, Florida State University, Tallahassee, FL, 1992

Employment History

1996–2000	**U.S. Navy,** received several promotions in rank
1994–1996	**Warehouseman,** Hilltop Press, Cocoa Beach, FL
1992–1994	**Assistant Foreman,** Datalink Computer, Moro, FL

References, including complete military records, are available upon request

TINA JONES

31 Bay Drive • Chicago, IL 60641 • (312) 555-6655

EXPERIENCE

8/95 - 5/00
Dwight Correctional Center, Dwight, IL
Pattern Maker

- Received training in fine tailoring and alterations.
- Developed expertise in pattern cutting and design.
- Created a line of women's wear retailed by three major stores
  in Dwight, IL.

9/92 - 6/95
Bay Drive High School student

EDUCATION

Correspondence courses in Liberal Arts
Dwight Community College
GED, 1998

SKILLS

- Organized and co-led self-help group.
- Wrote and published inmate newspaper.
- Trained and supervised five inmates in reporting, editing,
  and layout.

INTERESTS

Member of the DCC Choir

References enclosed

LUCILLE SIRIOS
392 Alturn Drive, Geneva, Illinois 60134
Home (815) 555-8372/Work (312) 555-3846

OBJECTIVE

Advertising staff of a major international publishing house. Particularly interested in a position that will utilize my written and verbal fluency in German.

PROFESSIONAL EXPERIENCE

Berlin American, Chicago, IL, Manager and Buyer, 1993 - present

- Develop, produce and implement direct main and newspaper advertising campaigns that have directly contributed to a 45% sales growth over four years.
- Buy and merchandise German textile and ceramic handcrafted items.
- Maintain financial control of $375,000 annual sales volume.
- Translate business-related documents, German/English and English/German.

Books, Etc., Bookstore, Minneapolis, MN, Manager/Regional Planner, 1989 - 1993

- Responsible for effective visual presentation for three area stores.
- Trained and supervised ten employees.
- Controlled inventory and financial planning of $300,000 annual sales volume.

La France, Edina, MN, Counter Manager, 1985 - 1989

- Supervised staff of twelve waiters.
- Supervised food preparation and distribution.
- Integrated daily cash receipts into restaurant financial budget.
- Wrote and engineered news programming and public service announcements.

EDUCATION

St. John's University, Collegeville, MN

Bachelor of Arts in Government and German, awarded June 1989

Institutes for American Universities, Berlin, Germany

German language coursework, 1993

References Available

JOEL S. COHEN

112 Anderson Avenue
Cliffside Park, NJ 07010
Home: (201) 555-8667
Cellular: (201) 555-1243

OBJECTIVE

To utilize my communication, problem-solving, and decision-making skills in conjunction with my knowledge of the law in relation to tenant-landlord issues.

EDUCATION

Bachelor of Arts in Music, June 1976
Rutgers, New Brunswick, NJ

EXPERIENCE

President, Tenants Union 4/96 - present
- Organized tenants of 112 Anderson Avenue.
- Performed detailed legal research.
- Conducted interviews.
- Prepared documents and correspondence.
- Succeeded in winning rebates three times in two years.
- Elected president last three years.
- Negotiated landlord-tenant disputes.
- Created "Anderson Avenue Newsletter."

Music Teacher   9/86-6/97
MANHATTAN SCHOOL OF MUSIC, New York, NY
- Taught courses in piano and guitar.
- Coordinated student events.
- Supervised student teachers.

Music Teacher   9/76-9/86
JULLIARD, New York, NY
- Taught undergraduate courses in piano.
- Organized yearly special events.

REFERENCES

Available upon request

JOAN KARLSON

456 West 107th Street • New York, NY 10025 • (212) 555-7788

OBJECTIVE

To obtain a position that will utilize my talents and interests.

EDUCATION

New York University, Master of Arts, Psychology
Graduated 1989

City College, City University of New York.
Bachelor of Arts, Early Childhood Education
Graduated *cum laude* 1987

EXPERIENCE

2000 - Present
Developed and managed a family day care program for 5 youngsters in my home.
- Planned and coordinated an instructional program that provided for the social, emotional, intellectual, and physical needs of children.
- Established goals and evaluated progress.
- Utilized stimulating activities such as creative storytelling, arts, and cooking.
- Created instructional lesson plans to enhance decision-making skills.
- Enlisted skilled volunteers in the areas of music and art.

1/95 - 6/00
Bank Street College, New York, NY
Adjunct Lecturer. Department of Education.
- Instructor for three undergraduate courses in early childhood education.

9/90 - 1/95
NYC Board of Education
Teacher, Common Branch
- Taught kindergarten through third grade.

PROFESSIONAL ACCREDITATION

New York State Certification, Common Branch.

REFERENCES

Available upon request.

SHARYL X. WILSON

84 Saratoga Avenue   Detroit, MI 48229   (313) 555-9388

SUMMARY

Sales and Marketing Manager with proven ability to conceptualize, structure, and achieve both market and profit objectives seeks to join the sales and marketing team of Fortune 500 manufacturer.

SALES

- Initiated sales incentive program to motivate the sales force to generate new product sales.

- Increased sales of recycled paper products from $250,000 to $600,000 in the first year. Successfully built sales to more than $3,000,000 over the next five years.

- Held total responsibility for sales of copy-type papers, which represented 40% of total sales volume. Supervised six sales professionals.

- Initiated aggressive sales efforts for additional volume, allowing increased production using idle equipment, which spread costs and substantially improved profits.

- Strongly successful in developing new corporate accounts.

MANAGEMENT AND MARKETING

- Created and implemented the Neighborhood Business Strategy concentrating sales efforts to develop business close to the mill, effectively reducing costs and improving profitability.

- Changed company image from volume supplier to a dedicated quality product producer and provider of top-level customer service, a strategy that enhanced repeat business.

- Assumed newly created position, established its purpose, and made it work profitably. Established specifications, pricing, and developed marketing strategies.

- Implemented advertising campaigns with assistance from ad agencies.

EMPLOYMENT EXPERIENCE

National Sales Manager, Starnes Paper, Subsidiary of Weyerhauser, Inc., Detroit, MI, 1994 - present

Regional Sales Manager, James River, Inc., Grand Rapids, MI, 1985 - 1994

page 1 of 2

(EMPLOYMENT EXPERIENCE cont.)

Regional Sales Manager, Specialty Papers, Greenfield Paper Company, Subsidiary of James River, Inc., Grand Rapids, MI, 1982 - 1985

Sales Manager, Greenfield Paper Company, Grand Rapids, MI, 1973 - 1982

EDUCATION

M.B.A., Harvard University, Cambridge, MA, 1973

B.S., Business and Economics, University of California, Berkeley, 1971

REFERENCES AVAILABLE UPON REQUEST

Resumes for Science, Technology, and Medical Careers

Charles D. Stiles
8765 South East Street
Ada, OH 45810
(419) 555-9876

CAREER OBJECTIVE

Position that requires technical knowledge in the areas of design, testing, and reliability of mechanical and electrical systems in order to produce a quality product.

EDUCATION

Ohio Northern University, Ada, OH
B.S. in Mechanical Engineering Technology, 1996

Ohio Northern University
Have completed 21 hours of electronics and 15 hours of computer programming.

WORK EXPERIENCE

Shepherd Engineering - Tulsa, OK
1998 to Present
Responsibilities include:

- Component designs

- Thermoset and thermoplastic molding

- Tooling evaluation

- Assembly line setups

- Adhesive development

- Robot feasibilities

- Supplier contacts

Ford Motor Company - Detroit, MI
1996 to 1998
Responsibilities included:

- Traveling to various engineering facilities to develop tests

- Setting up inventory systems

- Maintaining budget

- Supervising laboratory technicians

- Publishing testing manuals and reports

REGINALD D. DAWSON
4800 Johnson Plank Road • Albuquerque, NM 87819
505-555-4889 • r_dawson@xxx.com

JOB OBJECTIVE
To seek a position as a physical therapist assistant while continuing my studies in physical therapy.

EDUCATION
University of New Mexico/Albuquerque Campus
Physical Therapy curriculum; completed 2 years, received certification for Physical Therapy Assistant - 1995.
Continuing program in evening division commencing September 1999. Projected graduation date with a B.S. in Physical Therapy, December 2002.

Santa Fe School of Massage/Santa Fe
Certified in 1990. Course consisted of the study and application of Shiatsu and Swedish massage, hand and foot reflexology, therapeutic mineral massage, and deep heat massage.

Acupuncture School of New Mexico/Santa Fe
Certified in 1990. Studied Acupuncture application for remedy of headaches, bronchial conditions, bursitis, arthritis, tendinitis, and lower back ailments.

WORK EXPERIENCE
CITY OF ALBUQUERQUE, Department of Social Services
Paramedic, 1985 - 1990

U.S. NAVY, Basic Training/Great Lakes, IL
Hospital Corpsman, 1982 - 1985
Trained for rating of Hospital Corpsman in San Diego. Tour of duty served in Panama and Kuwait.

SEMINARS
- Rolfing, March 1992
- Healing properties of Raw Foods, Viktoras Kulvanskas, September 1992
- Goal Setting, Anthony Robbins, 1993

AWARDS & MEMBERSHIPS
- Dean's List, 1993 - 1994
- U.S. Paramedics Association
- Second-highest grade average, Hospital Corpsman School

REFERENCES
Available on request.

Jefferson Bird
3829 High Road
Warwick, RI 02887
(401) 555-9287

OBJECTIVE

A position in engineering in the public sector

BACKGROUND SUMMARY

Over twenty years experience in construction and mechanical engineering for private corporations, specifically: field engineer for installation of propulsion turbine plant on land-based test site; industrial and product engineering in the shipbuilding, material handling, chemical, and gas industries in construction, maintenance, engineering, and administrative capacities.

EDUCATION

M.S., Mechanical Engineering, 1975, Eastern University, Springfield, MA

B.S., Mechanical Engineering, 1971, Pennsylvania Institute of Technology, Pittsburgh, PA

EXPERIENCE

1992 - Present   Newport Shipbuilders, Inc., Warwick, RI
Senior Engineer

- Supported construction and operating personnel during installation, start-up, and testing of propulsion, generator, and hydraulic machinery.

- Performed facility survey, prepared technical reports, and provided engineering support during construction set-up, and testing of the propulsion turbine plant.

- Assisted in construction during structural and mechanical equipment support and foundation.

- Coordinated fabrication and installation of full-size mock-up for integrated sub-base turbo generator.

- Provided support to designers, draftsmen and construction personnel to ensure compliance with technical specifications and code requirements.

EXPERIENCE cont.

1984 - 1992   Shipbuilders Corporation, Providence, RI
Engineering Supervisor

- Designed various mechanical and fluid systems and assisted in procurement, installation, and testing of systems and equipment.

- Designed and assisted in construction and testing of flow-through crude oil handling system on 120,000-ton double-hull tanker, reducing initial cost and increasing operational efficiency.

- Organized a multidisciplinary team to develop and build an oil-water separator to meet pollution control requirements.

- Conducted equipment and system test at the factory and after completion of installation for various components, including pumps, heat exchangers, hydraulics, and control/monitoring devices.

- Assisted in installation and testing of bulk petrochemical heating system to maintain the product temperature.

1980 - 1984   TEC, Fiber Division, Boston, MA
Staff Engineer

- Assisted during installation, start-up, and testing of machinery for fiber, film, cellulose, and bulk material and processing equipment.

- Developed and assisted in installation of automated overhead conveying system to replace manual material handling operation for cellulose sheet.

- Supervised installation of the filling line to increase bagging output for micro-crystalline cellulose.

- Redesigned the PVC blown film machine and provided assistance during installation and start-up.

1978 - 1980   Pennsylvania Oxygen Corp., Ltd., Pittsburgh, PA
Assistant Engineer

- Supervised workforce of 120 with responsibility over production and maintenance for oxygen and acetylene plant and facilities.

- Conducted the economic analysis for relocating oxygen plant. Supervised erection of the plant at the new site.

References on Request

Ellen Janssen

724 Olympia Drive • Des Moines, IA 50265
Home: (319) 555-1284 • Pager: (319) 555-6744

Overview

Licensed Iowa RN with experience in private practice and community health. Excellent interpersonal, communication, and marketing skills. Strong rapport with patients. Holistic approach to health care.

Work Experience

Planned Parenthood, Des Moines, IA
Reproductive Counselor
1993 - Present

Provide reproductive counseling at walk-in clinic serving 500+ clients per year. Provide one-on-one patient education regarding birth control and pregnancy. Assist with general office management, including patient scheduling and maintenance of computer database and files. Participate in short- and long-term planning of program. Monitor changes in federal health care law and implement procedural changes as necessary.

LifeSource, Des Moines, IA
Blood Drive Coordinator
1990 - 1993

Contacted corporations to request off-site blood drives. Set up equipment and supervised blood drives at corporate sites. Took donor histories, supervised LPNs and RNs, provided discharge instructions to donors. Assisted with in-house donations as necessary, including patient intake, scheduling, and telemarketing efforts to increase donations.

Capital Medical Group, Iowa City, IA
Staff Nurse
1987 - 1990

General duty nurse for pediatric practice. Provided standard well-baby care, such as immunizations and oral polio treatments, as directed by physicians. Took patient histories, assessed and charted conditions, completed necessary paperwork, and maintained patient files.

Education

BSN   Public Health University of Iowa 1987

References

Rachel Stern, Director
Planned Parenthood
(319) 555-6102
E-mail: stern_pp@xxx.com

Dr. Michael Cooper
Capital Medical Group
(319) 555-6123
E-mail: michaelcoopermd@xxx.com

KEVIN SHANNON

P.O. Box 231, Bakersfield, CA 93301/805-555-9721

OBJECTIVE

Relocating to Los Angeles; seeking challenging employment with industrial engineering department of a large manufacturing company.

EDUCATION

A.A.S., Applied Engineering, 1984
College of Applied Technology, Los Angeles

Continuing education coursework (36 hours)
Bakersfield Technical College, 1988 - 1998

ACCOMPLISHMENTS

Named National Coordinator for corporation's P.A.R. system (Parts Action Request), which was an internal method of relaying information to manufacturer, purchasing, and others.

Instrumental in procedural change, using engineering drawings in lieu of sketches for the installation of customer-requested options not found on standard bills of material.

Approved or rejected engineering design variation requests, ensuring that appropriate changes comply with specifications and structural requirements.

Provided bills of material, worked with component vendors to secure special parts inventory, and compiled installation layouts.

Trained new employees in engineering drafting practices and standards.

Coordinated employee retraining program through local technical college.

Developed and implemented safety program that resulted in a 35 percent decrease in on-the-job injuries.

EXPERIENCE

Industrial Manufacturing, Inc., Bakersfield, CA

Departmental Coordinator, Parts Engineering/Dec. 1994 - present

Assistant Supervisor/1989 - 1994

Engineering Aide/1984 - 1989

REFERENCES AVAILABLE

SARAH ANN CHRISTIANSON

427 N. Spring Street
Park Ridge, IL 60068
(708) 555-3572

Summary

Programmer/analyst with extensive experience in DB2 database administration.

Technical Skills

DB2	MVS/ESA	IBM mainframes
COBOL	MVS/OS	Lotus 1-2-3
EASYTRIEVE	OS/2	CICS
SAS	IBM PCs	FileAid
VSAM	TSO/SPF	Panvalet

Employers

Crenshaw Insurance Group
Database Administrator   3/97 to Present
- DB2 testing and production activities
- Perform recovery and security functions
- Maintain compiles, sample programs, and subroutines

DuMont Financial Advisors
Systems Analyst/Programmer   6/95 to 3/97
- Performed systems analysis and programmed projects using batch COBOL and CICS applications
- Converted projects in VSAM, batch COBOL, and DB2

Affiliations

Women in Computer Programming
Midwest Programmers Association

Education

B.S. Information Science
Northwestern University, 1995

References Available

ADAM CANTOR

Work Address: Department of Chemistry
                     University of Vermont
                     Burlington, VT 16901
                     (802) 555-9811

Permanent Address: 2141 Rock Street
                     Alameda, CA 94501
                     (802) 555-1123

OBJECTIVE   To obtain a position as a senior research and development chemist
                 in the fields of polymer or physical chemistry.

EDUCATION   Ph.D., University of Vermont, 1999
                 in Physical Chemistry, Dynamic Light Scattering Study of
                 Ternary Polymer Solutions

                 B.S., Middlebury College, 1991
                 in Chemistry
                 Minors: Mathematics, Physics

EXPERIENCE   6/92 to 8/99
                 University of Vermont, Department of Chemistry

                 Research Assistant. Studied semi-dilute poly (n-alkyl isocyanate)
                 solutions containing a linear polystyrene probe polymer. Examined
                 concentration, molecular weight, and temperature dependences of
                 the ternary solutions. Performed dynamic and static light scattering
                 measurements. Characterized solutions using FTIR, UV,
                 viscometry, and differential refractometry. Assisted in design,
                 assembly, and maintenance of experimental instruments.
                 Administered laboratory computer systems (UNIX, VMS, Macintosh,
                 MS/DOS).

                 2/93 to 1/98
                 University of Vermont, Department of Chemistry

                 Health and Safety Representative. Implemented laboratory safety
                 measures, prepared chemical inventories, and provided personal
                 safety instruction. Aided in development of departmental safety film.

                                                                    Page 1 of 2

Adam Cantor
Page 2 of 2

EXPERIENCE (cont.)   6/90 to 12/90
                      Middlebury College, Department of Chemistry

                      Teaching Assistant for Physical Chemistry, Laboratory
                      (Head TA and Course TA), First-year Chemistry, Organic Chemistry

HONORS   Member, Eta Kappa Nu Fraternity
                      Recipient, Chemical Engineering Scholarship of America
                      National Merit Scholar

REFERENCES   Furnished on Request

CLARENCE T. JACKSON

3316 Westview Road
Lake Forest, CA 92630
tjackson@xxx.com
(714) 555-6150

OVERVIEW

Experienced EMT capable of responding to wide variety of trauma cases at scene. Currently seeking RN licensure. Strong commitment to career in trauma services.

EDUCATION

BSN   Nursing
University of California, degree expected 2002

AS   Emergency Medical Technology
Lake Forest Community College, 1993

Board-Certified EMT

CPR Instructor

EXPERIENCE

Lake Forest Community Rescue Team   *1995 to Present*

Team leader for urban mobile trauma unit. Interface with hospital ER staff by phone to provide trauma management en route from accident scenes. Stabilize patients for transport. Train dispatchers to answer calls and document critical information.

Warren County Fire and Rescue Service   *1993 to 1995*

CPR instructor for firefighters and EMTs. Provided CPR certification programs for community groups as requested.

REFERENCES AVAILABLE

Warren Owen Pierce

12 Boxwood Lane
Oakwood, Illinois 60335
(815) 555-2368

Job Objective	A professional position in engineering safety with a local government agency, with emphasis on fire protection.
Education	Bachelor of Science in Chemical Engineering, University of Illinois, Chicago, 1999. GPA 3.86. Minor Fire Protection Engineering.
	Major coursework included structures chemistry, chemical engineering, fire protection engineering, thermodynamics, hydrology, and electromagnetics.
Experience	Intern, Oakwood Fire Department, Oakwood, Illinois, Summer 1999.
	Employed full-time as assistant to the fire chief. Underwent rigorous three-week training in fire fighting, prevention, and protection. Participated in site clearances and arson investigations. Proposed new procedures for responding to college dormitory fire alarms, which resulted in a 25 percent quicker response time.
	Assistant Safety Technician, University of Illinois Public Health and Safety Department, Fall 1998 to Winter 1999.
	Worked part-time providing on-site training in public health and safety issues. Worked with safety specialists in fire, electrical, chemical, and nuclear emergency preparedness. Trained in recognizing potential fire, health, and safety hazards.
	Residential Adviser, University of Illinois Student Housing Department, Fall 1997 to Spring 1998.
	Supervised residential hall wing that housed 75 students.
	Responsible for safety surveillance, counseling, and coordinating building maintenance.
References	Available upon request.

• *Cindy Cannon* •

3344 N. Western Ave.
Chicago, IL 60625
773-555-1998
cindycannon@xxx.com

Data Analyst

•

• *Summary*

Exceptional organizational skills. Over seven years business experience in a variety of settings. Proven ability to utilize extensive knowledge of information systems.

• *Employment*

Programmer Analyst
Midcom Legal Consultation, Chicago, IL   9/96 to present

Responsible for support of an integrated legal practice system, which includes subsystems for rate filings and document orders from federal, state, and local government agencies. Develop project standards and procedures as well as train others.

Programmer Analyst
InterDesign, Inc., Evanston, IL   6/94 to 9/96

Oversaw maintenance of batch and online systems. Trained and supervised junior employees using DPPX/DSX programs. Analyzed business systems to identify conversion, interface, and technical requirements. Redesigned company mailing system.

• *Technical Knowledge*

IBM 3090 and 4381, PS/2, Windows, DB2, TSO/ISPF, QMF, MVS-ESA, CICS, VSAM, and Pascal.

References available at your request

ALLEGHENY COLLEGE
CAREER PLANNING AND PLACEMENT CENTER
MEADVILLE, PENNSYLVANIA 16335

Name: Allen Day
Address: 88 State Street
               Carmel, IN 46032

Phone: (317) 555-3175

OBJECTIVE: To obtain a position in information systems, software
               design/development, or related area utilizing computer programming
               language skills.

EDUCATION: Allegheny College, Meadville, PA
               B.S., Computer Science
               Graduation Date: June 2002

EXPERIENCE:

Summer 2001   City of Reading, Reading PA, *Management Information Systems Intern:*
               Duties included personal computer assembly and setup (hardware &
               software installation) as well as system troubleshooting. Involved
               significant user interaction and operating system knowledge. Worked
               on IBM PC AT's and XT's, HP Bectra PC's using MS DOS 3.3.

Summer 2000   Indiana University, Indianapolis, IN, *Student Programmer:* Developed
               application that aids in vision/perception research by performing linear
               transformations to bitmap images. Consultant to supervisor.

Summer 1999   Indiana University, Indianapolis, IN, *Research Programmer:* Developed
               an IBM application for desktop security and screen-saver.

SKILLS SUMMARY:

Computers: C, Pascal, Lisp. Also familiar with Ada, SmallTalk, Prolog, 68000
               Assembly Language. Procedural, Functional Object-oriented
               programming. LightSpeed, MDSenvironments.

REFERENCES: Available on Request

allison moore
Computer Repair Technician

6556 Crosstown Pkwy.
Cherry Hill, NJ 08003
(609) 555-6189
allisonmoore@xxx.com

goal

To apply my new education in computer repair to a new challenge in a company focused on quality.

education

Stevenson Technical School, Newark, NJ
Received certificate 9/2000. Curriculum included: Mathematics, Basic Electricity, AC & DC Circuitry, Power Supplies, Semiconductor Theory and Troubleshooting, Operational Amplifiers, Boolean Algebra, Combination Logic Circuits, Flip Flops, Memory Systems, D/A Conversion, and Microprocessors.

professional experience

DoubleTech, Inc., Newark, NJ
11/96 to Present
Field Service trained on high-speed check processing unit, which included optical reader, magnetic ink character reader, and ink jet printer. Also worked on 80 megabyte Pertec disk drives, line printers, and Harris PC6 controllers.

Schector Electronics, Princeton, NJ
04/95 to 11/96
Worked from blueprints, pictorials, and schematics reading and interpreting changes made by engineers in regard to the modification of circuits. Worked well alone and in groups to ensure all changes were made. Awarded two certificates of achievement for lowest failure rate two quarters in a row.

References Available

SARALYNNE KVITKA
654 S.W. Marshall Street
Jackson, Mississippi 39215
(601) 555-4932

EDUCATION:

Bachelor of Arts in Architecture, with a minor in Environmental Studies. University of Mississippi, March 1999.
Areas of Emphasis:
Structures, Geology, Geography
Environmental Control Systems
Public Planning, Policy, and Management
Jackson Community College, certified August 1999
AutoCAD, Release 12, AutoDesk Training Center

EXPERIENCE:
Engineering Specialist
State of Mississippi, Engineering Division, Jackson (April 1999 - present)
Proofread, compiled, and distributed specifications. Designed files for drawing storage and organized current system. Conducted drawing research for various projects. Created database files for several Port accounts.

Engineering Intern
State of Mississippi, Engineering Division, Jackson (June 1998 - Sept. 1998, Dec. 1998)
Prepared and submitted permit applications. Received, processed, and distributed requests for utility locales. Updated house addressing maps for all facilities. Organized microfilm for all drawings from 1891 to 1985.

Draftsperson
Smithson, Davis & Forbes, Architects, Jackson (Jan. 1998 - March 1998)
Drafted preliminary through construction drawings. Researched building codes and product information. Practicum experience for academic credit.

Customer Service and Cashier
Howell's Supply Store, University, Mississippi (Sept. 1995 - March 1999)
Served 500 to 750 customers daily. Solitary employee in Art & Architecture Supply Store on weekends. Advised customers about product usage and brand comparison. Handled returns, exchanges, and personal/business charge accounts.

ADDITIONAL SKILLS:
Intermediate skills and experience with IBM software, including: AutoCAD, Paradox, MS DOS, MS Windows 3.0 - 3.1, MS Word, WordPerfect, Excel, and Lotus 1-2-3.
Some Macintosh experience including MS Word.
Art Media, Model Making, and Photography.

REFERENCES:
Available on request

MARCIA BLAKE

5082 Merrick Street • Union, KY 41091 • Cellular: (606) 555-6315

Background
- BSN with more than 10 years of nursing experience
- Staff RN for pediatric and med/surg units
- Mental health counselor for psychiatric hospital
- MSN in progress

Employers
UNION HOSPITAL
Staff RN
1994 - Present

Perform primary nursing duties for 30-bed pediatric unit. Rotate to med/surg unit as needed.

BRENTWOOD PSYCHIATRIC INSTITUTE
Mental Health Nurse
1990 - 1994

General nursing, patient assessment, and counseling duties for psychiatric hospital specializing in pediatric and adolescent psych cases.

Education
Kentucky Nursing License #484-123026
MSN   in progress Union College, degree expected 2002
BSN   St. Catherine's College, 1990

Computer Skills
Familiar with current computer programs used in regional medical facilities for documenting patient insurance information, recording stats, and logging medical history. Extensive work with patient database maintenance at Union Hospital. Also proficient in Microsoft Office 2000, including Word, Excel, Access, and PowerPoint.

REFERENCES AVAILABLE

STEVE MADISON

2728 Clark Street
Ann Arbor, MI 48766
(313) 555-9874
stevemadison@xxx.com

BACKGROUND

Computer programmer/analyst with extensive experience installing, testing, and maintaining financial systems.

TECHNICAL SKILLS

COBOL	DB2	MS/OS
EASYTRIEVE	IDMS	MS/DOS
BASIC	RAMIS	TSO/ISPF
Pascal	Oracle (PC)	CICS
C	FileAid	Telon
Panvalet	Roscoe	INFOPAC

APPLICATIONS

- Installation and maintenance of financial systems for general ledger, check reconciliation, inventory, and cash management systems
- Creation of program specifications
- Installation of bug-fix tapes and hand fixes
- Design and writing of interfaces from in-house systems to M&D systems
- Maintenance and development of mainframe systems

EMPLOYERS

Quinn Automotive, Ann Arbor
9/98 to Present, Programmer/Analyst

Small Business Council, Ann Arbor
9/96 to 9/98, Consultant

Best Foods, Detroit
6/94 to 9/96, Systems Analyst

LT Chemical, Detroit
6/92 to 6/94, Systems Analyst

EDUCATION

B.S. Information Technology
University of Michigan, 1990

M.I.S.
Stanford University, 1992

REFERENCES AVAILABLE

Antonia Harasmus
456 Shady Glade
Pepin, WI 54759
715-555-9898 home and voice mail
harasmus@xxx.com

EMPLOYMENT OBJECTIVE

To obtain a position in computer support services

SKILLS AND EXPERIENCE

- Experienced in writing, analyzing, testing, and implementing computer programs
- Competent in a wide variety of computer languages
- Expert inventor of interactive computer games for the adult market
- Qualified to conduct data systems studies involving meta-analysis techniques
- Skilled in advanced programming techniques
- Fluent in Spanish, including technical terms of the computer industry

WORK BACKGROUND

Programmer/ Analyst
United States Army
1998–2002

Computer Operator
United States Army
1994–1998

Video Gaming Consultant
Minnesota Technology Consortium
1992–1994

Youth Advisor to the Govenor's Task Force on Youth and Technology
Appointed by State of Wisconsin Governor Tommy Thompson
One of two young people asked to serve on task force from 1991 to 1992. Helped write a proposal to improve computer access for young Wisconsinites through schools and libraries statewide. Proposal eventually became a bill and was passed in 1993.

Antonia Harasmus—page one of two

TRAINING/EDUCATION

Bachelor of Science, University of the Pacific, Sacramento, CA, 1992
Major: Computer Science
Minor: Mathematics

Army training courses at Information Systems Software Center, Fort Belvoir, Virginia

VOLUNTEER/TRAVEL EXPERIENCE

- Traveled in Latin America after graduation from high school
- Became fluent in Spanish and was trained as a medical aide by Catholic Charities in order to assist in emergency post-hurricane relief work
- Received Medal of Honor from Mayor of El Capitan, Peru

COMPLETE MILITARY, EDUCATIONAL, AND EMPLOYMENT RECORDS ARE AVAILABLE AT YOUR REQUEST

JASMINE K. LAKE

Present Address: Permanent Address:
P.O. Box 04834   5606 Castle Avenue
Baltimore, MD 21218   Langston, OK 73050
(301) 555-0523   (405) 555-3247

OBJECTIVE: To obtain a position in the entering class of a top medical school
                        and pursue a career in research-oriented medicine.

EDUCATION: Johns Hopkins University, Baltimore, MD
                        Bachelor of Science, Biology, with honors, June 2000
                        Overall GPA: 3.83   Science GPA: 3.89

RESEARCH EXPERIENCE:

Research Investigator, Molecular Endocrinology Lab, Johns Hopkins Medical
Center (1998 - 2000). Studied the relationship between stem cell factor protein
and the Sertoli cell only and germ cell arrest male infertility syndromes.
Assisted on projects studying inhibin protein transcription and translation rates.
Helped plan, coordinate, and carry out research. Learned and used techniques
such as Southern blots, cell cultures, reverse transcriptase polymerase chain
reactions, and single-stranded conformational polymorphism. Prepared data
and reports for publication.

Research and Clinical Assistant, Department of Neurology, Baltimore
Veteran's Administration Outpatient Clinic (1997). Studied neuromuscular
diseases and the ability of human muscle to survive different methods of
storage. Learned a variety of pathology techniques. Assisted with neurological
examinations such as EEGs.

OTHER WORK EXPERIENCE:

Tutor, Johns Hopkins University, Baltimore, MD (1997 - 1998).
Assisted other students with English, mathematics, physics, and biology.

ADDITIONAL INFORMATION:

- *Member,* Student Radio Board of Directors,
  Johns Hopkins University.
- *Volunteer,* "Tiny Tots" Nursery School, Johns Hopkins Special
  Olympics, Drunk Driving Prevention Program,
  and Free Peer Tutoring.
- *Member,* Committee on Housing and Residential Education,
  Johns Hopkins University.

REFERENCES: Available upon your request.

CHARLES ANDAWA

4783 West Maple • Baltimore, MD 21218 • 410 555-2983

Objective   A position in chemical engineering with an environmental engineering organization.

Recent Experience

1993 - Present   Senior Project Manager, PPD, Inc., Baltimore, MD

Report to senior vice president of engineering. Supervise 32 employees. Direct, supervise, administer, and manage projects from inception to startup, including new chemical process equipment manufacturing. Assist sales department in reviewing the system process design, scheduling, engineering, and costs before final proposal is presented to client.

Conceive, initiate, and develop chemical formations for nontoxic solutions for use in oil recovery and recycling. Formulated empirical equations and design criteria for the system, which resulted in increasing company sales seven-fold over the last five years.

Train project engineers and project managers to design and manage projects.

1991 - 1993   Senior Project Engineer, Moreland Chemical, Annapolis, MD

Project experience included pulp liquor evaporation system operations, sand reclamation systems, waste wood utilization to manufacture charcoal, sewage sludge oxidation, waste oxidation, and heat recovery. Responsible for planning, scheduling, process design, and specifications.

Education   B.S., M.S., Chemical Engineering, Minnesota Technical University, Houghton, MN, 1984

References   Available by request.

EARLE F. ABLE
6255 Maple Drive
Chicago, IL 60636
———
Telephone (312) 555-4948
Fax (312) 555-4897

OBJECTIVE   To attain a position as a designer drafter with a
                     highly aggressive, goal-oriented architectural
                     engineering firm.

SKILLS   Design and detailing of commercial, mechanical,
                     electrical, and plumbing systems

                     Architectural plan and details and site layout

CAREER EXPERIENCE

May 1997 to Present ENGINEERING DEVELOPMENT DESIGN
                     Position: Designer Drafter

                     Duties: Design development of mechanical,
                     electrical, and plumbing systems within
                     commercial projects. Produce final bid documents
                     on multiple medias and AutoCAD software.
                     Develop construction details for architectural and
                     engineering concepts. Also responsible for pictorial
                     sections used in development and layout.

EDUCATION   B.S. Mechanical Engineering Technology
                     University of Illinois, Champaign, 1997

                     A.S. Mechanical Design and Drafting Technology
                     Indianapolis Community College, 1995

REFERENCES   Furnished upon request

Benjamin Yoav

1558 Hilsdale Dr.
Los Angeles, CA 90068
(213) 555-2318
Cell: (213) 555-8893
benyoav@xxx.com

Data Analyst

Superior organizational and analytical skills. More than ten years business experience in a variety of settings. A consistent record of systems analysis and programming applications that are easily maintained and consistent in outstanding performance.

Employment

Herron Systems, Los Angeles, CA, April 1998 to Present
Responsible for support of all integrated systems, including subsystems. Developed software configuration management procedures for a variety of systems. Utilize Application Development Workbench to maintain logical and physical data models, data flow diagrams, and structure charts for PC-based system.

Lockhart, Inc., Santa Barbara, CA, June 1996 to April 1998
Developed project standards and procedures as well as trained other employees on system. Conducted modeling sessions with development and user teams for delivery to executive management.

Denali Systems, Inc., Fullerton, CA, October 1993 to June 1996
Coordinated program and CLIST maintenance, testing and implementation for remote users. Trained and supervised junior programmers to maintain and monitor data integrity.

Education

B.S. University of California–Los Angeles, 1993

References Available

RASHAD AHMED
_____

1287 NW Vine Avenue, Jonesboro, Arkansas 72403 / 501/555-9846

OBJECTIVE

To work with a major engineering specialty firm in the development of new start-up enterprises.

PROFESSIONAL EXPERIENCE

January 1997 to present
VARITECH
Jonesboro, Arkansas
Position: Director

Developed a new business, which includes managing the engineering, development, design, production, and marketing of a new product in the field of personal protection for women. The product was tremendously successful and marketed internationally.

February 1993 to December 1997
TURBOMAG CORPORATION
Dallas, Texas
Position: Director

Secured funds for venture capital from private sources in order to initiate the start of an energy research firm under the direction of the Technical Education Department (TED Center), Ft. Worth Community College. Upon receipt of the initial funds, I developed and managed the project as director and engineer. I was responsible for effective time and financial management, clear and precise project direction, research coordination, experimental results, consultant activity, machine shop fabrication, and working models.

July 1989 to February 1993
SOUTHWEST PIPELINE CORPORATION
Jonesboro, Arkansas
Position: Project contractor

Developed property and subdivisions and remodeled homes as a sideline, including land clearing, street construction, building, and utility installation as contractor.
Emphasis on utility and road construction.

EDUCATION

Edison Technical Institute   Automation Institute
Dallas, Texas   Little Rock, Arkansas
B.S., Electrical Engineering, 1989 Electrical Engineering Technology Certificate, 1996

Robert Capa

42 Park Avenue • New York, NY USA • (212) 555-7783 • robertcapa@xxx.com

Web Designer

I design eye catching, innovative websites that engage the user, promote the client's brand, and create a buzz. I seamlessly integrate functionality into form.

History

Sloan Digital, New York City

In my three years at Sloan, I have designed award-winning websites for 8 Fortune 100 companies and 14 other industry leaders. Two sites I designed were featured in *Fast Business* and *Wired* magazines. My attention to detail and eye for design has made me the lead designer on my company's biggest projects.

Sunday Media Solutions, Denver

Over the course of four years, I proved myself as an innovative designer with a watchful eye on deadlines and was promoted from Junior Designer to Lead Designer. My expertise in e-commerce made me an invaluable asset to Sunday Media. My desire to live in New York led me from my native Denver to bigger clients and more responsibility.

Carter Consulting Group, Denver

Carter is where my career began as an intern at one of Denver's most respected and established consulting firms. Under the tutelage of Don Balmore I honed my skills as a designer and established myself as a key staff member.

Education

Swift School of Visual Arts, Denver, CO
New York University, Masters of Visual Arts

References and samples available

NOLAN BRIAN KERR

---

930 North Leland Road
Flint, Michigan 48502
(313) 555-7623

CAREER OBJECTIVE

Position that requires technical knowledge in the areas of design, testing, and reliability of mechanical and electrical systems in order to produce a quality product.

EDUCATION

Purdue University, West Lafayette, Indiana
Attended: August 1987 - June 1989
Bachelor and Associate degrees in Mechanical Engineering Technology

Indiana State University, Terre Haute, Indiana
Attended: August 1985 - May 1987

Education included 20 hours of electronics and 10 hours of computer programming.

WORK EXPERIENCE

Michigan Lighting, Manufacturing Engineer.
M.L. is a joint American and Japanese automotive lighting company. Experience includes these areas: component designs, thermoset and thermoplastic molding, tooling, material evaluation, assembly line set-ups, adhesive development, robot feasibilities, and customer/supplier contacts. Familiar with foreign and domestic manufacturing concepts. Received Taguchi Design of Experiments training.

page 1 of 2

WORK EXPERIENCE *(cont.)*

**Mercury Lamp Division of Ford Motor Company,
Project Engineer.**
Five years' experience in working with automotive lighting systems. Performed the following functions: developed tests and implemented changes from test car and laboratory data; set up inventory systems; maintained budget, timing, and payroll records on computer; designed hardware parts for lamps; coordinated prototype parts; and designed layouts for the Forward Lighting facility. Supervised laboratory technicians, published testing manuals and reports, performed costs savings analysis on computer, and developed systems to monitor product performance in the field.

REFERENCES

Furnished upon request.

CATHY SMITH

546 Elm Street
Chicago, IL 60645
312-555-3894
cathysmith@xxx.com

GOAL

Computer science professional with experience in customer service and technical writing seeks customer service position with potential for supervisory responsibility.

WORK HISTORY

2-96 to Present:
Technical Writer
Superior Software Products, Chicago, IL

Prepare technical manuals for end users of Superior Software Products. Obtain program feature specifications from programmers and systems engineers to develop step-by-step instructions, written in clear, nontechnical language. Supervise ongoing revision and updating of manuals. Implement and test user experience guidelines to ensure directions are understood. Product line includes desktop publishing, graphic arts, word processing, and database products.

4-92 to 2-96:
Customer Service Technician
Worthington Software, Palatine, IL

Served as customer support contact for end users of Worthington Software and as telephone troubleshooter for clients, providing step-by-step solutions for online difficulties. Maintained phone log of customer problems. Worked with systems engineers and technical writers to modify systems designs and revise instructional manuals as necessary.

EDUCATION

University of Illinois at Chicago
Computer Career Training Program, One-year Graduate Certificate, completed 1-96

Northern Illinois University
B.S. Degree, completed 1-95

References Available

DENNIS P. WARDEN

152 Hogarth Avenue, Apt. #7D
Flushing, NY 11367
(718) 555-5401
warden@aol.com

BUSINESS EXPERIENCE

4/96 - Present   Industrial Engineer, Needham Cable
Flushing, NY

- Assist with world-class manufacturing and cell technologies implementation for rapid and continual improvement.

- Designed and programmed computerized suggestion system using dBase III, reducing clerical duties.

- Coordinated cost reduction program.

10/93 - 9/95   Plant Design Engineer, Coastal Cable
New Orleans, LA

- Justified and submitted cost reduction projects.

- Served as project engineer for OSHA safety project supervising completion of the project on time and under budget.

- Designed spreadsheet and database programs to create monthly master production schedules and material requirements for capacity analysis and JIT planning.

6/92 - 8/93   Plant Industrial Engineer, Lawrence Metals
Tampa, FL

- Established engineering standards to increase productivity.

- Reduced scrap and rejected shipments by writing detailed process sheets for operator use.

EDUCATION

Columbia University, 1991
School of Engineering and Applied Science
B.S. in Mechanical Engineering

JEFFERSON BIRD
3829 HIGH ROAD
WARWICK, RI 02887
401-555-9287

OBJECTIVE	A POSITION IN ENGINEERING MANAGEMENT IN THE PUBLIC SECTOR
BACKGROUND SUMMARY	More than twenty years experience in construction and mechanical engineering for private corporations, specifically: field engineer for installation of propulsion turbine plant on land-based test site; industrial and product engineering in the shipbuilding, material handling, chemical, and gas industries in construction, maintenance, engineering, and administrative capacities.
EDUCATION	M.S., Mechanical Engineering, 1975, Eastern University, Springfield, MA B.S., Mechanical Engineering, 1971, Pennsylvania Institute of Technology, Pittsburgh, PA

EXPERIENCE

1988 - Present   **Newport Shipbuilders, Inc.,** Warwick, RI
Senior Engineer

- Support construction and operating personnel during installation, start-up, and testing of propulsion, generator, and hydraulic machinery.

- Perform facility survey, prepare technical reports, and provide engineering support during construction, start-up, and testing of the propulsion turbine plant.

- Assist in construction during structural and mechanical equipment support and foundation.

- Coordinate fabrication and installation of full size mock-up for integrated sub-base turbo generator.

- Provide support to designers, draftsmen, and construction personnel to ensure compliance with technical specifications and code requirements.

1980 - 1988   **Shipbuilders Corporation**, Providence, RI
Engineering Supervisor

- Designed various mechanical and fluid systems and assisted in procurement, installation, and testing of systems and equipment.

EXPERIENCE (continued)

- Designed and assisted in construction and testing of a flow-through crude oil handling system on 120,000-ton double-huff tanker, reducing initial cost and increasing operational efficiency.

- Organized a multidisciplinary team to develop and build an oil-water separator to meet pollution control requirements.

- Conducted equipment and system test at the factory and after completion of installation for various components, including pumps, heat exchangers, hydraulics, and control/monitoring devices.

- Assisted in installation and testing of bulk petrochemical heating system to maintain the product temperature.

1975 - 1979   **TEC, Fiber Division**, Boston, MA
                   Staff Engineer

- Assisted during installation, start-up, and testing of machinery for fiber, film cellulose, and bulk material and processing equipment.

- Developed and assisted in installation of automated overhead conveying system to replace manual material handling operation for cellulose sheet.

- Supervised installation of the filling line to increase bagging output for micro crystalline cellulose.

- Redesigned the PVC blown film machine and provided assistance during installation and start-up.

1971 - 1973   **Pennsylvania Oxygen Corp., Ltd.**, Pittsburgh, PA
                   Assistant Engineer

- Supervised a workforce of 120 with responsibility over production and maintenance of oxygen and acetylene plant and facilities.

- Conducted the economic analysis for relocating oxygen plant. Supervised erection of the plant at the new site.

- Designed and assisted in the fabrication of the filtering system for acetylene. Supervised start-up and the testing of the system.

- Developed the test procedure for high pressure cylinders to meet regulatory requirements.

REFERENCES ON REQUEST

Martin K. Meade
411 West Street • (617) 555-6786 Home • (617) 555-5600 Work • Boston, MA 02129

Skills
IMS/DB & DC, CICS and DB2 using COBOL, RAMIS, IFPS, EASYTRIEVE, EASYTRIEVE Plus, and TELON. IBM8100/DPPX, Prime 750, Honeywell GCOS6.

Professional Experience
Eleven years systems experience in IBM operating systems, IBM machines, and IBM PC/LAN work-stations. Extensive use of Standard TAPS Code and converted TAPS on IBM8100/DPPX. A proven record of delivering computerized systems under tight deadlines to meet exacting requirements.

Taylor Healthcare Corporation   1989 - Present
Senior Programmer Analyst   1994 - Present
- Lead a team of seven analysts in installing the INFOPAC report distribution system, which reduced Freight printed output by 85 percent. Responsible for work plans, headcount utilization, program specifications, and user training
- Developed software to interface with IFPS (Interactive Financial Planning System) and ran graph system
- Convert all CICS programs from one system to another, updating JCL and complying with new systems standards
- Provide application support of the Freight/DCMS (Distribution Center Management System)

Programmer Analyst   1990-1994
- Converted interface to general ledger system from MSA to M & D. Created all necessary program specifications
- Developed program specifications, trained APAs and Co-op students, produced programs necessary for marketing of the Dealer Business System to an external division
- Designed, implemented, and supported additional Dealer Business Subsystems using CICS, VSAM, TELON, COBOL, EASYTRIEVE, and EASYTRIEVE Plus

Associate Programmer Analyst   1989-1990
- Provided user interface for METAPHOR system. Designed databases, managed query processing using SQL, and provided all necessary user training
- Completed training in IMS DB/DC, VSAM, and DB/DC BAL
- Completed continuing education course in COBOL programming and Method One structured methodology techniques

Education
A.A. in Computer Studies
Boston Junior College, graduated 1989

B.T. in Technical Writing
Massachusetts Institute of Technology, graduated 1991

References Available

SHER POONA
48 Lawrence Hall
University of California
Berkeley, CA 94720
(510) 555-0568

OBJECTIVE Development of computer and communication networks

EDUCATION University of California at Berkeley, Berkeley, CA
M.S. in Electrical Engineering, December 1998
G.P.A.: 3.8/4.0

Chambal Regional College of Engineering, Kanpur, India
B.S. in Electrical Engineering, May 1997
Senior Project: Simulated a PC-based protection relay and
verified various algorithms for line and phase faults on power
transmission lines.

One-month industrial training at Delhi Electronics Limited,
Lahore, India, in the areas of data processing,
communication, and electronics.

BACKGROUND Design, modeling, and analysis of centralized and distributed
networks, routing and flow algorithms, switching techniques,
multiple access for broadcast networks, data communication
hardware and software, packet-stitched and circuit-switched
networks, and satellite and local area networks.

Scientific Programming on VMS, UNIX, and MS-DOS in C,
Pascal, FORTRAN 77, Basic, and Assembly languages.

EXPERIENCE **Adjunct Lecturer,** Department of Computer Science,
University of California at Berkeley. Instructor for an
undergraduate course in FORTRAN programming.
(1/98 to 7/98)

ACTIVITIES **Treasurer,** IEEE Student Chapter, Kanpur, India
(1990 - 1991)
Coordinator, National Symposium on Applications of
Telecommunication in the Indian context, Kanpur, India
(September 1998)

Beverly Jackson

1800 West Sheridan Avenue • Atlanta, Georgia 30356
(770) 555-6978 Work • (770) 555-5836 Home
beverlyjackson@xxx.com

Goal

Systems Analysis and Programming Projects

Experience

Independent Contractor from 8/91 to Present

Recent Projects:

University of Georgia, Programming Consultant
Two-month project testing and executing SQL statements in QMF, SPUFI, or CANDLE EXPLAIN. Fine-tuned statements for efficient execution by the Optimize, using QMF or CANDLE EXPLAIN. Wrote all programs and all specifications for batch processing.

New World Packaging Inc., Independent Systems Analyst
One-year contract. Responsibilities included development, specifications writing, modification of existing programs as necessary, and design and coding of new programs. Performed structural procedure testing. Responsible for data and program modifications, recompiling and rebinding, testing and debugging.

Georgia Chemical Corporation, Independent Programmer
Assisted with set up of 30-member data processing department in Georgia branch office. Assignment included analyzing, coding, debugging, and implementing business applications, including payroll, general ledger, and inventory control. Implemented scientific applications such as process modeling and engineering. Performed troubleshooting. Expanded and interconnected system hardware.

Technical Knowledge

Languages	Systems	Software
COBOL	MVS/JCL	VSAM
COBOL II	MVS/ESA	IBM DB
FORTRAN	EASYTRIEVE	CICS
SQL	DOS/VS/VSE	DB2
BAL	MS DOS	QUICKEN
BASIC		EASE

Education

B.S. in Computer Science, Roosevelt University, 1991

References

Available on Request

Stephen Monetti
34 South Avon Street
Charleston, South Carolina 29411
603-555-2236

Career Achievements and Responsibilities

- Direct, supervise, and administer turn-key projects from inception to start-up for equipment manufacturing firm.
- Coordinate with sales department to review system process design, equipment sizes, schedule, and engineering costs before presenting final proposal to the client.
- Negotiate purchases and advise corporate president and CEO of pending contracts and negotiations.
- Supervise four project management teams, including twelve engineers and sixteen draftsmen.
- Completed seventeen domestic projects and twenty international projects in Latin America, South America, Spain, and Africa.
- Conceived, initiated, and successfully sold design of two new equipment products that resulted in a 40 percent increase in corporate sales over two years.
- Completed all projects on or ahead of schedule. All projects resulted in corporate profits; many produced higher profits than anticipated.
- Trained project engineers and project managers to design and manage assigned projects.
- Instituted program for college interns and developed training program that culminated in job offers to those graduates whose performance met challenges of the position. After seven years, all students thus hired are still with the company and highly productive.
- Acted as site project engineer during construction of $250 million plant.
- Registered professional engineer in the states of South Carolina and Arkansas.

Career Experience

Senior Engineer, DRG Inc., Charleston, South Carolina, 1984 - present
Senior Project and Process Engineer, Hopewell Systems, Charleston, 1980 - 84
Consultant Engineer, Toverston Dryers, Little Rock, 1977 - 80
Process Development Engineer, James River Corp., Neenah, Wisconsin, 1973 - 77

Education

M.S., Chemical Engineering, Georgia Institute of Technology, Atlanta, 1984
B.S., Engineering, University of Wisconsin, Milwaukee, 1973

EDGAR PETERS

9 De Soot Drive
Baton Rouge, LA 70805
(504) 555-1388

OBJECTIVE: Industrial engineering position with involvement in a manufacturing environment and opportunities to advance into production management.

EDUCATION: Master of Engineering
Tulane University, 1996
Major: Industrial Engineering

Bachelor of Science
Tulane University, 1995

EXPERIENCE:

1996 to present   Alexander Steel Company, Baton Rouge, LA

Associate Industrial Engineer
Provide identification and implementation of computer applications for analysis and control. Activities include computer modeling and economic and statistical analysis. Originated an operating change to increase furnace hot-blast temperature. Developed diagnostic, routing, quality control, and unit scheduling expert systems.

1995 to 1996   Packaging Systems, Inc., New Orleans, LA

Part-time Supervisor
Responsible for ten people in package-sort activities. Supervised, evaluated, and trained sort and audit personnel.

1993 to 1995   Production Facilities, New Orleans, LA

Student Assistant
Assisted project managers in development of new production and test facilities. Developed and documented procedures for initiating component repairs.

REFERENCES: Available upon request.

CHARLES W. WHITE
45 Cedar Pines Lane
Logan, Utah 84322
(801) 555-7516

OBJECTIVE	Capitalize on my experience in surveying and develop new skills in related fields.
EDUCATION	Utah State University, Logan, Utah Bachelor of Science Degree in Earth Science, May 1997

AREAS OF KNOWLEDGE

Physical Geography	Meteorology
Chemistry	Geomorphology
Structural Geology	Glacial Geology
Mineralogy	Oceanography
Calculus	Physics
Wave Optics	Petrology
Paleontology	Astronomy

WORK EXPERIENCE

1/95 - Present   L. HARVEY WILL, Logan, Utah - Party Chief

Responsible for three-person crews. Work involves new subdivisions, construction layout, grade work, roads, boundary surveys, stakeouts, and title and deed research.

3/94 - 1/95   PRICE AND CASPER, Ogden, Utah - Party Chief
Performed surveys of residential and commercial property.

9/93 - 3/94   L. HARVEY WILL, Logan, Utah - Transit Man

1/93 - 9/93   ROBERT BECK AND ASSOCIATES, Provo, Utah - Assistant Surveyor

Participated in field work utilizing theodolite and transit, aerial photographs, tax maps, deeds, and sophisticated field instruments.

REFERENCES   Furnished upon request

RICARDO SMITH
15 Orchard Court Drive
Baltimore, Maryland 21202
Home: (301) 555-1218
Cellular: (301) 555-9087

SUMMARY OF QUALIFICATIONS

Experienced and highly competent dental hygienist.
Adept at interacting with people and creating a nonthreatening environment.

ACCOMPLISHMENTS

Served successfully on active duty with the United States Navy as a dental hygienist.
Received outstanding performance evaluations. Helped unit earn citation for excellence,
2000 and 2001. Served in volunteer capacity through special program providing dental
care for disadvantaged children, 2001 - 2002.

EMPLOYMENT HISTORY

1993 - 2002 Dental Hygienist, United States Navy.
Rank: Petty Officer First Class
Locations of service:

U.S. Naval Station, Agana, Guam, 2001 - 2002

Naval Medical Command, Bethesda, MD, 1993 - 2001

EDUCATION

Associate in science degree (Dental Hygiene), 1993
Towson State University
Baltimore, MD 21204
GPA: 3.75 (4.0 scale)
Member, student government

CERTIFICATES/LICENSES

Certified, National Dental Hygiene Board
Certified, Mid-Atlantic Regional Dental Hygiene Board

MEMBERSHIPS

Member, American Dental Hygiene Association
Member, Maryland Dental Hygiene Society
Member, Local United Way Advisory Committee

REFERENCES

Provided on request

Lisa K. Evans

1596 Piedmont Road • Durham, NH 03824

(603) 555-4206 • Pager: (630) 555-8237

GOAL:

Geriatric Nursing Position

OVERVIEW:

- Talented RN with experience on orthopedic surgery ward
- Compassionate pre- and postoperative care
- Proven ability to develop successful discharge plans, including strategies for coping with altered mobility
- Experience in hospital and skilled care settings
- Nursing preceptor

WORK RECORD:

11/98 to Present
Level II Staff RN
Durham Community Hospital

10/92 to 11/98
Staff RN
Leighton Skilled Care Center

CREDENTIALS:

New Hampshire Nursing License #108-57410
RN, Durham School of Nursing, 1992
Member, American Nurses Association

References Available

WILLIAM J. SHAW

1810 Cedar Crest Boulevard
Evansville, IN 47722
(812) 555-1479

CAREER SUMMARY

More than twenty years' experience in manufacturing, production, and assembly of medium- and high-volume stamping and fabrication operations. Supervised activities in fabrication, stamping, welding, and finishing of automotive and agricultural equipment as well as appliances. Responsible for training, scheduling, safety, work quality, material movement, and discipline.

TECHNICAL QUALIFICATIONS

Experienced with JIT, MRP, Statistical Process control, and automated visual inventory/scheduling concepts. Proficient in high speed light stampings, transfer press operations, heavy stamped assemblies, welding, and testing instrumentation/procedures.

EMPLOYMENT HISTORY

Whirlpool Corporation, Evansville, IN   8/91 to present
Operations/Finishing Manager

Ford Motor Company, San Leandro, CA   6/79 to 8/91
Positions held: Supervisor of Cab Fabrication/Finishing, Maintenance Supervisor, and Finished Vehicle Assembly Supervisor.

EDUCATION

B.S. in Business Administration, Carnegie Mellon University, 1989

References available on request.

Barbara Danbury

9950 Brockport Road • Houston, Texas 77386
(713) 555-1947 • (713) 555-8590 • barbd@xxx.com

Overview

Commercial applications programmer familiar with large operating environments, database management, direct access technologies, and remote processing. Some exposure to CRT drivers, virtual systems, and database handlers.

Skills

COBOL, BASIC, RPG II, Pascal, C, C Plus

Job Responsibilities

• Program Design
• Coding
• Systems Testing and Debugging
• Creation of Program Documentation

Employers

Houston Savings & Loan, Houston, TX
Programmer/ Analyst
June 1995 - Present

Security Insurance, Dallas, TX
Systems Analyst
May 1993 - June 1995

S & J Manufacturing, Dallas, TX
Programmer
April 1990 - May 1993

Education

B.S. Baylor University, 1990

Major: Computer Science
Minor: Accounting

References Available

PETER DAWSON

420 Calumet Avenue, Gary, IN 46408　　　　　**219/555-6457**

OBJECTIVE

Position in process metallurgy/quality control.

CAREER SUMMARY

Fifteen years' service with a major manufacturer of flat-rolled and tubular products in various functional areas. Highly developed skills in work organization, metallurgical process control and applications, and expertise in finishing and management of basic manufacturing.

WORK EXPERIENCE

United States Steel Corporation, Gary, IN 1996 - present

Hot Mill Metallurgist (1998 - present)
Responsible for all aspects of hot strip mill quality including thermal practice, customer product and processing requirements, testing, and claims.

- Established new product/grade hot-rolling standards.
- Supervised hot strip mill quality control work force, including metallurgical turn supervisor, observers, and testing personnel.

High Carbon/Alloy Metallurgist (1996 - 1998)
Responsible for quality and thermal process control for all high carbon and alloy grades/products.

- Directed and coordinated slabbing and hot-rolling of customer conversion material.
- Established and developed standard operating and testing procedures for high-tech alloy application.

page 1 of 2

Peter Dawson
page 2 of 2

WORK EXPERIENCE (cont.)

United States Steel Corporation, Cleveland, OH   1988 - 1996

Shipping Supervisor (1994 - 1996)
Responsible for processing of various sizes, lengths, and grades of tubular products.

EDUCATION

B.S. Metallurgical Engineering, Purdue University, West Lafayette, IN, 1988

AFFILIATIONS

American Steelworkers Association
Professional Metallurgical Engineers Guild
Steelworkers Union #458

REFERENCES

Available on request.

STEPHANIE MORRIS
11917 NORTH MERIDIAN
CARMEL, IN 46032
(317) 555-6463

OBJECTIVE:

Seeking a challenging position in the areas of systems analysis, database management, and programming that will utilize my technical and interpersonal skills.

EDUCATION:

University of Texas
Austin, Texas
B.S. in Computer Technology, Computer Information Systems
Minors in Business and Industrial Operations
Fall 1990, Fall 1995

WORK EXPERIENCE:

Carl James Associates, Indianapolis, Indiana
Associate (February 1997 to Present)
Converted all operations for an Indiana municipality from Burroughs ISAM/COBOL/RPG to HP3000 IMAGE/COOL. Redesigned, rewrote, developed, and implemented all applications and new development.

Mayflower Van Lines, Indianapolis, Indiana
Programmer/Analyst (February 1996 to February 1997)
Designed, developed, and implemented reporting applications for operations including financial and operational reporting. Responsible for PC hardware and software setup and support for 25 PCs. Provided user support for applications written in FOCUS on an Amdahl mainframe.

Hardware Wholesalers, South Bend, Indiana
Programmer/Analyst Trainee (summer 1995)
Programmed COBOL with IDMS, created an on-line application using CICS and COBOL, and wrote documentation and created new applications using Easytrieve Plus and Keymaster.

REFERENCES AVAILABLE

Christopher Wiley

862 Oak Street
Santa Clara, CA 95051
Home (408) 555-3948
Pager (408) 555-9881

Goal: Full-time pediatric nursing position

Background: Eight years of hospital nursing experience serving pediatric and geriatric patient populations. Direct patient care from assessment through discharge planning. Excellent peer reviews. Active committee member. Four years as home health case manager.

Employers: Santa Clara Community Hospital   1/97 – Present
Pediatric Staff Nurse

St. Andrew's Hospital for Children   2/94 – 1/97
Pediatric Staff Nurse

Quality Home Health Inc.   6/91 – 2/94
Case Manager

Credentials: BSN, San Diego State, 1991
California Nursing License 843682
Pediatric Advanced Life Support Certification
CPR Certification
Member, American Nurses Association

Computer Skills: Microsoft Excel, Word, and Outlook
Lotus Notes
Meeting Maker
Proficient in using Internet medical search engines

References: Available

RAY PIERCE

3102 HOPPER STREET • CAMBRIDGE, MA 02139
(617) 555-3862 • CELL: (617) 555-9943
E-MAIL: RAYPIERCE@XXX.COM

- ## OVERVIEW

More than 12 years of experience in R&D, programming, and systems design. Successful supervisor, recruiter, and trainer.

- ## SKILLS

COBOL, PL/1, RPG III, C, C+, BAL, Ada, CAD/CAM, CICS, IMS/DLI, and VSAM

- ## EXPERIENCE

Triton Electronics
Programmer
6/96 - Present

Assigned to Research and Development Division. Develop and monitor projects, select software and vendors. Recruit and train new employees. Corporation has annual budget of 2.1 million. Currently developing a language interface for E-mail.

Patterson Development Corporation
Computer Technician
4/92 - 6/96

Assisted in development of software package for inventory control. Coded programs for retail use. Experienced in both microcomputer and mainframe environments.

Technical Data Corporation
Systems Designer
5/89 - 4/92

Created custom software for clients requiring specialized business applications. Met with end users to define needs. Designed software and assisted with coding and debugging as requested. Designed and implemented revisions and upgrades based on feedback from product support personnel.

- ## EDUCATION

B.S. Computer Science
Rochester Institute of Technology, 1988

M.S. Computer and Information Science
Dartmouth, 1990

- ## AFFILIATIONS

American Society for Information Science
Data Processing Management Association

References available upon request

DARRYLA MacKENZIE
442 N.W. Sunset Place
Corvallis, Oregon 97330
(503) 555-9227

CAREER OBJECTIVE

Civil engineering staff position in corporation or government organization responsible for large-scale civil construction projects.

DEGREE ACHIEVED

- B.S. Degree in Civil Engineering, 2000
- Oregon State University, Corvallis, Oregon
- Graduated 15th in class of 221; GPA 3.92
- Concentration: Major Project Design and Construction (Highways, Dams, Bridges)

SPECIALTY COURSES COMPLETED
(in addition to standard civil engineering requirements)

- Highway Engineering
- Highway Location and Design
- Reinforced Concrete Construction
- Low-Volume Road Design
- Asphalt Technology
- Advanced Concrete Technology
- Traffic Flow Analysis and Control
- Public Transportation Facility Design
- Transportation Systems Analysis and Planning
- Pre-stressed Concrete
- Traffic Operations and Design
- Bridge Design
- Construction Engineering Management and Methods
- Pavement Evaluation and Management
- Municipal Planning and Urban Engineering

EXPERIENCE

Student Internship, Summer 1998
State of Oregon Highway Division

- Worked with highway engineers on traffic pattern study and analysis.
- Conducted research in current traffic management theory and technology.
- Prepared written report for presentation to chief highway engineer.
- Assisted with planning and preparation for public hearings on proposed change in traffic flow.

REFERENCES on request.

Michael G. Block
75 Eldridge Court   Home (617) 555-4813
Cambridge, MA 02138   Work (617) 555-6741

OBJECTIVE   To utilize my communication, problem-solving, and decision-making skills in
                   a professional position that offers development and increasing levels of
                   responsibility.

EDUCATION   Ivy Technical Institute - Associate Degree
                   Material Requirements Planning Seminars - Certificate
                   ITT Technical Institute - Certificate

EXPERIENCE

10/99 - Present   *Lincoln Engineering - Cambridge, MA*
                   Service Technician Assistant - Assist service technicians in installing heating
                   and air-conditioning units in various city-wide industrial and residential
                   applications. Provide pick-up and delivery service. Operate hydraulic forklift.
                   Use acetylene/oxygen cutting torch and other related trade tools.

4/94 - 9/99   *Taylor Components Group - Concord, NH*
                   Programmer Technician - Developed and maintained applications for various
                   departments. Created screen formats for program access using FOCUS
                   Report Writer language.

                   Trainer - Provided end users with working understanding of computer.
                   Taught in-house seminar on creating Bills-of-Material using Cullinet on-line
                   software package.

                   Help Service - Allocated, created, and deleted data sets for end users.
                   Provided troubleshooting assistance. Served as liaison between Management
                   Information Service and various departments.

                   Documentation - Prepared and provided end users with step-by-step
                   procedures for using computer. Prepared user manual for Bills-of-Materials
                   seminar.

4/89 - 4/94   *Taylor Components Group - Concord, NH*
                   Drafter - Prepared detailed drawings of parts from layouts and sketches
                   using standard drawing and drafting and measuring tools and instruments.

KEVIN G. ACKROYD
438 BEAVER DRIVE, APT. 67
UNIVERSITY PARK, PA 16802
(814) 555-9478

EMPLOYMENT GOAL

Full-time employment in a medium-size company that does earthwork and/or heavy construction.

EDUCATION

Penn State University - Senior 1997 - 98, Graduate June 1998
Degree - Bachelor of Science in Construction Engineering Management

RELATED EXPERIENCE

ENGINEER INTERN - Williamsport Paving Co., Williamsport, PA, June to September 1997. Responsible for upkeep of the job-costing system on all projects and time and material billings. Some estimating, job supervision, signing, and laboring.

PROJECT OFFICER - 125th Engineer Battalion, PAANG, 1995 to present. The Officer-in-Charge of a road construction project and a haul-in project. Duties include coordination of materials, equipment, and direct supervision of project.

GRADE CHECKER/LABOR - White Construction Co., Wilkes-Barre, PA, July to September 1996. Gained experience in grade checking, pipe-laying, chip-seal, and flagging.

EQUIPMENT OPERATOR - Barron's Trenching, Altoona, PA, July to September 1995. Operated a CASE 580 Backhoe and 450 dozer in excavation for farm drainage systems and private contract work.

LEADERSHIP, ACTIVITIES, HONORS, & AWARDS

MEMBER - AGC Student Chapter, Penn State
COMMANDER - ROTC Drill Team
PLATOON LEADER - Heavy Equipment Platoon, National Guard
SCHOLARSHIP - AGC, 3-year, undergraduate

THERESA FOSTER
916 South Wilkins Avenue   **Home: (617) 555-6879**
Reynoldsburg, Ohio 43068   **Pager: (617) 555-6655**

GOAL   Community mental health nursing

OVERVIEW   • Five years of community mental health nursing
                  • BSN, MSN in progress
                  • Extensive experience with pediatric and adolescent
                    psychiatric cases
                  • Strong clinical assessment skills

EXPERIENCE   Glenview Hospital
                  Mental Health Nurse
                  September 1998 to Present

                  Northwest Community Mental Health Center
                  Outpatient Mental Health Counselor
                  July 1994 to September 1998

EDUCATION   Ohio Nursing License #583-126052
                  RN, St. Catherine's School of Nursing, 1994
                  BA, Psychology, Ohio State, 1990

REFERENCES   *Personal and professional references on request*

George Kusaka

4470 Grant Street • San Francisco, CA 94107
(415) 555-8635 Home • (415) 555-4800 Office • gkusaka@xxx.com

Objective: A senior programmer/analyst position developing and maintaining computer applications, with opportunity to develop skills in PC-based applications

Skills: MVS JES 3, Expediter, FileAid, Endeavor, COBOL II, DB2, IBM 3033 DOS/VSE, EMC2 Disk, CICS 1.7/VSAM, CS-Sort, CA-DART, System Manager, FALCON, COBOL, IBM 3083 MVS-XA TSO/ISPF, COBOL, IMS-DB, VSAM, PANVALET, JCL, Utilities, EASYTRIEVE, ABEND-AID, MS DOS 6.22, Windows, Office 97 & 2000, WordPerfect, ABC Flowchart, SuperProject Plus, Lotus 1-2-3 & Notes

Experience: BIGELOW BROTHERS 8/98 to Present

Developed and revised online management tool used to calculate bonus pay for sales associates. Created other customer service reports. Nonproduction applications under INFORMIX 46L.

SOFTWARE MONTHLY 8/96 to 8/98

Developed Ad Ticket application and order conversion for the ADMARC computer package, used to centrally administer 150,000 magazine advertisements annually, plus receivables. System replaced four separate legacy systems.

PASCAL PRINTERS 2/93 to 8/96

Handled maintenance and enhancement of labor/cost system for ten plants. Developed online job-class-exception subsystem and the online file maintenance for the same system. Developed credit approval system for Accounts Receivable to help track customer credit profiles and customers' parent corporations. The customer credit approval report became the internal executive level document for credit administration.

Education: B.S. Information Science
Kenyon College
January, 1993

References: Submitted upon request

JEAN A. JENKINS

216 S. Fulton Street • Park Ridge, IL 60068
708-555-2461 • Cell: 708-555-5463 • jeanjenkins@xxx.com

PROFESSIONAL BACKGROUND

DB2 Database Administrator/Programmer/Analyst

TECHNICAL EXPERTISE

Databases:	DB2
Languages:	COBOL, Easytrieve Plus, SAS, C, PASCAL, Lisp, Assembler
Systems:	MVS/ESA, MVS/OS, OS/2, IBM/370 (VM/CMS), VAX/VMS, UNIX, PC (Windows, DOS)
Hardware:	IBM mainframe and PCs
PC Software:	System Architect, Word Perfect, Lotus 1-2-3, Dbase IV, Microsoft Office
Other Tools:	Omegamon for DB2, ICandle DB2 tools, OS JCL, TSO/SPF, CICS, VSAM, FileAid, Panvalet, SYSD, SYSM

EDUCATION

B.S. from Northeastern Illinois University
Major: Information science   Minor: Business

Total GPA: 4.9/5.0   GPA in Major: 5.0/5.0

WORK HISTORY

MUNROE INSURANCE, Lincolnwood, IL   4/91 to Present
Senior Database Administrator   2/94 to Present

Support DB2 testing and production activities. Build and maintain Enterprise Data Model for all group systems DB2 applications, using System Architect. Monitor and tune DB2 system and applications to prevent resource shortages and shorten the execution times of long-running queries. Manage DB2 datasets to ensure proper sizing, back-up, organization, and record keeping, preventing problems with space, recovery, and performance. Perform recovery and security functions as required; some involvement with master disaster recovery plan. Maintain common procs (compiles), sample programs, and subroutines (error routines, date functions).

MUNROE INSURANCE (continued)
ACHIEVEMENTS
- Revised DB2 programming standards as member of DB2 development committee.
- Wrote and maintained in-house System Architect programmer training manual and shop data modeling standards.
- Most recently involved in year-long joint effort between Systems and Actuarial to build a DB2-based financial system. Focused on data design, writing SAS macros, and implementing special scheduling system.

Programmer/Analyst   4/91 to 1/94

Supported various group insurance applications.

ACHIEVEMENTS
- Designed and implemented covered person dependents function for administration system, using batch COBOL and CICS applications.
- Converted premium and claim statistical system from sequential files to DB2, for end-user query.
- Rewrote VSAM-based batch COBOL interface to copy covered persons data from administration system to Claimfacts system files.

REFERENCES AVAILABLE

Leo Cervetto
18 Cliff Road
Portland, Oregon 97205
(503) 555-3546

PROFESSIONAL EXPERIENCE

COORDINATOR OF TECHNICAL SERVICES, ALLIANCE OREGON, INC.
December 1999 to present

   In charge of asbestos program for more than 100 school buildings,
   involving review of existing asbestos management programs and
   extensive contact with school administrators in planning and
   implementation of timely and budget-sensitive management programs
   for environmental issues.

   Regularly conducted field surveillance and inspection activities at all
   sites. Trained school personnel on various environmental issues
   including asbestos, lead, and radon.

   Wrote company hazard communication, respiratory protection, and
   medical surveillance programs as well as standard operating
   procedures manuals for functions within the asbestos management
   program.

INDUSTRIAL HYGIENIST, ENVIRONMENTAL CONSULTANTS
March 1998 to October 1999

   Project manager position involving coordination of industrial hygiene
   and asbestos-related projects: bulk sampling, technical report writing,
   abatement project specification development, environmental
   compliance monitoring, and project design. Supervised technician
   pool and client services.

   Carried out wet chemistry procedures applicable to analysis of
   priority pollutants, both organic and inorganic, for solid and liquid
   matrices.

LABORATORY TECHNICIAN, BEAVER ANALYTICAL SERVICES
June 1997 to February 1998

   Responsible for preparation of solid and liquid samples for the
   analysis of tetrachlorodibenzodioxin. Duties included sample check-in,
   solid/liquid extraction, various clean-up procedures, and standards
   preparation.

EDUCATION

PORTLAND STATE UNIVERSITY, May 1997
    Bachelor of Science, Biology
    Chemistry minor

TRAINING/ACCREDITATION

OSHA compliance training

EPA-accredited building inspector, asbestos

EPA-accredited asbestos management planner, asbestos

Sampling and Evaluating Airborne Asbestos Dust certification

SPECIALTIES

All aspects of asbestos management in residential and commercial
buildings

Air sample analysis by Polarized Light Microscopy

Indoor air quality evaluation

Industrial Hygiene sampling

Scott Williams

1062 West Lemont Road • St. Louis, MO 63146 • 314-555-2269

OVERVIEW

Nurse advocate and labor relations specialist. Act as a collective bargaining representative and health care lobbyist. Personally and professionally committed to furthering the best interests of registered nurses and licensed practical nurses.

RECENT EXPERIENCE

1996 - Present
Director
Missouri Nurses Association
Primary focus is drafting and lobbying for legislation to protect collective bargaining rights of nurses and LPNs.

1993 - 1996
Labor Relations Specialist
Midwest Nurses Alliance
Represented alliance members in grievance procedures and contract negotiations. Investigated grievances. Educated chairpersons to assist them in representing their bargaining units.

1989 - 1993
Director of Education
Breslin Memorial Hospital
Responsible for staff orientation and certification programs, in-service workshops, nursing preceptor programs, and community health initiatives.

PUBLICATIONS

- "Job Security in the Age of Downsizing," *The Nurse Advocate*, November 1994.
- "Collective Bargaining: The Newest Strategies," *Journal of Holistic Health*, July 1997.
- "The Politics of Public Policy," *American Nurse*, February 1999.

EDUCATION

MSN	University of Texas Health Science Center	1989
BSN	St. Catherine's College	1987

CERTIFICATIONS

National Labor Relations Board

ANCC Advanced Nursing Administration

REFERENCES

Available upon request.

CORBIN DREYFUS
7530 Cypress Street • Midlothian, VA 23113 • (804) 555-7154 • corbind@xxx.com

---

Overview

- Successful computer consultant
- Knowledge of BASIC, C Language, MS/DOS, COBOL, FORTRAN, Pascal, DOS/VSE, IBM 370 under OS/MVS and JES3
- Specialize in long-term corporate consulting/training projects
- B.S., University of Virginia, Information Sciences, 1995

Recent Projects

QDC INTERNATIONAL
6/98 to Present

Provide freelance technical support. Job has included systems analysis to determine needs, selection of microcomputers and peripheral equipment, installation of hardware, design of custom software. Train employees in use of commercial packages, including file-handling program.

MIDLOTHIAN COMMERCIAL BANK
4/97 to 6/98

Hired to devise and implement quality control procedures. Designed, staffed, and implemented program. Trained and evaluated in-house staff in use of new procedures.

SAWYER BUSINESS SYSTEMS
3/95 to 4/97

Successfully designed and implemented schema and subsystem flow for inventory subsystem. Created and documented microcomputer hardware and software standards, saving the company more than $50,000 in first year of implementation.

VIRGINIA PUBLIC SCHOOLS,
Districts 62 and 14
3/93 to 3/95

Designed computer labs for four public high schools and six elementary schools. Project included developing and presenting proposal, selecting equipment, soliciting bids, supervising installation of hardware, and training teaching staff.

References Available

JERRY RESTON

8204 W. Bishop Street • Atlanta, Georgia 30356
(770) 555-7089 Office • (770) 555-6947 Home
jerryreston@xxx.com

OBJECTIVE: **SUMMARY:**	Systems Analysis/Programming Projects • Independent contractor for past 10 years • Specifications writing • Programming for batch processing • Design and coding of new programs • Structural procedure testing • Data and program modifications • Systems testing and debugging • Implementation of business and scientific applications
CLIENTS:	Culver Technical Institute Tredmont Industries Georgia Telecommunications ATP Business Systems Adler Financial Group
TECHNICAL **EXPERTISE:**	Languages: COBOL, COBOL II, FORTRAN, BAL, Pascal, BASIC Systems: MVS/JCL, MVS/ESA, EASYTRIEVE, DOS/VS/VSE, MS/DOS Software: VSAM, IBM, DB, DB2, CICS
EDUCATION:	M.I.S. University of Georgia 1992 B.S. North Park College 1990
REFERENCES:	Bob Carrington Vice President/General Manager ATP Business Systems Telephone: (707) 555-2984 Carol Sawyer Human Resources Director Adler Financial Group Telephone: (707) 555-2280

JOHN K. LAI

20 West Concord Street
Dover, NH 03820
(603) 555-1703

EDUCATION: B.S., Civil Engineering, University of New Hampshire

CAREER SUMMARY:

Extensive experience in program management on complex construction projects. Managed all phases of project administration, contract development, and claims negotiation. Proven knowledge and skills to interact with professionals, contractors, and labor personnel.

EXPERIENCE:

1997 - Present Johnson, Inc.
Position: Resident Engineer, North Shore Interceptor, Phase IV.
Location: Concord, New Hampshire
Duties: Supervise performance of construction contractors. Project includes tunnels, deep shafts, chambers, odor control structures, and appurtenant facilities.

1996 - 1997   Bechtel
Position: Project Manager
Location: Hanford, Washington
Duties: Special consultant to the Department of Energy and Rockwell International for design and construction of underground and shafts facilities for storage of nuclear waste.

1994 - 1996   Bechtel
Position: Project Manager Construction Services
Location: Los Angeles, California
Duties: Prepared division budgets, long-range plans, and project proposals. Assigned construction personnel to projects. Acted as area construction manager on the proposal for Los Angeles Subway Construction. Supervised preparation of procedures for construction of power generation plant and coal mine in China.

Page 1 of 2

REGISTRATION: Registered to work in New Hampshire

AFFILIATIONS: American Management Association
Society of American Military Engineers
Society of Mining Engineers

REFERENCES: Available upon request

KAREN S. ADAMS
1685 MOUNTAIN DRIVE
TUCSON, AZ 85720
(602) 555-8960

PROJECT MANAGEMENT

Project management for medium-sized company. Working toward international construction management with an eye on environmental compatibility.

PROFESSIONAL EXPERIENCE

1998 - Present   University of Arizona Physical Plant, Tucson, AZ
                  Position: Project Coordinator
                  Responsibilities include:

- Start-to-finish management of construction projects.
- Estimating, assembling technical teams, surveying and layout, some design/drafting/ACAD, specs, job supervision, and inspection.
- Redesign of local "problem" intersection.

Prior to 1998   Thirteen years in the construction industry, starting as a laborer in 1982, ending as a journeyman, formsetter, and concrete finisher. Experience as crew supervisor, tractor operator, job supervisor, and estimator. Other experience includes many other construction jobs, motorcycle mechanic experience, waitressing, and owning and operating a woodworking shop.

STRENGTHS AND CAPABILITIES

- Detail and big picture-oriented.
- Anticipating and solving problems.
- Very good with numbers in the field and with people.
- Bringing projects in on time and within budget without sacrificing quality.

page 1 of 2

Karen S. Adams
page 2 of 2

ACADEMIC BACKGROUND

1990 - 1994   Senior in Civil Engineering at the University of Arizona,
Tucson, AZ. G.P.A. of 3.85. Outstanding Junior and
Outstanding Service Awards for 1990. Honors recipient
every year from 1991 - 1994. Coursework stressing
construction management, environmental and
geotechnical engineering, IBM and MAC computer
literacy, and French. Graduated May 1994.

REFERENCES Available upon request.

ROBERT ELLISON

414 Jefferson Street

New Orleans, LA 70119

504-662-9973

SUMMARY

Environmental scientist with ten years' experience. Have held both private sector and government agency positions.

CAPABILITIES

- Experienced in visual inspection and chemical analysis of suspicious effluents
- Comprehensive knowledge of EPA methods and procedures
- Detailed understanding of state industrial pollution and toxin standards
- Experience in land management and reclamation research
- Project management and supervisory experience

EMPLOYERS

Environmental Defense Fund
Staff Environmentalist
(1998 - Present)

U.S. Environmental Protection Agency
Environmentalist III
(1994 - 1998)

United Chemical Corporation
Environmental Consultant
(1991 - 1994)

Louisiana Department of Fish and Wildlife
Field Inspector II
(1989 - 1991)

EDUCATION

B.S.
Chemistry
University of Illinois, Chicago

REFERENCES

Available Upon Request

Resumes for Executive and Management-Level Careers

DARREN TREVOL
43433 N. Melrose Ave.
Elmhurst, IL 60189
708/555-4328
708/555-1010
trevol2000@xxx.net

OBJECTIVE:

Senior vice president of sales and marketing for Vincent Electronics, Inc.

PROFESSIONAL ACHIEVEMENTS:

Marketing

- Researched computer market to coordinate product line with current public tastes and buying trends.
- Developed new approaches to marketing software products, including in-store displays and Internet advertising.
- Organized and planned convention displays and strategies.

Sales

- Introduced new and existing product lines through presentations to major clients.
- Increased sales from $27 million to $50 million in five years.
- Initiated and developed nine new accounts.
- Supervised five sales agencies throughout the United States.

EMPLOYMENT HISTORY:

Vincent Electronics Inc., Elmhurst, IL
Sales and Marketing Manager, 1994 - present

Porcelana Inc., Melrose Park, IL
Product Coordinator, 1989 - 1994

Radio Shack, Inc., New York, NY
Sales Representative, 1984 - 1989

EDUCATION:

New York University, New York, NY
B.S. 1984
Major: Business Administration
Minor: Computer Science

REFERENCES:

Available upon request.

Daniela A. Jamas

71 S.W. 15th Street, Sacramento, California 95814 (916) 555-7321

Objective

A staff management position in a human resources firm or in a corporate human resources department.

Related Experience and Skills

- Developed and provided one-day seminars and a ten-week adult education class in social services advocacy through Pacific Community College.
- Experienced with group participation, lecture, and one-on-one instructional techniques.
- Supervised a staff of ten to develop community-wide needs assessment; set training goals and objectives; developed an audience-appropriate curriculum; coordinated speaker schedule; evaluated training results.
- Tutored middle-school students with special needs on a one-on-one basis.
- Coordinated social services to help individuals meet their needs for support, counseling, resources, and information in other support services.
- Worked closely with government, private social service agencies, and businesses to integrate services that best met individual needs.
- Implemented, produced, and edited various newsletters; wrote articles for several magazines.
- Familiar with IBM computers, well versed in Macintosh word processing and database programs.
- Semifluent with both written and spoken Spanish.

Work History

- *Office Manager,* Environmental Consultants, Inc., Sacramento, CA, 1995 - present
- *Marketing Director,* All Seasons Windows, Sacramento, CA, 1991 - 1995
- *Telemarketing Director,* Raymond Bros., Inc., San Jose, CA, 1989 - 1991
- *Manager,* The Book Cover, San Jose, CA, 1986 - 1989
- *Manager,* Information and Referral Department of Public Affairs, Sacramento, CA, 1982 - 1986
- *Teacher's Aide,* Highland View Middle School, San Jose, CA, 1981 - 1982

Education

San Jose State University, B.S., 1981
Recreation and Leisure Studies, with minor in English

References available upon request

EDWARD J. FISHER
1456 Burlington Ave.
Cincinnati, Ohio 45642
(513) 555-8976

CAREER OBJECTIVE

A cost-effective performer with a proven record of accomplishment, my career objective is to utilize my management, marketing, and computer service experience to make an immediate contribution as a member of a professional management team.

OPERATING SYSTEMS EXPERTISE

MVSIXA, CICS, Vtam, CA/I, CA/7, NCP, SURPA, VPS, ACF2, Omegamon

HARDWARE

IBM 309X, 308X, IBM 4331, StorageTek 4400 ACS

CAREER SUMMARY

OPERATIONS MANAGER: 1994 - Present
Genair Corporation, Cincinnati, OH

Achievements:

Directed implementation of new data center and hired and trained operations and network personnel. Brought on-line ten months under scheduling.

Reduced printing costs by 50% resulting in an annual savings of $1.5M by managing a project team through the analysis, design, development, and implementation of new printing systems and procedures.

Installed corporate telecommunication systems, including PBX'S, key systems, and national contract with a major carrier, resulting in a savings of over $1M.

Planned and monitored annual operating budget, supervising technical staff consisting of 25 supervisors, analysts, operators, and remote schedulers.

Page 1 of 2

EDWARD J. FISHER
Page 2 of 2

CAREER SUMMARY (cont.)

OPERATIONS MANAGER: 1985 to 1994
Information Services Agency, Dayton, OH

Achievements:

Initiated automated problem resolution system resulting in reduction of recurring problems and elimination of tedious manual system.

Developed position titles and pay scales that resulted in identifiable career paths for operations personnel.

EDUCATION

Computer Science Degree from Rose-Hulman Institute of Technology, Terre Haute, Indiana

Master in Business from University of Notre Dame, South Bend, Indiana

PROFESSIONAL TRAINING

Managing Data Processing/IBM

Data Processing Operations Management/IBM

Turning Telephone Costs into Profits/University of Notre Dame

PROFESSIONAL AFFILIATIONS

ITUA - Indiana Telecommunications User Association

AFCOM - Association for Computer Operations Managers

REFERENCES AVAILABLE UPON REQUEST

HENRY JAZZINSKI
3000 Big Mile Road
Dallas, TX 84038
214/555-8888 (Daytime)
214/555-3839 (Evening)

OBJECTIVE

A management position in the sales and marketing field.

ACHIEVEMENTS

Sales

Increased watch sales from $3 million to $12 million during the past six years. Introduced new and existing product lines through presentations to marketing directors of major manufacturers. Developed 15 new accounts. Supervised five sales agencies throughout the United States and Canada.

Marketing

Developed new products expanding from watches to other accessories, which resulted in increased sales. Researched the watch market to coordinate product line with current fashion trends. Increased company's share of the market through improved quality products.

WORK HISTORY

Culture Shock Watch Co., Dallas, TX
Vice President of Sales and Marketing, 1988 - present

Nabisco Food Co., San Francisco, CA
Sales and Product Manager, 1983 - 1988

Avis, Inc., Los Angeles, CA
Sales Representative, 1978 - 1983

EDUCATION

University of Southern California, Los Angeles, CA
B.S. in Business Administration, 1977

SEMINARS

Dallas Sales and Marketing Seminar, 1996 - 1999
National Marketing Association, 1991 - 1993

References available on request.

MARGARET FONG

16201 Blossom Hill Road
San Jose, CA 95008
(408) 555-2985 cell phone
(408) 555-8923 home phone

SUMMARY

Experienced financial lending professional with strong analytical skills in all areas of banking. Background in commercial and construction lending, branch management, and new business development.

EXPERIENCE

December 1997–Present
COMMUNITY BANK OF LOS GATOS, Los Gatos, California
Vice President/Regional Manager

- Manage portfolio of new and existing commercial loans.
- Negotiate and structure loans for financial feasibility, industry analysis, and collateral evaluation.
- Implemented new construction lending department.
- Improved credit quality of substandard loan portfolio.
- Established 80 new commercial accounts during fiscal year 2000 in new Saratoga branch.

October 1994–November 1997
SANTA CLARA BANK, Santa Clara, California
Vice President/Manager

- Directed a $20 million branch; supervised all operations, new business development, and lending.
- Developed branch into a profitable entity in four years.
- Increased total deposits 30 percent annually.
- Increased commercial loan portfolio 400 percent in three years.

July 1992–October 1994
FIRST NATIONAL BANK, San Jose, California
Branch Manager

- Consistently met or exceeded branch goals and profit projections.

EDUCATION

San Jose State University, B.S. in marketing

COMMUNITY SERVICES

Chamber of Commerce, Los Gatos
Finance Committee, Los Gatos Methodist Church
City of Los Gatos Business Development Committee

Susan Lund

1225 Camden Road
Columbus, Ohio 43266
(614) 555-8316

Background

Dedicated, experienced RN seeking supervisory nursing position that uses my clinical, organizational, and human relations skills.

Previous Employment

November 1995 - Present
Covington General Hospital, Columbus, Ohio
Level IV Staff RN
Intensive Care Unit Supervisor

Charge nurse for 10-bed ICU. Supervise RNs, LPNs, and therapists. Facilitate implementation of multidisciplinary care plans. Schedule, train, and evaluate nursing staff. Carry out day-to-day directives of hospital administration.

April 1991 - November 1995
Good Shepherd Hospital, Milwaukee, Wisconsin
Level III Staff RN
Medical/Surgical Nurse

Observed, charted, and monitored patients' conditions. Assisted MDs with assessment and treatment. Provided general pre- and postoperative care. Developed discharge plans and instructed patients in home care.

May 1989 - April 1991
Lincoln Medical Center, Milwaukee, Wisconsin
Staff RN

Provided general nursing care at walk-in clinic, including community referral services, mental health and substance abuse interventions, and well-baby care. Instructed patients in home care and preventive health measures.

Credentials

University of Wisconsin, BSN, 1989
Licensed in Wisconsin (394-362392) and Ohio (775-760381)
Member, American Nurses Association

References

A list of references will be provided on request.

KEVIN L. BAUER

3890 43rd Avenue
Ann Arbor, Michigan 48106
(313) 555-3892

CAREER SUMMARY

General management executive with significant broad-based experience in consumer, manufacturing, and publishing businesses. Technical background in publishing, graphic arts, printing, and systems. Proven leadership skills and expertise in:

Sales   Strategic Planning

Marketing   Business Development & Acquisitions

Operations Management   Financial Analysis

PROFESSIONAL EXPERIENCE

D.D. WILLIAMS CORPORATION, 1993 - Present

A $1 billion Fortune 500 public corporation serving niche printing and graphics/video markets.

Executive Vice President, Santo Catalog and Commercial Group, Ann Arbor, Michigan, 1997 - Present

- Directed sales, marketing, customer services, estimating, and distribution for a two-plant, $125 million sales printing operation.

- Combined two acquired companies into the second largest corporate business group, eliminating $250,000 in duplication.

- Designed a national, market-driven strategy which delivered a 17% increase in sales.

- Generated new business sales of 30% in response to expanded and upgraded manufacturing equipment requirements.

- Increased profits 28% through focus on prospecting and pricing control. Improved control and productivity by reorganizing sales assignments and centralizing sales support functions.

Corporate Officer and Vice President, Oshkosh, Wisconsin, 1993 - 1997

- Key member of Corporate Management (executive) Committee with broad strategic, acquisition, business development, and marketing responsibility and authority in lean and highly autonomous corporate structure.

- Directed major capital expenditures, business plans, and incentives for 12 autonomous business units. Key board member for venture subsidiaries.

Page 1 of 2

(PROFESSIONAL EXPERIENCE continued)

- Formulated corporate mission and market strategy which led to major restructuring decisions.
- Completed the purchase and transitionally directed the Peters Companies, adding five new subsidiaries and two new print markets and expanding sales by more than $200 million.
- Accomplished other acquisitions and strategic divestitures, including the sale of the Flexible Packaging Group (two plants, $50 million sales) and the decision to divest the video group (five companies, $45 million sales).
- Established the long-range strategy for the D.D. Williams Publications Groups (two plants, $43 million sales) and the strategic plan to create the D.D. Williams Pre-Press Group (three plants, $18 million sales), including the group management organization and start-up of Color Response-Minnesota.
- Spearheaded a corporate identity campaign which emphasized D.D. Williams's national scope; developed a new corporate name which sparked investor and Wall Street interest.

GREETING CARDS, Inc., 1975 - 1993

A $1.5 billion market leader in consumer and publishing products.

Director of Corporate Development, Kansas City, Missouri, 1989 - 1993

- Spearheaded four-year diversification program resulting in Greeting's first major acquisitions of Beel & Craig ($254 million sales) and SSN (educational, specialty, and consumer software publisher).
- Managed all business/venture development, including acquisitions, new technologies, start-ups, joint ventures, and licensing agreements.
- Directed an electronics venture and an acquired educational software subsidiary.

Manager of Graphic Arts Engineering, Kansas City, Missouri, 1985 - 1989

Operations Manager, Kansas City, Missouri, 1980 - 1985

EDUCATION

University of Massachusetts, Amherst, M.S., Industrial Engineering, 1979

University of Tennessee, Knoxville, B.S., Mechanical Engineering, 1977

MICHELLE WOODS
1201 W. Porter Ave.
Oak Park, IL 60302
708/555-9000
708/555-9492

OBJECTIVE

Vice President of Operations at Osco Drug Co.

WORK EXPERIENCE

Osco Drug Co., Oak Park, IL
Manager of Operations, 1990 - present
Supervised marketing, production, distribution, and accounting. Introduced and developed a computer system to provide accurate inventory controls. Achieved efficiency savings of over $100,000 during system's first year of operation.

Product Manager, 1988 - 1990
Initiated several new products that resulted in high profit margins for the company. Coordinated research, production, and promotional programs. Introduced new packaging concepts.

Regional Sales Manager, 1986 - 1988
Supervised 34 brokers and salespeople. Increased sales 40 percent through special marketing programs. Developed better customer distribution at lower costs.

District Manager, 1985 - 1986
Handled sales in Chicago area. Increased profits 19 percent in my first year. Promoted to Regional Manager after one year.

Jewel Food Stores, Inc., Melrose Park, IL
Sales Representative, 1982 - 1985
Sold to wholesalers and chain stores in the Midwest. Opened many new accounts that previous sales representatives could not open.

OTHER ACHIEVEMENTS

Marketing consultant for private businesses.
Wrote a book on product efficiency.
Contributed to various trade journals.

page 1 of 2

EDUCATION

University of Michigan, Ann Arbor, MI

B.S., 1980
Major in business, minor in economics

Attended seminars at Simmons Institute, Cleveland, OH, and J. L. Kellogg School of Management, Evanston, IL

PROFESSIONAL MEMBERSHIPS

National Management Association
Lion's Club, Board of Directors
Midwest Sales Affiliates

REFERENCES

Available upon request.

Lee Ann Kusaka

3984 Briar Street
Oakland, California 94609
Home: (414) 555-2837
Cell: (414) 555-0098
E-mail: lakusaka@xxx.com

EDUCATION

M.S. in Public Health Administration, 1991
University of Hawaii

B.S. in Psychology, 1989
University of California, Berkeley

EXPERIENCE

General Manager
St. Mary's Medical Center
Oakland, California
1998 - Present

Direct day-to-day operations and long-range planning for medical clinic with annual budget of $2.5 million. Areas of responsibility include financial planning, cost containment, and staffing.

Achievements
- Increased first-year profits by 10 percent
- Continue to maintain steady financial growth
- Implemented marketing plan that resulted in a 15 percent increase in patient referrals from private physicians

Assistant Director
Lakehurst Recovery Center
San Francisco, California
1995 - 1997

Supervised medical records, admissions, and billing departments for substance abuse center with staff of 60.

Page 1 of 2

EXPERIENCE (cont.)

Achievements (Lakehurst Recovery Center)
- Streamlined billing procedures
- Reduced annual operating expenses by 5 percent

Assistant Administrator
Northwest Mental Health Center
Berkeley, California
1992 - 1995

Assisted general manager of 60-bed psychiatric center. Participated in all aspects of health management: educational, therapeutic, and personnel. Involved in hiring and training of new staff members and volunteers. Assisted in direct patient care and emergency intervention as needed. Responsible for all billing.

Achievements
- Successfully recruited and trained group of 12 new volunteers
- Secured a $250,000 federal grant for research in obsessive compulsive disorders
- Implemented HELP computer program for the entire center

AFFILIATIONS

California Public Health Council
American Management Association
National Academy of Office Administrators

REFERENCES

Available on request

AMY RANDALL

4967 Front Street
Gallup, New Mexico 87321
(505) 555-7761
E-mail: randall@xxx.com

GOAL

A position as food and service manager.

EDUCATION

B.A. Hotel Management, University of Santa Fe, New Mexico, 1982

ACCOMPLISHMENTS

1998 - present
- Created recipes that appeared in the 1998 *New York Times Cookbook*
- Taught adult education cooking courses
- Entered and won several cooking contests
- Created and sold recipes for:
    Green bean walnut pate
    Carrot yam soup
    Salmon in ginger-soy sauce
    Sauteed spinach with garlic and red pepper
    Semolina pizza with zucchini and pesto topping
    Gluten-free pizza with onions, rosemary, and roasted garlic
- Competed for a cooking program on a major TV network

CAREER EXPERIENCES

1990 - 1998   Hilton Hotel, Santa Fe, New Mexico
Food and beverage manager
- Directed the food services for the hotel manager
- Supervised the operation of the hotel's restaurants and banquet facilities
- Scheduled and supervised food and beverage preparation
- Directed the work of 32 service workers
- Planned meals, estimated costs, and ordered supplies

1982 - 1990   Comfort Inn, Santa Fe, New Mexico
Assistant to F&B manager
- Assisted in training and supervising the food service staff
- Inspected hotel's restaurant and banquet facilities
- Planned menu
- Directed food supply office

REFERENCES AVAILABLE UPON REQUEST

Lance Jacobson

1243 Prince Road
Arlington, VA 87554
(508) 555-8834 cellular
(508) 555-3545 home

Objective:

A senior human resources management position that would effectively utilize my experience and legal education.

Employers:

Young & Barkley International
1998 - Present
Corporate Manager, Human Resources Department

General Dynamics
1993 - 1998
Associate Manager, Human Resources

Expertise:

Employment, Staffing & EEO

- Experience in managing the employment, staffing, and EEO functions.
- Planned, developed, and implemented several EEO initiatives that increased the company's visibility among minority groups and women.
- Successfully screened, interviewed, tested, and recruited both exempt and nonexempt personnel.
- Responsible for the successful introduction of the company's relocation policy.
- Developed alliances with professional recruiters, advertising agencies, and temporary services.
- Designed and implemented job posting programs.
- Authored affirmative action plans and policies.
- Successfully defended employers against charges of discrimination.

Education:

California State College of Law
J.D., 1993

University of Southern California
B.A., Business Administration, 1978
Minor in Sociology

JOHN JAMES HYMAN III
5555 Euclid Avenue • Ft. Lauderdale, FL 33053
305/555-8982 (Day) • 305/555-6001 (Evening)

OBJECTIVE: A management position with a machine tool manufacturer where I can apply my abilities and experience in sales and marketing.

WORK EXPERIENCE:

Florida Hydraulics, Inc., Miami, FL

Assistant Sales Manager, January 1994 - present

Managed a staff of seven sales representatives. Supervised the production of a marketing newsletter that has circulation throughout the company. Cowrote the annual marketing plan. Served as a liaison between sales staff and upper management.

Peaston Machine Tools, Inc., Tampa, FL

Sales Representative, March 1991 - November 1993

Sold machine tools to business and industry. Wrote articles on sales techniques for monthly newsletter. Handled seven accounts in which sales rose 29 percent during my tenure.

EDUCATION:

B.S. in Civil Engineering

Miami University, Miami, FL, 1990

PROFESSIONAL MEMBERSHIPS:

Society of Civil Engineers, New York, NY
1992 - present

Machine Tools Sales Organization, Chicago, IL
1993 - present

SPECIAL SKILLS: Fluent in Spanish and French.

REFERENCES: Available on request.

JUAN C. GARCIA
2103 Afton Street
Temple Hill, Maryland 20748
Home (301) 555-2419

EDUCATION:

Columbia University, *New York, NY*
Majors: Business, Philosophy
Degree expected: Bachelor of Arts, 2000
Grade point average: 3.0
Regents Scholarship recipient
Columbia University Scholarship recipient

EXPERIENCE:

7/99 - 9/99   Graduate Business Library, Columbia University, NY
General library duties. Entered new students and books into computer system. Gave out microfiche. Reserved and distributed materials.

9/98 - 5/99   German Department, Columbia University, NY
Performed general office duties. Offered extensive information assistance by phone and in person. Collated and proofread class materials. Assisted professors in the gathering of class materials.

6/98 - 9/98   Loan Collections Department, Columbia University, NY
Initiated new filing system for the office. Checked arrears in Bursar's Office during registration period.

9/97 - 5/98   School of Continuing Education, Columbia University, NY
Involved in heavy public contact as well as general clerical duties.

SPECIAL ABILITIES:

Fluent in Spanish. Currently studying German. Can program in Virtual Basic. Excellent research skills.

REFERENCES:

Available on request.

THEODORE WELLINGTON
34 W. Washington Drive
New York, NY 10019
212/555-4904

JOB OBJECTIVE

A senior management position in sales and marketing.

RELEVANT ACHIEVEMENTS

- Introduced new and existing product lines through presentations to marketing directors.
- Developed new products, which resulted in increased sales.
- Increased sales from $3 million to $12 million during the past six years.
- Supervised five sales agencies throughout the United States and Canada.
- Developed fifteen new accounts.
- Researched the market to coordinate product line with current trends.
- Increased company's share of the market through improved quality products.
- Oversaw programming and development of company website.

EMPLOYMENT HISTORY

Surf City Skateboard Co., New York, NY

　　Vice President of Sales and Marketing, 1987 - present

Nike, Inc., San Bernardino, CA

　　Sales and Product Manager, 1982 - 1987

Vons Ltd., Los Angeles, CA

　　Sales Representative, 1977 - 1982

EDUCATION

University of Southern California, Los Angeles, CA

　　B.S. in Marketing, 1975

SEMINARS

Manhattan Sales & Marketing Seminar, 1995 - 1998

National Marketing Association, 1996 - 1997

Webnoize, 1999

REFERENCES

Provided on request.

DARREN SCHWARZWALTER
1001 Park Avenue
New York, NY 11201
212/555-1113
darrens@xxx.com

JOB SOUGHT

A position in circulation management within the publishing field.

WORK EXPERIENCE

PARKER PUBLISHING CO., NEW YORK, NY

Circulation Director, 1997 - present

Developed and implemented all circulation and related programs. Devised and coordinated merchandise marketing promotions. Oversaw subscription promotion, direct response, graphics buying, fulfillment, E-commerce, budgets, agency sales, and newsstand sales.

NORTHEAST MAGAZINE, WHITE PLAINS, NY

Circulation Director, 1991 - 1997

Directed all circulation areas, direct response programs, agency sales, subscription programs, budgets, and fulfillment. Assisted in advertising and promotion.

OMNI MAGAZINE, NEW YORK, NY

Assistant Circulation Director, 1988 -1991

Assisted Circulation Director in circulation, including subscription promotion, newsstand, fulfillment, budgets, and direct-response programs.

SARRIS & SARRIS PUBLISHING, NEW YORK, NY

Assistant Operations Manager, 1984 - 1987

Assisted in magazine, book, direct-mail, and merchandise fulfillment services.

EDUCATION

Forest College, Forest Lawn, NY

B.A. in English, 1983

Forest College School of Business Administration

Forest Lawn, NY, 1984

REFERENCES PROVIDED UPON REQUEST.

ANGELINA BERGMAN

884 N.W. 12th Avenue
Fort Worth, Texas 76109
(214) 555-1985 (daytime)
(817) 555-9712 (evening and weekend)

SUMMARY OF QUALIFICATIONS

General management executive with 15 years experience in corporate sales, marketing, customer service, development, and distribution.

EXPERIENCE

DaMark-Dolin America Corp.   *1990 - present*

A $640 million Fortune 500 public corporation serving the cosmetics industry.

EXECUTIVE VICE PRESIDENT, Dallas, Texas
1994 - present

Catalog and Commercial Division. Direct sales, marketing, customer relations, and distribution for a two-plant, $180 million sales operation. Combined two acquired companies into the second-largest corporate division. Eliminated $325,000 in duplication costs. Designed national marketing strategy that produced a 15 percent sales increase. Generated 30 percent increase in new-business sales by expanding and upgrading product production. Increased profits by a margin of 23 percent in one year by enlarging client base and controlling prices. Improved quality control and productivity by reorganizing departments and centralizing support functions.

CORPORATE OFFICER AND VICE PRESIDENT, Houston, Texas
1990 - 1994

Corporate Management Division. Directed strategic acquisition business development, marketing, and venture subsidiaries. Directed major capital expenditures, business plans, and incentive programs for twelve business units. Formulated corporate mission and established long-range strategic plan, which led to supervision of major restructuring decisions. Completed several acquisitions and strategic divestitures that expanded the corporate profit margin approximately 18 percent.

Angelina Bergman
Page 2

EXPERIENCE, CONTINUED

DIRECTOR OF CORPORATE DEVELOPMENT, Houston, Texas
1983 - 1990

Corporate Management Division. Spearheaded four years of product design and diversification, resulting in the corporation's first major market breakthrough in the pharmaceutical industry. Managed all business and venture development, including acquisitions, new technologies, start-ups, joint ventures, and leasing agreements. Directed development of a new manufacturing line of medicinal lotions through acquisition of Soltero, Inc. Improved plant productivity by 15 percent.

EARLY CAREER POSITIONS   1975 - 1983

Operations Management, WemCo Inc., Houston, Texas
Design Module Leader, Patterson Corporation, Houston, Texas
Project Team Leader, Patterson Corporation, Shreveport, Louisiana

EDUCATION

Louisiana State University, M.S., Chemical Engineering & Business, 1983
University of Montana, B.S., Mechanical Engineering, 1975

REFERENCES AVAILABLE ON REQUEST.

YOLANDA RICHARDS

6600 Manhattan Ave.
Brooklyn, NY 10090
718/555-9656
yolanda@xxx.com

JOB OBJECTIVE:

Vice President of Focus Lens, Inc.

PROFESSIONAL EXPERIENCE:

Focus Lens, Inc., New York, NY
Regional Manager, 1992 - present

Sold custom-designed point-of-purchase elements and product displays. Researched target areas and developed new account leads. Placed advertising in national publications and on websites. Made sales presentations to potential customers. Participated in lens industry trade shows.

Redheart Lawn Co., Forest Lawn, NY
District Sales Manager, 1989 - 1991

Planned successful sales strategies to identify and develop new accounts. Supervised seven sales representatives. Increased sales by at least 20 percent in each of my four years. Researched and analyzed market conditions to seek out new customers. Wrote monthly sales reports.

Ace Office Supply Co., Brooklyn, NY
Account Executive, 1986 - 1989

Managed accounts in the New York metropolitan area. Expanded customer base 30 percent in four years. Maintained daily contact with customers by telephone to ensure good customer/company relations. Wrote product information flyers and distributed them through a direct-mail program.

EDUCATION:

Northwestern University, Evanston, IL
M.B.A. with honors, 1985

Drake University, Des Moines, IA
B.A. in Accounting, 1982

PROFESSIONAL MEMBERSHIPS:

Brooklyn Sales Association, 1991 - present
New York Merchants Group, 1989 - present

REFERENCES:

Available upon request.

James K. Melton

784 Crest Avenue • San Antonio, TX 78284 • Jamesmelton@xxx.com • (723) 555-1889

Goal

Management of daily operation and long-range planning for midsize medical clinic or nonprofit health care corporation.

Abilities

- Financial Planning
- Cost Containment
- Staffing
- Marketing
- Systems Analysis
- Grant Writing

Work Experience

General Manager, 1997 - Present
Ridgeway Medical Clinic

Director, 1993 - 1997
Garner Medical Center

Assistant Administrator, 1990 - 1993
Dallas Community Mental Health Program

Education

MBA   University of Texas, 1989
RN   Larrabee School of Nursing, 1985
Member, Texas Nurses Association
Member, National Academy of Health Management
Red Cross CPR Certification
Texas Nursing License #214-476182

Computer Experience

Proficient in Microsoft Office 2000, including Access, PowerPoint, Excel, and Word. Familiar with PageMaker, Adobe Photoshop, and QuarkXpress. Also familiar with a variety of database management systems and other office management software.

References Available

WILLIAM ROBERT GARRETT

5050 W. Palatine Road
Palatine, IL 60067
708/555-3789 (Home)
708/555-1000 (Work)
bill.microtech@xxx.net

JOB OBJECTIVE

A management-level position in computer sales where I can use my sales and technical experience in the computer industry.

RELEVANT EXPERIENCE

Sales

- Handled sales accounts for northwest suburban Chicago area.
- Expanded customer base by 25 percent during my tenure.
- Conducted field visits to solve customers' problems.
- Maintained daily contact with customers to ensure good customer/company relations.
- Wrote product information flyers and sales manual.
- Contributed content to company website.

Technical

- Installed and maintained operating system.
- Defined and oversaw network lists and tables.
- Coordinated problem solving with phone companies.
- Performance-tuned subsystems and networks.
- Planned and installed new hardware and programming techniques.

Systems Analysis

- Documented procedures for mechanization of payroll department.
- Created standards and procedures for main accounting system.
- Developed test procedures for reverification of new application.
- Developed distribution lists, user IDs, and standards for electronic mail system.

EMPLOYMENT HISTORY

MICROTECH COMPUTERS, Northbrook, IL
Account Executive, 1987 - present

APPLE COMPUTERS, Berkeley, CA
Technical Support Specialist, 1980 - 1987

DATALOG, INC., St. Louis, MO
Systems Analyst, 1969 - 1979

EDUCATION

UNIVERSITY OF CHICAGO, Chicago, IL

M.S. in Mathematics, 1967
Honors graduate

NORTHWESTERN UNIVERSITY, Evanston, IL

B.S. in Communications, 1964

PROFESSIONAL AFFILIATIONS

Computer Sales Association
Illinois Business Chapter
Citizens for a Cleaner Environment

SEMINARS

Microtech Sales Seminars
Apple Technical Workshops

REFERENCES AVAILABLE ON REQUEST.

Robert A. Figueroa
2175 Broadway
Morganton, North Carolina 28655
(704) 555-3795
(704) 555-0908 cell phone/voice mail

OBJECTIVE: A senior management position requiring leadership, decisiveness, and vision.

PROFESSIONAL BACKGROUND

Career military officer, United States Army
Active service: June 1976–present
Rank: Major General

Career summary:

- Began service as a Second Lieutenant.
- Served as a combat infantry officer in South Vietnam.
- Progressed through officer ranks with consistently high evaluations.
- In addition to Vietnam, stationed in West Germany, South Korea, and several postings in the continental United States, including the Pentagon.
- Specialized in infantry leadership with secondary specialty in tactical/strategic intelligence.

AWARDS/ACCOMPLISHMENTS

Received numerous medals, ribbons, and other recognitions including Bronze Star, Purple Heart, Meritorious Service Medal, and others.
Consistently earned praise from superior officers for outstanding performance.

EDUCATION

B.S., United States Military Academy, West Point, New York, 1976.
Graduated in top 25 percent of class.

M.B.A., University of Texas, Austin, Texas, 1984.
Completed additional studies at U.S. Army Command and General Staff College, Fort Leavenworth, Kansas, and at Army War College, Carlisle Barracks, Pennsylvania.

Additional details regarding Army career available on request.

References provided on request.

PETER SIMMONS

678 Park Street #546
Noblesville, IN 46060
pesimm@xxx.com

OBJECTIVE:

To obtain an executive position in marketing with an emerging company that is dedicated to a long-term program.

EXPERIENCE:

5/98 - Present   DCS SOFTWARE, INC., Noblesville, IN
Senior Partner
Contingency marketing agency

- Designed marketing strategies for local and national companies
- Directly responsible for meeting payroll of 25 full-time employees
- Improved sales for one company by over 25 percent in a 12-month period
- Developed marketing programs for corporations

1/97 - 5/98   BLAUVELT ENGINEERS, New York, NY
Regional Sales Manager
Business communications systems

- Set regional sales record in six months
- Procured ten national accounts
- Exceeded company goals for the 1997 fiscal year
- Developed sales marketing program for the northwest regional area

8/93 - 1/97   EDWARDS AND KELCEY, Livingston, NJ
Marketing Director

- Implemented international marketing program
- Promoted from sales executive to marketing director
- Company's sales increased over 100 percent in a 12-month span
- Successful in developing database and reselling directly

EDUCATION:

Stevens Institute of Technology, Hoboken, NJ
Bachelor of Arts degree in Technical Marketing Design, 1993

DAVID ALLEN POPE
7806 Paso Robles Road
San Antonio, TX 78284
(512) 555-4948
E-mail: dap@xxx.net

Summary of Experience:

- Chief Financial Officer of a $90 million privately held company and a start-up e-commerce business.

- Controller of $300 million group, generating $150 million in earnings yearly.

- Thirteen years' experience in software, telecommunications, disk drive, and manufacturing companies.

- Specialist in internal controls, MIS, and cost containment programs.

Experience:

Chief Financial Officer, Focus Computers, San Antonio, TX, 2000–2001
Manufacturer of tape, disk, and solid state disk drives. The company has annual revenues of $90 million and employs 500 people worldwide.

- Sold discontinued operation with annual revenues of $10 million.

- Reduced accounts receivable balances by 35 percent.

- Wrote corporate strategic business plan.

- Raised $15 million in new financing offering.

- Eliminated unnecessary operating and manpower costs.

Chief Financial Officer, Games, Inc., Los Angeles, CA, 2000
Start-up company developing a handheld interactive computer game module and retailing games on company website.

- Implemented computerized financial system and new chart of accounts.

- Responsible for all administrative functions.

- Developed 401(k) benefit plans.

- Provided advice on distribution channels and marketing strategy.

Controller, Houston Systems, Houston, TX, 1998–2000
Seller of UNIX operating systems and other software applications. The family-operated company has annual revenues of $150 million and employs 1,250 people worldwide.

- Installed new general ledger and accounts payable systems and new chart of accounts.

- Defined financial job descriptions, salary levels, and career paths.

- Implemented monthly departmental, sales, and product line profitability reporting.

- Developed intercompany transfer cost strategy.

Page one of two

David Allen Pope—Page two of two

Consultant, Compucom, Austin, TX, 1996–1998
Manufacturer and distributor of modem boards.

- Developed corporate business plan and managed banking and investor relationships.
- Improved computerized financial systems.

Scott Paper Products, Los Angeles, CA, 1988–1996
Worked in the packaging group, which included food packaging, plastic film manufacturing, and chemical products.

Group Controller
Group included five divisions and 12 manufacturing locations.

- Developed strategic, annual, and capital plans as well as accounting policies and procedures.
- Performed financial valuation for division spin-off.

Plant Controller

- Developed plant financial reporting package.
- Increased output by 40 percent and reduced staff by 10 percent.

Management Consultant, McKinsey and Company, Los Angeles, CA, 1986–1988
- Developed the consulting practice in Hong Kong.
- Audited and assisted in the preparation of financial and SEC statements.

Education:

MIT Sloan School of Management, Cambridge, MA: M.B.A., 1986
Princeton University, Princeton, NJ: B.A. in History, 1984

DEREK STRONG

1501 N. Polk Ave.
Springfield, IL 66660
217-555-5552

POSITION DESIRED:

Financial Management Director.

SKILLS & ACHIEVEMENTS:

Research

- Conducted consumer surveys.
- Coordinated policy formulation.
- Developed advertising concepts and strategies.
- Controlled transportation and distribution costs.

Development

- Handled costs forecasting and pricing policies.
- Implemented costing techniques.
- Oversaw research and development budgeting.
- Conducted feasibility studies.

Planning

- Handled long- and short-range financial forecasting.
- Managed capital investment opportunities.
- Made financial projections.
- Directed tax reductions and budgets.

Analysis

- Involved in statistical methodologies and analysis.
- Administered trend analysis.
- Conducted media evaluations and survey designs.

WORK EXPERIENCE:

Control Data, Inc., Springfield, IL
Senior Financial Analyst, 1998 - present

Warner Co., Jackson, MS
Financial Analyst, 1988 - 1998

EDUCATION:

Howard University, Washington, DC
M.A. in Financial Planning, 1988

Thelonious College, Jackson, MS
B.A. in Economics, 1986

References available on request.

REBECCA ROBINSON

1801 Kirchoff Rd.
Rolling Meadows, IL 60007
708/555-3839
rebrob@xxx.net

JOB OBJECTIVE

Public relations director for Hot Fun Sunglasses Co.

ACCOMPLISHMENTS & ACHIEVEMENTS

- Managed a sales/marketing staff that included account managers and sales representatives.
- Represented company to clients and retailers.
- Monitored and studied the effectiveness of a national distribution network.
- Organized and planned convention displays and strategy.
- Designed and executed direct-mail campaign that identified marketplace needs and new options for products.
- Oversaw all aspects of sales/marketing budget.
- Conceived ads, posters, and point-of-purchase materials for products.
- Initiated and published a monthly newsletter that was distributed to current and potential customers.
- Handled design and programming for www.hotfunsunglasses.com website.

WORK HISTORY

Hot Fun Sunglasses Co., Schaumburg, IL

National Sales Manager, 1996 - present

Account Manager, 1994 - 1996

Assistant Account Manager, 1993 - 1994

Research Assistant, 1991 - 1993

Secretary, 1987 - 1991

EDUCATION

Indiana University, Bloomington, IN

B.A. in Economics, 1987

SEMINARS

National Marketing Association Seminars, 1994 - 1998

SPECIAL SKILLS

Computer programming experience, including HTML, database, and spreadsheet skills.

REFERENCES AVAILABLE.

JANE P. HARPER
8395 Beaumont Drive
Lincoln, Nebraska 68508

OBJECTIVE: A managerial position in a major Midwest private corporation that will maximize my proven abilities in:

- Administrative Management
- Organizational Development
- Corporate Affairs
- Public and Community Relations

SKILLS/EXPERIENCE

- Recruited, trained, and developed management teams of up to 15, supervising up to 2,800 employees.
- Successfully prepared and administered operating and capital budgets totaling up to $133 million.
- Experienced in initiating and overseeing all operating functions associated with capital improvement projects totaling $150 million.
- Developed marketing and public relations programs that generated significant private-sector business. Created public and private-sector partnerships that fostered substantial commercial and entrepreneurial growth.
- Guided operations analyses resulting in significant efficiency improvements and cost savings through changes in work processes and operating procedures, upgrades to management methods and systems, and reallocation and downsizing of workforce.

CAREER HISTORY

Chief Executive Officer, City of Lincoln, NE

- Recruited in 1996 to improve the financial situation, strengthen organizational planning and development as well as establish better communication and information management systems. Responsible for administrative and business affairs including management staffing, budgeting, finance, employee relations, service programs, and community relations.
- Initiated multilevel operations analysis used as basis for creating new strategic plan.

CAREER HISTORY continued

- Identified and led planning, design, and completion of capital improvement projects totaling more than $150 million.
- Supervised development of business plan that reduced operating costs $800,000 in key corporate component.
- Initiated analysis and guided development of internal organization to better manage labor relations and employee benefits functions. Eliminated two-year backlog of unresolved worker compensation cases.
- Prepared and implemented reorganization that resulted in creation of central data processing and management information services functions.
- Led and implemented reorganization that resulted in creation of central data processing and management information services functions.

General Manager, City of Greeley, Colorado

- Recruited in 1994 to unify and upgrade administrative systems/procedures and gain better control of finances. Responsible for all day-to-day operations.
- Introduced coordinated management reporting system which yielded significant improvements in internal/external communications, management decision making, and organizational efficiency.
- Adapted existing budget to modified zero-base budgeting system.
- Reversed trend of economic base erosion by working with existing businesses to foster expansion and improved competitiveness.

Previous Experience: Includes progressive general management positions in public sector organizations in Florida, Oklahoma, and Maine.

EDUCATION

Master's Degree, Marcus Graduate School, University of Ohio, Athens, 1990
Bachelor's Degree, Bates College, Lewiston, Maine, 1985

References provided on request

THOMAS GEORGE UHR

4220 Woodridge Drive
Ft. Lauderdale, FL 30898
305/555-2898 (Home)
305/555-2900 (Work)
thuhr@xxx.com

OBJECTIVE

A career in business management in the technical industry.

SKILLS & ACHIEVEMENTS

MANAGEMENT

- Hired consultant engineers and trained them in technical and interpersonal communications.
- Oversaw the expansion of the department.
- Developed a career path strategy with management, which was successfully implemented.

ADMINISTRATION

- Supervised seven employees responsible for running the central communications operation.
- Handled the inventory of the product development department.
- Wrote and developed a proposal that led to the implementation of a streamlined communications system.

PERSONNEL

- Trained over 300 people, including vice presidents, managers, salespeople, and field engineers.
- Developed course objectives and a task analysis for trainees.
- Oversaw personnel evaluations and made appropriate recommendations.

EMPLOYMENT HISTORY

PORTER & HAWKINS, INC., MIAMI, FL

General Manager, Communications Department, 1994 - present
Assistant Director of Personnel, 1990 - 1994
Technical Instructor, 1987 - 1990
Technician, 1982 - 1987

EDUCATION

UNIVERSITY OF FLORIDA, MIAMI, FL

B.A. in Management, Evening Division, 1989

MIAMI-DADE COMMUNITY COLLEGE, MIAMI, FL

Certificate in Electronics, 1981

REFERENCES

Available upon request.

PAULA STEVENSON
2782 W. 57th St.
Washington, DC 02390
202/555-8908
202/555-7200

OBJECTIVE:

A management position in the import business.

WORK EXPERIENCE:

Sandler Imports, Washington, DC

Manager of Operations, 1994 - present

Managed ten field representatives. Handled information dissemination and distribution. Codesigned a full-color catalog. Placed advertising in major trade publications. Promoted products at trade shows and on company website. Maintained inventory status reports and personnel records.

HTO Publishing Co., Owings Mills, MD

Distribution Assistant, 1987 - 1994

Developed new distribution outlets through cold calls and follow-up visits. Increased distribution in my district by 45 percent over a three-year period. Coordinated a direct-mail program that increased magazine subscriptions 120 percent.

Eastman Kodak Co., Atlanta, GA

Sales Representative, 1982 - 1987

Sold and serviced office copiers to businesses and schools in the greater Atlanta area. Maintained good customer relations through frequent calls and visits. Identified potential customers.

EDUCATION:

Georgetown University, Washington, DC

B.S. in Communications, 1981

PROFESSIONAL MEMBERSHIPS:

National Association of Importers

DC Community Association

Lion's Club

REFERENCES:

Available on request.

ROBERT COSTANZA
1711 N. Gurman Ave.
Atlantic City, NJ 02110
609/555-8971

CAREER OBJECTIVE: Restaurant Management.

EXPERIENCE:

Food Service

- Supervised kitchen staff of eight.
- Conducted business with a local catering service.
- Interviewed, hired, and trained student food service workers.
- Catered banquets.
- Served dining patrons as a waiter.

Management

- Ordered and maintained inventory of all food and beverages for a college cafeteria.
- Planned budget and strictly adhered to it.
- Organized work schedules for student workers.
- Managed computerized purchasing, bookkeeping, and payroll.

Food Preparation

- Assisted in the preparation of meals for 90 children and adults at a summer camp.
- Planned meals for 250 resident students.

EMPLOYMENT HISTORY:

Szabo Food Service/Jersey College, Atlantic City, NJ
Food Service Director, 1998 - present

Jersey College, Atlantic City, NJ
Assistant Cafeteria Director, 1997 - 1998

North Shore Children's Camp, Skokie, IL
Dining Hall Director, 1996 - 1997

Paco's Restaurant, Atlantic City, NJ
Waiter, 1995

Tacky's, Garden City, NJ
Busboy, 1994

EDUCATION:

Jersey College, Atlantic City, NJ
B.S. in Business, June 1998

REFERENCES FURNISHED ON REQUEST.

WILLIAM ACUNA

202 Bedford Lane
Roselle, Illinois 60172
(708) 555-8162 Home
(708) 555-3571 Cellular

Background: Professional health care manager who provides sound business leadership while creating an environment conducive to compassionate patient care.

Skills:

Business
- Sales
- Budgetary Control
- Marketing
- Purchasing

Supervisory
- Employee Recruitment
- Performance Evaluations
- Training
- Scheduling

Employers: 1996 - Present
Director, Harrison Home Health
Elmhurst, Illinois

Direct all aspects of agency. Develop and implement marketing plan. Ensure compliance with all state and federal regulations. Purchase all durable medical equipment. Develop and monitor annual budget.

1991 - 1996
Personnel Director, St. Catherine's Skilled Care Center
Mount Prospect, Illinois

Responsible for all aspects of human resources for staff of 20+ health care workers. Duties included hiring, training, supervising, scheduling, and evaluating employees.

Page 1 of 2

1989 - 1991
Level III RN, Rosary Hospital
Park Ridge, Illinois

Provided direct patient care in pediatrics and medical/surgical departments.

Education: BSN, University of Illinois, Chicago, 1989
Minor in Accounting

Affiliations: Illinois Nurses Association
Society of Health Care Managers

References: Available on request

IVAR T. KOPESKI
501 W. Glendale Blvd.
Kansas City, MO 51132
816/555-3524
816/555-9090
kop2000@xxx.com

OBJECTIVE

Regional sales manager for a national manufacturer/distributor.

EXPERIENCE

REB Pharmaceuticals, Kansas City, MO

District Sales Manager, 1992 - present
Directed the selling and servicing of accounts to physicians, pharmacies, and hospitals in the Kansas City area. Increased sales by 50 percent in three years. Initiated an incentive plan that resulted in 21 new accounts. Worked with production department to improve product quality.

Jacobs & Jacobs Advertising, Trenton, NJ

Display Coordinator, 1989 - 1992
Coordinated and supervised the installation of displays in men's clothing stores in the Trenton area. Managed a five-person office in all aspects of display planning and production. Worked to help place the firm in the syndicated display advertising field.

Mark Shale, Inc., Schaumburg, IL

Retail Store Manager, 1985 - 1989
Promoted from salesperson to assistant manager to manager within two years. Supervised the designing of display for interior and windows. Handled all aspects of personnel, sales promotions, inventory control, and new products. Interacted with corporate management frequently.

EDUCATION

Harper College, Palatine, IL

Attended two years (1983 - 1985) and majored in advertising.

American Institute, Putnum, NJ

Completed course on sales and marketing techniques, 1991

MEMBERSHIPS

American Display Advertisers
Kansas City Sales Association
Kansas City Community Development Association

REFERENCES

Available upon request

CARLOS MARCOS
45 TABOR HILL RD.
TULSA, OK 55678
(406) 555-7865 HOME
(406) 555-2453 CELLULAR/VOICE MAIL

EXPERIENCE:

1994 to Present
Morton Enterprises
Vice President Law and Administration
- Report to the chairman and CEO of this multistate holding company and investment firm.
- Supervise a staff of 17 responsible for three critical administrative company functions.
- Successfully defended the company in a $23 million product liability charge alleging unsafe manufacturing practices.

1992 to 1994
Rossi, James & Pasternack, CPAs
Partner
- Was responsible for managing the firm's investment banking practice.
- Utilized my accounting and legal training to advise clients on financial and legal implications of various business decisions.
- Developed $45 million in new business and repeat assignments from established clients.

1998 to 1992
Able, Swain and Pritchard
Partner
Senior Associate
- Worked on legal issues affecting the financial service industry.
- Successfully defended Silverman Partners in a $34 million insider trading case.
- Developed seven new clients and generated $1,130,000 in new business.

EDUCATION:

Yale University
  J.D., 1988

University of Tulsa
  B.S., Business, concentration in Accounting

References Available

RANDALL COURY
62 Collins Place, #43
New Orleans, LA 33290
504/555-3490
504/555-3999

OBJECTIVE

A position as manager of a record store.

EMPLOYMENT HISTORY

WEST RECORDS, New Orleans, LA

Assistant Manager, 1997 - present

Sold records, waited on customers, assisted in product selection and ordering, handled special orders and returned merchandise. Designed window displays. Oversaw the placement of ads for a major advertising campaign. Represented the store at conventions. Implemented and maintained store website (www.westrecords.com) and E-mail database.

THE BELT STORE, West Lake, LA

Salesperson, 1995 - 1996

Sold accessories to customers, filled special orders, organized and arranged inventory. Handled customer returns and special requests. Assisted in the design of window displays.

EDUCATION

EAST CENTRAL HIGH SCHOOL, New Orleans, LA

Graduated June 1996
Ranked 12th in a class of 200
Tennis Team
Homecoming Committee

REFERENCES

Available on request.

RANDALL BERTRAND KENNEDY
7901 Martella Ave.
New Orleans, LA 29920
504/555-2900 (Day)
504/555-2810 (Evening)
rbk@xxx.net

WORK EXPERIENCE

Johannson, Inc., New Orleans, LA

Industrial Relations Manager, 1994 - present

Oversaw all labor relations between the corporation and the union. Worked with the personnel department to plan labor policy, negotiate contracts, review hiring practices, and maintain records. Participated on grievance committees. Advised Vice President of Personnel on legal matters. Supervised a staff of ten employees.

Target Discount Stores, Inc., Los Angeles, CA

Assistant Personnel Manager, 1989 - 1994

Supervised a staff of eight interviewers and testers for hiring of office and warehouse personnel. Assisted Personnel Manager with all department operations. Oversaw all records for warehouse personnel. Developed a successful training and evaluation program for all company employees.

Republic Telephone, Inc., Detroit, MI

Personnel Intern, 1988 - 1989

Assisted with testing and evaluation of prospective employees. Scheduled interviews. Maintained records.

EDUCATION

University of Michigan, Ann Arbor, MI

Juris Doctor, 1989
Admitted to the Michigan Bar Association, 1989

University of Virginia, Norfolk, VA

B.S. in Management, 1985

REFERENCES

Available on request

BRIAN P. MILLER

212 Brookside Avenue East • Portland, Oregon 97786
503/555-2238 • bmiller@xxx.com

OBJECTIVE

A responsible and challenging managerial position where my extensive supervisory background can be utilized to achieve company goals.

EDUCATION

University of Oregon - Portland, Oregon; MBA in Business Management, 1983 Honors: Dean's List, 1981 - 1983

Hooper-Paterson College, Eugene, Oregon; B.S. in Marketing, 1981
Honors: Dean's List, 1978 - 1981

PROFESSIONAL EXPERIENCE

Operations Manager, Euro Auto Car Leasing Company
London, England, 1990 - 1999
Responsible for the largest region in the country, with a $2.5 million USD per month revenue and 250 fleet accounts. Servicing all lease customers with respect to purchasing new vehicles and facilitating delivery. Implemented preventive maintenance program, established a dealer network for cost effective purchasing of new vehicles. Supervised a staff of twelve maintenance and purchasing coordinators. Conducted program planning and presentation, projected account profitability, maintained profitability reports and analyses.

Account Manager, Dictaphone Corporation
Salem, Oregon, 1983 - 1990
Established service agreement accounts, prospected for leads and referrals, maintained branch inventory on all stock. Monitored activity and technological advancements of competitors and emphasized similar features in sales presentations.

AWARDS

- Manager of the Year, European Division, Euro Auto Car Leasing, 1994 and 1999.
- Best Performance New Sales Representative, Dictaphone Corporation, 1983.

SUMMARY OF ACHIEVEMENTS

- Developed training programs that have enhanced sales performance and directly increased sales revenue by 15 percent.
- Have decreased maintenance expenses 20 percent by implementing preventive check-ups at each delivery port-of-call transfer.
- Established an incentive program for station managers that rewarded outstanding employee achievements and recognized employee efforts for positive public relations.
- Initiated a monthly news report to keep all stations abreast of company administration, personnel, and internal affairs information and changes.

REFERENCES

Furnished upon request.

ADRIAN KASIMOR
389 NORTH BEND
IOWA CITY, IOWA 52240
(319) 555-2243

OBJECTIVE:

A position involved in the management of a conference center or conference services

EXPERIENCE:

Assistant Director, Iowa Summer Quarter, 1990 - present, University of Iowa, Iowa City

- Direct administrative operations, University of Iowa Summer Quarter.

- Make policy decisions and direct long-range planning.

- Responsible for program development and communications with vice-presidents, academic deans, department chairs, and academic unit personnel.

- Manage the development, preparation, justification of budgets and accounting operations.

- Direct marketing and publicity campaign.

Conference Administrator, 1985 - 1990, University of Iowa, Iowa City

- Managed biannual international seminars.

- Produced brochures, made registration and site arrangements, developed and maintained operating budget.

- Coordinated additional conferences, seminars, workshops.

Administrative Assistant, 1982 - 1985, University of Iowa, Iowa City

- Managed/supervised Academic Records Department.

- Assisted in start-up operations of University Conference and Performing Arts Center.

EDUCATION:

University of Iowa, Iowa City

B.A., Psychology, 1981

OTHER COURSES AND WORKSHOPS:

- Supervision
- WordPerfect Desktop Publishing
- The New Supervisor/Manager
- Practical Ways to Improve Your Communication

REFERENCES:

Available on request

ROBERT HAMMOND

16119 Sea View Drive

La Jolla, CA 91201

619/555-2221

robhamm@xxx.net

WORK EXPERIENCE
La Jolla Motel, La Jolla, CA

Manager, 1996 - present
Handled all bookkeeping, payroll, personnel, advertising, and public relations. Developed a successful advertising campaign that increased convention business 33 percent. Oversaw the implementation of an expansion program.

Assistant Manager, 1993 - 1996
Managed front office, switchboard, groundskeepers, and housekeepers. Hired and trained all personnel. Handled all purchasing and payroll activities. Directed convention and banquet facilities.

Desk Clerk, 1992 - 1993
Handled all registration, reservations, and billing. Informed housekeeping of arrivals and departures of guests. Issued keys and distributed mail.

EDUCATION
San Jose High School, San Jose, CA

Graduated 1991

REFERENCES

Available on request

CARMEN McRAE

7 E. Magnolia

Atlanta, GA 24990

Phone: 404/555-7449

ACCOMPLISHMENTS

- Managed administrative activities of a staff of 250.
- Designed improved administrative, clerical, and payroll systems, which resulted in significant savings.
- Oversaw operational studies of the activities and organizational structure of client companies.
- Introduced new purchasing, shipping, and billing procedures.
- Received a high percentage of acceptance on recommendations to upper management.
- Conducted a study of clerical operations in the purchasing department and attained a 20 percent reduction in department budget.
- Revised printing operations, which increased cost efficiency.
- Oversaw the installation of a computer network for the department.

EMPLOYMENT HISTORY

1995 - present	NUMARK SYSTEMS, INC., Atlanta, GA *Administrative Manager*
1990 - 1995	PARKER LEWIS, INC., New York, NY *Accounting Consultant*
1984 - 1990	AMERICAN NATIONAL CORP., White Plains, NY *Systems Analyst*
1981 - 1984	SANDERSON CO., New York, NY *Assistant Systems Analyst*
1978 - 1981	AT&T, Chicago, IL *Accountant*

Page 1 of 2

EDUCATION

UNIVERSITY OF GEORGIA, Atlanta, GA
M.B.A., 1977
B.A. in Economics, 1975

REFERENCES

Available upon request.

Sophia Resta
76 Oscar Drive
Spring Valley, WI 54767

(715) 555-3498

Summary: *Bright and motivated legal assistant with over ten years experience in law offices. Effective and efficient. Looking to relocate to an urban environment.*

Experience: **Britta, Holmes and Henderson**
Glenwood, WI
1996 - Present
Legal assistant: Managed secretarial staff and student interns, created interoffice E-mail system. Gathered information and attended daily staff briefings. Prepared legal memoranda and correspondence.

McNoughton, Fife, Anderson and Brown
St. Paul, MN
1992 - 1996
Secretary: Performed clerical duties for busy law firm while attending weekend college full time.

Education: Associate's Degree in English and Pre-Law, 1996
MetroState University, Minneapolis, MN
Graduated with Honors

Other Abilities: Fluent in American Sign Language and Spanish
Well-traveled and comfortable in wide variety of environments
Familiar with website development and upkeep
Enjoy canoeing, kayaking, and bouldering

H. BRIAN PAINTER

507 Sunnyview Place
Boulder, CO 80306
(303) 555-4557

CAREER OBJECTIVE

To obtain a position requiring excellent organizational and leadership skills

MILITARY SERVICE/PROFESSIONAL EXPERIENCE

2001–2003 Fleet Marine Force, Atlantic. Norfolk, Virginia.
        Rank: Captain

1994–2001 First Marine Amphibious Force. Camp Pendleton, California.
        Rank: First Lieutenant (promoted from Second Lieutenant 1997)

1990–1994 Student member, Reserve Officer Training Corps (ROTC), University of
        Colorado. Boulder, Colorado.

DUTIES/SKILLS

In all positions as Marine Corps officer, provided key role in training, preparing, and leading combat-ready troops.

Specialized in amphibious operations. Duties required assertiveness, mental and physical vigor, highly developed leadership qualities, loyalty, and excellent skills in planning, organizing, and managing.

EDUCATION

Bachelor of Science, University of Colorado, 1994.
Major: Business Management
Minor: Marketing
24 credits toward master's degree, Old Dominion University, Norfolk, Virginia

REFERENCES PROVIDED ON REQUEST

ALICE SANSONE   6576 Elizabeth Court   Home: (508) 555-8325
                     Falmouth, MA 02541   Office: (508) 555-9415

BACKGROUND

- Experienced hospital administrator
- Strong employee relations and arbitration skills
- Proven record of cost containment and quality control
- Successful facilities management

WORK HISTORY

1997 - Present
Administrative Director
Falmouth General Hospital, Falmouth, MA

Assist chief administrator in directing all activities of this 300-bed facility. Duties include personnel management, fiscal management, and public relations.

Achievements

- Initiated fund-raising effort that increased hospital endowment by $1.5 million

- Designed new community outreach projects to enhance hospital's visibility and image in the community

Page 1 of 2

1991 - 1997
Assistant Hospital Administrator
Perkins Memorial Hospital, Richmond, VA

Responsible for fiscal management, human resources, and facilities management projects under supervision of chief administrator.

Achievements

- Instituted new data processing procedures that increased collections and facilitated third-party reimbursements.

- Directed construction of $25 million maternal/child care wing that increased admissions by 20 percent. Responsible for all aspects of project: funding, contract negotiations, project management. Project completed on time and within budget.

EDUCATION

MBA   Harvard University   1991
BSN   University of Virginia 1989

References Available

PATRICK H. McCOY
1701 N. Hampshire Pl.
Miami, FL 33126
305/555-3909
305/555-9099

OBJECTIVE

A management position for a furnace manufacturer.

WORK EXPERIENCE

NEWMARK FURNACE CO., Miami, FL
Account Executive, 1995 - present

Handled accounts for southern Florida area. Expanded customer base by 28 percent during my tenure. Conducted field visits to solve customer complaints. Maintained daily contact with customers to ensure good company/customer relations. Wrote product information flyers and distributed them to potential customers.

POTISCO, Terre Haute, IN
Sales Representative, 1991 - 1995

Sold to customers, particularly contractors. Priced bid estimates as required. Oversaw customer and public relations, which helped to build company's image. Set up office procedures where necessary.

HONOCO, INC., Chicago, IL
Sales Representative, 1988 - 1991

Developed and managed new territories. Built sales through calls on physicians, hospitals, retailers, and wholesalers. Developed creative techniques for increasing product sales. Maintained current knowledge of competitive products.

EDUCATION

WHEATON COLLEGE, Wheaton, IL
B.S. in Business, 1987

SEMINARS

Sales and Marketing for the 90s
Florida Business Association
Marketing for the Furnace Industry

REFERENCES

Available upon request.

INDIRA PAX   988 Gavin Road
Newport News, VA 23606
Home (904) 555-8214
Cellular (904) 555-9602

Goal: Management position in home health industry that will use supervisory and marketing skills.

Experience:

9/98 to Present   **Director of Recruitment, NurseTemps Inc.**
Direct marketing/recruitment program. Design direct mail campaigns. Produce promotional literature. Developed employee screening process currently in use. Monitor employee performance. Have increased staffing by 15 percent during past year.

8/95 to 9/98   **Educational Director, St. Anne's Hospital**
Responsible for staff orientation, peer review, and community outreach programs.

7/91 to 8/95   **Director of Nursing, Morgan County Hospital**
Supervised RN staff for 260-bed county hospital. Chaired shared governance and public health committees. Promoted after four years service as level III RN.

Education: MSN   Wake Forest University   1991
BSN   Western New England College   1989
AA   Newport Business College   1986

References: On request.

JOEL JAMES III
1441 S. Goebert
Providence, RI 00231
401/555-1234
401/555-3782

Objective

President of a publishing corporation where I can apply my management, promotion, and marketing experience.

Employment History

JOHNSON PUBLISHING CORPORATION, Providence, RI

Vice President, Advertising, 1988 - present

Promoted from Marketing Manager to Vice President of Advertising after three years. Managed all phases of publishing properties including

> *Furniture Magazine*
>
> *Home Improvement Weekly*
>
> *Scuba Digest*
>
> *Travel Age Magazine*
>
> *Pharmacy News*

Established and developed the first newspaper advertising mat service in the furniture industry. Increased distributors and retailers using this service by 55 percent in three years. Improved the effectiveness and volume of all retail advertising.

REBUS PUBLISHING COMPANY, Boston, MA

Advertising Manager, 1979 - 1987

Serviced and developed accounts throughout the eastern United States. Handled advertising for publications in the restaurant industry. Increased sales in my territories every year by at least 21 percent.

TIME MAGAZINE, New York, NY

Assistant Advertising Promotion Manager, 1975 - 1979

Spearheaded original promotion program that increased revenue 33 percent in two years. Developed new markets. Helped to improve company/customer relations.

ROYAL CROWN COLA CORPORATION, Chicago, IL

Division Sales Manager, 1972 - 1975

Promoted from salesman to sales manager after one year. Organized sampling campaigns and in-store and restaurant displays. Directed bottlers' cooperative advertising and point-of-purchase displays.

Education

DRAKE UNIVERSITY, Des Moines, IA

B.A. in Economics, 1971
Graduated Phi Beta Kappa
Top 5 percent of class

Professional Affiliations

ROCKING CHAIR, social and professional organization of the furniture industry, President, 1996 - 1998

BEVERAGE ASSOCIATION of AMERICA
Board of Directors

PUBLISHERS ASSOCIATION
Advisory Committee

References

Available upon request.

DENNIS R. RILEY

606 Tall Oaks Lane
Helena, MT 59624
(406) 555-6540

CAREER OBJECTIVE

Position as a civilian pilot or in a management/support role within the aviation industry

EDUCATION

B.S. United States Air Force Academy, 1990

Graduated in top 20 percent of class

M.S. in Management, Georgetown University, Washington, DC, 1998

MILITARY EXPERIENCE

- Highly experienced as accomplished pilot on active duty with the U.S. Air Force (1990–2003)
- Experienced in flying a variety of aircraft, with emphasis on the F-16, and comprehensive training as a combat pilot
- Active participant in Operation Desert Storm with several medals/citations (complete list available)
- Highly skilled in all aspects of aircraft operation
- Exemplary military record with option to continue in service still available at time of leaving military

SPECIAL KNOWLEDGE & SKILLS

Outstanding analytical skills

Highly flexible in taking on new assignments

Diligent in applying sound safety skills to all aspects of aviation practice and management

MEMBERSHIPS

Aviation Society of America

Rotary International

REFERENCES AVAILABLE ON REQUEST

TERRENCE LEONG
9021 W. Cedar Lane
Grand Rapids, MI 50399
616-555-2002

OBJECTIVE

To become manager of a Thai-Chinese restaurant in the Grand Rapids area.

WORK EXPERIENCE

SHANGHAI RESTAURANT, Grand Rapids, MI

Assistant Manager, 1996 - present

Supervised kitchen, dining, and bar staff of 25. Maintained food and linen stocks. Hired waitstaff and busboys. Approved menus. Assisted in the placement of advertising.

PANCAKE WORLD, St. Louis, MO

Assistant Quality Control Director, 1992 - 1996

Evaluated and maintained performance standards at several restaurants. Oversaw food, service, and cleanliness. Prepared reports and made recommendations for improvements.

CALIFORNIA CAFE, East St. Louis, IL

Assistant Manager, 1990 - 1992

Supervised breakfast service at a busy neighborhood cafe. Hired and evaluated employees. Maintained food stocks. Handled various financial matters.

ROSE'S, Chicago, IL

Cook, 1987 - 1990

Prepared various deli-style meals for a local restaurant.

EDUCATION

WHEATON COLLEGE, Wheaton, IL

Studied for two years, 1985 - 1987

Majored in business

REFERENCES

Available upon request.

HARRISON G. BUNWADDIE

55 E. Huron St.
Chicago, IL 60601
708/555-2900 (Day)
708/555-2810 (Evening)
bunwaddie@xxx.com

WORK EXPERIENCE

Sandler Electronics Inc., Chicago, IL
Industrial Relations Manager, 1993 - present

Oversaw all labor relations between the corporation and the union. Worked with the personnel department to plan labor policy, negotiate contracts, review hiring practices, and maintain records. Participated on grievance committees. Advised Vice President of Personnel on legal matters. Supervised a staff of ten employees.

Good Cereal Co., Battle Creek, MI
Assistant Personnel Manager, 1988 - 1993

Supervised a staff of eight interviewers and testers for hiring of office and warehouse personnel. Assisted Personnel Manager with all department operations. Oversaw all records for warehouse personnel. Developed a successful training and evaluation program for all company employees.

IBM, Chicago, IL
Personnel Intern, 1987 - 1988

Assisted with testing and evaluation of prospective employees. Scheduled interviews. Maintained computer database.

EDUCATION

Northwestern University, Evanston, IL
Juris Doctor, 1988
Admitted to the Michigan Bar Association, 1988

Garrison College, Terre Haute, IN
B.S. in Management, 1984

REFERENCES PROVIDED ON REQUEST.

MARLENE MAREGO
55 E. Wood St.
White Plains, NY 10604
914/555-1234
914/555-2938

WORK EXPERIENCE

ITC, INC., WHITE PLAINS, NY

Executive Vice President, Special Projects, 1996 - present

> Managed all administrative operations. Directed the work of several project units simultaneously. Created and implemented organizational policy. Planned and developed programs and publications. Designed promotional materials. Oversaw website development.

AMERICAN DEVELOPMENT, INC., MIAMI, FL

Director of Operations, 1990 - 1996

> Managed all educational and personnel projects. Prepared proposals for public and private funding. Assisted in technical management functions. Evaluated operations to ensure effective implementation of contractual requirements. Negotiated contracts.

CERTA CORPORATION, JACKSON, MS

Account Executive, 1985 - 1989

> Handled accounts for all of Mississippi. Expanded customer base by 30 percent during tenure. Conducted field visits to solve customer complaints. Maintained daily contact with customers to ensure good company/customer relations. Wrote product information flyers and distributed them to potential customers.

EDUCATION

NEW YORK UNIVERSITY, NEW YORK, NY

M.B.A. with Honors, 1985

UNIVERSITY OF MISSISSIPPI, JACKSON, MS

B.A. in Economics, 1983

MEMBERSHIPS

New York Association of Business Executives

National Business Association

REFERENCES

Provided upon request.

ANTHONY RUTHERFORD

7900 Mile High Ave.   807-555-4949
Salt Lake City, UT 84126   807-555-2911

GOAL:

Vice President of Operations at a reputable banking institution.

ACHIEVEMENTS:

- Assisted Senior Vice President in day-to-day operations.
- Directed work procedures in light of bank policy.
- Managed assets, securities, and bank records.
- Established all operating procedures and policies in the department.
- Oversaw restructuring of MIS Department.
- Coordinated duties of department personnel.
- Served on bank policy review board.
- Assisted in the planning of branch locations.
- Handled accounting and financial analysis.
- Approved and declined credit for loans.

WORK HISTORY:

FIRST NATIONAL BANK OF UTAH, Salt Lake City, UT
Assistant Vice President, 1998 - present

FIRST NATIONAL BANK OF UTAH, Provo, UT
Branch Director, 1994 - 1998

SANTA FE BANK, Santa Fe, NM
Teller, 1992 - 1993

EDUCATION:

WASHINGTON STATE UNIVERSITY, Tacoma, WA
B.S. in Accounting, 1990

References available on request.

Resumes for Skilled Trades

Donald B. Davidson

13 Williams Estates
Cedar Rapids, IA 52406

Home: 319-555-2354
Mobile: 319-555-9087

Summary of Qualifications

Experienced in operating a variety of construction equipment and other heavy and light equipment. Highly skilled in earth moving processes.

Accomplishments

Equipment Operator, active duty, United States Navy

• Operated multipurpose excavators and cranes

• Operated clamshells, backhoes, pile drivers, and other equipment

• Assisted in a variety of construction projects

• Advanced from Constructionman (E-3) to Equipment Operator First Class

• Earned excellent evaluations from superiors

• Held a perfect on-the-job safety record

Employment History

U.S. Navy, 1994–2002
Naval Construction Center
Gulfport, Mississippi

Cook Construction, 1992–1994 (summers)
Cedar Rapids, Iowa

Education

Diploma, South High School, 1992
Completed Navy training courses in equipment operation, safety, and related topics

References provided on request

MIKE BOYLE

288 PALISADE AVENUE
JERSEY CITY, NEW JERSEY 07306
201-555-2938

Job Desired   Apprentice mechanic with automotive repair company with opportunity to train as auto mechanic.

Education   Dickinson High School, Jersey City, 1999 to present
                         Hudson Regional Junior-Senior High School, Highlands, NJ
                         1994–1996

Skills   Mechanically inclined with skills ranging from basic auto mechanics to very technical electrical diagnostics.

                         Experienced with engine overhaul, suspension, brakes, fuel, power train, and motor detailing.

                         Some auto-body repair experience.

Work Experience   Dickinson High School Auto Shop, 2000–present
                         Duties: Tune-ups, oil changes, general check-up and trouble shooting in student-run auto mechanics shop. Diagnose and repair mechanical problems on cars, trucks, and vans.

                         East Jersey Radiator, 2000–present
                         Duties: Cleaning and testing radiators, installing replacement radiators, and motor detailing. Shop services both foreign and domestic cars. Assisted with stock warehouse.

                         Northern Landscape Maintenance, 1999–2000
                         Duties: Planting, mowing, pruning, and hedging for three apartment complexes and four office complexes. Responsible for maintaining nursery inventory.

References   Available upon request.

JASON RASKIN

1005 University Blvd.

Fort Collins, CO 80523

(303) 555-6922

CAREER OBJECTIVE

To obtain a position in auto body repair

RELATED EXPERIENCE

Experienced in repairing frames and bodies of trucks, automobiles, and other vehicles

Skilled in using a wide range of tools and equipment

Experienced in tasks such as
> Replacing damaged body parts
> Straightening frames, doors, hoods, and fenders
> Welding damaged frames and auto body parts
> Installing glass windows
> Refinishing body surfaces
> Completing other related tasks

WORK BACKGROUND

Served in United States Army, 1996–2003
> Specialized in providing auto body repair services for Army vehicles
> Worked well with diverse personnel

Webb Auto Repair, 1994–1996 (part-time and summers)

Fort Collins, CO
> Provided general services ranging from cleanup to assisting in basic auto body repair functions; range of duties progressed during job tenure

TRAINING

Completed certificate in auto body repair, Rocky Mountain Technical College, 1995

Completed additional training through military courses

REFERENCES PROVIDED ON REQUEST

Dwight Miller

3425 East Broad Street
Columbus, Ohio 43213
(614) 555-9078

Experience

1998 - present
Self-employed automobile mechanic

1995 - 1998
S&W Auto, Columbus, Ohio
Auto Mechanic/Manager

- Produced and implemented performance and quality development program
- Established additional efficiency and reliability standards
- Improved response time of repairs by 2 days
- Improved customer service by cutting costs and reducing prices
- Changed company image to that of a reputable, dependable neighborhood auto repair shop
- Increased client accounts by 60 percent

1989 - 1995
Texaco Auto Service
Auto Mechanic

Education

1988 - 1990   Cooperative Technical Education Institute for Automobile Mechanics Columbus, Ohio

1986 - 1988   Columbus Community College
Courses in Marketing, Economics, Customer Relations, Advertising, Accounting

1981 - 1986   Samuel Gomper's High School for Vocational Training

References furnished upon request

Thomas H. Akers
1109 Old Depot Street
Stone Ridge, New York 12484
(914) 555-4124

Summary of Qualifications

Highly experienced sheet metal worker with seven years' experience in United States Army. Adept at using proper techniques for top-quality sheet metal work.

Highly dependable and productive.

Experience

• Served in United States Army, 1992–2003.

• Specialized in sheet metal work.

• Assisted in major projects including base expansion at Fort Lee, Petersburg, Virginia, 1994–95.

• Performed comprehensive duties requiring a broad range of sheet metal construction skills. These included

    —Fabrication and installation of air ducts

    —Installation of aluminum siding

    —Repair of various structures made of sheet metal

Education

Diploma, Washington County Vocational-Technical Center, Stone Ridge, New York, 1992.

Additional education through Army training courses.

References

Available on request.

John Von Hamer

963 Lake Drive
Philadelphia, PA 19104
Home: (215) 555-5352
Pager: (215) 555-8890

Experience

Small appliance mechanic - Self-employed (1995 - present)
Repair cords, connections, and switches.
Replace plugs and install terminals of all types.
Adjust, repair, or replace temperature controls.
Analyze the performance of compressors, dehumidifiers, humidifiers, and air conditioners.
Restore switching circuits, thermostats, relays, solid state components, and SCR.

Warehouse Foreman - The Seamack Corporation (1985 - 1995)
Managed 85,000 square-foot facility.
Supervised 30 employees.

Achievements

Increased storage capacity by 15 percent.
Expanded warehouse output by 10 percent.
Designed and implemented new inventory procedures.
Promoted to foreman in 1989.
Named supervisor of the year for three consecutive years.

Education

Washington High School for Electronics
Completed 10 seminars in personnel management.

References

Furnished upon request.

JUAN SANCHEZ
3838 16th Street
San Bernardino, CA 92401
(714) 555-6155

OBJECTIVE

Responsible position requiring proven mechanical skills.

ACHIEVEMENTS

• Provided comprehensive mechanical services for military aircraft.

• Received excellent evaluations from superiors.

• Earned three promotions in rank based on job accomplishments and overall performance.

WORK EXPERIENCE

United States Coast Guard, 1996–2002
Specialty: Aircraft maintenance and repair
Rating: Aviation Structural Mechanic First Class (E-6)
Responsibilities:
• Performed comprehensive duties related to handling, inspecting, servicing, and maintaining aircraft structures and components.

• Fabricated and assembled metal parts.

• Made repairs.

• Performed nondestructive testing.

• Painted and maintained painting equipment.

• Maintained hydraulic systems, landing gear, fuel tanks, and other components.

• Performed related duties.

EDUCATION

Graduate, Aviation Training Technical Center, USCG, Elizabeth City, North Carolina, 1997

Diploma, Warren High School, San Bernardino, California, 1996

REFERENCES

Available on request

JAMES P. WODYNSKI
212 Harding Avenue
Evanston, IL 60201
(312) 555-2530
E-mail at: jwody@xxx.net

EXPERIENCE

Enlisted Personnel, United States Coast Guard
Ratings held: Progressed from Seaman Recruit (E-l) to Radarman First Class (E-6)
Active Service: 1995–2003
Reserve Duty: Present
Duties: Operated radar and associated equipment

Representative tasks completed:

- Collected, processed, displayed, evaluated, and disseminated information related to movement of ships, aircraft, and other objects
- Performed duties related to navigation and piloting
- Prepared and maintained records and logs for Combat Information Center operations and operating equipment
- Understood and used Nautical Rules of the Road
- Prepared requisitions for supplies
- Computed statistics necessary for operational reports
- Prepared preventive maintenance schedules

EDUCATIONAL BACKGROUND

Graduate, Yorktown Training Center, VA
Successfully completed additional Coast Guard courses including Radioman First Class (Course No. 139-5) via Coast Guard Institute, Oklahoma City, OK

SPECIAL SKILLS

Excellent quantitative skills
Adept at use of various computer software

REFERENCES PROVIDED ON REQUEST

Carl Pujol   *Photographer*

22-B W. 44th Street
Wilmington, Delaware 19835
302-555-9080
carl_pujol@xxx.com

Education
- Cooper Union, New York City, M.A. Photography, 2000
- New York University Tisch School of the Arts, B.A. Photography, 1993

Objective
To secure employment as a fashion photographer for a major magazine

Experience
1998 - present
Self-employed photographer
- Developed a profitable portrait business
- Designed and shot record album cover for the rock group Dream Scape
- Hired to photograph models for the book *Men* by Sandcastle Productions
- Assisted head photographer in Havana, Cuba, for a documentary developed in London by Wildcat Productions

1995 - 1998
Photographer
Sears, Chicago, Illinois
- Assisted head photographer in all aspects of shooting print work for the 1995 and 1996 catalogues
- Promoted to head photographer 1997
- Designed, shot, and developed 1997 and 1998 catalogues
- Resigned to attend a special invitational fashion photo class in London

1993-1996
Photographer's assistant
Victoria's Secret, London, England
- Designed and shot 50 percent of the 1995 autumn portfolio
- Shot and developed 50 percent of the 1996 spring portfolio
- Assisted team in developing marketing strategies and campaigns

Demonstrated Skills
- Ability to work under pressure and meet deadlines
- Ability to work independently or collaborate

References
Furnished upon request.

MARILYN DAUGHERTY

405 Warren Street
Mt. Pleasant, TX 75455
(903) 555-8631 (voice)
(903) 555-9091 (fax)

SUMMARY OF QUALIFICATIONS

Highly experienced in maintaining and repairing aircraft electrical, instrument, and power systems. Skilled and well trained in performing with efficiency and diligent attention to safety standards. Also experienced in effective management and supervision.

ACHIEVEMENTS

• Served effectively for a ten-year tour with the United States Navy

• Reached rating of E-7, Chief Aviation Electrician's Mate

• Demonstrated highly developed technical skills

• Worked with a variety of aircraft types

• Received excellent evaluations of performance

• Supervised over fifteen personnel

• Performed a variety of planning, management, and reporting functions

WORK HISTORY

1993–2003   United States Navy. Progressed from Airman to Chief Aviation Electrician's Mate. Served aboard U.S.S. *America.* Specialized in repair and maintenance of aircraft electrical systems.

1991–1993   Electrician's Assistant, Cox Electrical Service, Mt. Pleasant, TX.

EDUCATION

Certificate, Tidewater Community College, Portsmouth, VA, 1997 (included 18 semester credit hours in electricity/electrical systems).

Completed additional training at Naval Air Technical Training Center, Memphis,TN, 1993 and 1998. Courses covered electrical, electronic, and engine instrument systems; aviation weapons systems; physics; technical mathematics; and related topics.

REFERENCES

Available on request

JOSEPH W. CALDWELL

346 Buena Vista
Pocatello, Idaho 83251
(208) 555-6682 or E-mail: jwc@xxx.com

Job Goal:

Construction foreman for housing construction company.

Skills:

Experienced in a wide range of construction and wood products occupations.

Thorough knowledge of indigenous woods and their suitability for construction.

Twenty years of supervisory experience.

Work History:

Supervisor, Twin Peaks Plywood, Pocatello, ID

Trained and supervised mill workers in all areas of mill operation. Scheduled shifts of 24 workers each, three shifts a day. Worked relief schedule on weekends. Developed safety awareness program. Monitored safety procedures. Consulted with SAIF inspectors for methods of improving working environment safety. Employed continuously from 1988 to present.

Shift Foreman, Idaho Lumber Supply, Boise, ID

Supervised splitters, pullers, and saw operators on day shift. Trained workers in all aspects of lumber mill operation. Monitored safety procedures. Employed initially as mill worker; worked seasonally from 1982 to 1988 (moved).

Carpentry Crewman, Dales Construction, Boise, ID

Worked on carpentry crew building residential dwellings and office complexes in Boise and environs. Experienced with foundation work, roofing, sheetrocking, and finish carpentry. Worked seasonally from 1979 to 1988 (moved).

Woodworker, Ames Oak Furniture, Boise, ID

Operated lathe, power saw, miter saw, drill press, scroll saw, burnishing sander, and other power equipment in the manufacture and finishing of oak furniture. Employed full-time from 1977 to 1979 (business relocated out of state).

Education:

Boise Central High School, graduated 1977

Memberships:

International Mill Workers Local #655; Carpenters Local #2815

TYRONE H. ROBERTS

17 N. Franklin St.
Valencia, CA 91355
(805) 555-5145

EMPLOYMENT OBJECTIVE

To obtain a position involving installation or repair of electrical systems and components

CAREER HISTORY

Ten years' outstanding service maintaining and repairing aircraft electrical systems in the United States Marine Corps

Honorably discharged at rank of sergeant (E-5) after service as Aircraft Electrical Systems Technician, 2002

WORK BACKGROUND

Installed and repaired electrical components and systems on military aircraft

Inspected and tested electrical components

Diagnosed equipment malfunctions

Demonstrated thorough working knowledge of diodes, transistors, integrated circuits, motors, and other electrical components

Performed Level 3 tasks including conducting pre-flight and post-flight operational tests on electrical systems

REFERENCES WILL BE PROVIDED ON REQUEST

JOSHUA GOLDSTEIN

205 Pendleton Street
Apartment 16-B
Americus, Georgia 31709
(912) 555-2918

CAREER OBJECTIVE

To obtain a position in service and repair of electronic data equipment

EDUCATION

Associate of Applied Science in Computer Electronics, Greenville Technical College, Greenville, South Carolina, 1995.

Additional training through U.S. Navy training courses at Combat Systems Technical School, Mare Island, California, 1996–1997.

RELATED EXPERIENCE

- Served as Data Technician First Class, U.S. Navy
- Performed general maintenance and repairs on computers, data link devices, and other electronic data equipment
- Inspected and tested equipment and components
- Diagnosed and repaired malfunctions in computers, data storage devices, and other equipment
- Performed troubleshooting and adjustment of electromechanical devices in digital systems
- Prepared maintenance schedules for electronic data equipment
- Effectively utilized various hand tools and electronic equipment

SPECIAL SKILLS/MEMBERSHIPS

Highly skilled in troubleshooting process

Member, Professional Electronic Technicians Association (ETA)

Currently undergoing ETA certification process

REFERENCES PROVIDED ON REQUEST

ROGER NEWTON 765 Murphy's Lane • Arlington, VA 22207 • (703) 555-3099

OBJECTIVE: To become a full-time auto mechanic.

EDUCATION: 2000 Graduate of Arlington High School
                        GPA 3.5/4.0
                        Relevant course work:
                        • Auto shop   2 years
                        • Auto shop student supervisor   1 year
                        • Business math   1 year

EXPERIENCE:

6/99 to present   ARLINGTON SHELL, Arlington, VA
                        Station Attendant
                        Responsible for operating the cash register, assisting
                        customers, checking oil, washing windows, checking tire
                        pressure, and fixing flat tires.

Prior to 6/99   ODD JOBS
                        Gardening, dog walking, catering, cleanup work, and car
                        repair.

ACTIVITIES: 4-year member high school morning weight-lifting club
                        2-year member high school spirit club
                        1-year member high school business club

INTERESTS: Customizing vans
                        Attending NASCAR races
                        Racing motorcycles

REFERENCES PROVIDED ON REQUEST

John R. Fleming, Jr.

4215 Pilot Creek Road
Clinton, MS 39058
(601) 555-7228

Career Objective

A position in aviation mechanics or a related field

Work Experience

- Served as Gunnery Sergeant (E-7), United States Marine Corps.
- Completed twelve years of active service concluding July 2002.
- Performed highest level tasks (Level 4) in helicopter maintenance and repair.
- Planned and scheduled activities of aircraft maintenance work centers.
- Performed a wide range of inspection and maintenance duties.

Training and Education

Certificate, Aircraft Maintenance, Lansing Technical College, Lansing, MI, 1991

Completed Marine Training courses in aviation mechanics (Air Ground Combat Center, Twentynine Palms, California), 1992 and 1997, and in personnel management (correspondence), 2000.

References Available

ROGER E. NUNN

707 Washington Terrace
Concord, NH 03301
(603) 555-2152

CAREER OBJECTIVE

To obtain a position in machining, machine tool technology, or related field.

EDUCATION

A.S. degree, New Hampshire Vocational-Technical College, Manchester, NH, 1990.
Emphasis area: machine tool technology.

Additional education through U.S. Army training courses. Subjects covered included personnel supervision, records management, and organizational management.

RELATED EXPERIENCE

Allied Trades Technician, U.S. Army, 1997 - 2003.

Machinist, U.S. Army, 1989 - 1997.

Rank at end of Army service: Chief Warrant Officer

- Set up and operated machine tools

- Made and repaired metal parts, mechanisms, and machinery

- Supervised subordinates in setting up and using equipment

- Managed shop operations

- Interpreted regulations and orders

- Performed comprehensive duties requiring firsthand knowledge of metalworking techniques and practices, as well as effective supervisory techniques

SPECIAL ACCOMPLISHMENTS

Contributed to several issues of *Preventive Maintenance Monthly*, 1994 - 1998.

Selected to serve on special review team for revision of technical manuals, 1999.

REFERENCES PROVIDED ON REQUEST

ROSAMARIA C. ALVAREZ
255 Outlook Drive
Twin Falls, ID 83303
(208) 555-3242

OBJECTIVE

A position as a senior or supervising receptionist providing efficient, high-quality typing, clerical, and word processing services to a business firm.

EDUCATION

College of Southern Idaho - 1999
- Certificate in Business Practices
- Typing: 80 WPM
- Office practice
- Business machines

EXPERIENCE

Manpower Temporary Services, Twin Falls, ID
June to August 1996, 1997, and 1998
General office worker
- Filed applications, greeted applicants, and answered phones.
- Assisted with administration and grading of applicants' tests and completed all test paperwork.
- Gained experience in light invoicing, setting up files, typing, and data entry.

Idaho State Automobile Association, Twin Falls, ID
June to August 1995
Assistant cashier, relief PBX, and relief DMV
- Assisted customers with paperwork.
- Entered data in computer system.

COMPUTER EXPERIENCE

- Windows 98
- Microsoft Office 2000
- WordPerfect
- NEC PowerMate 8100 Series
- Microsoft Excel
- Microsoft PowerPoint

REFERENCES

Available upon request.

NATASHA L. WOODBINE

21101 Locust Valley Rd.
Marlburg, TN 37223
615/555-3684

Job Objective

A position that will best utilize my secretarial experience.

Professional Experience

U.S. Naval Station, Rhodes, Greece
Secretary to the Commander, 1990 - 1993
Organized meeting places for the Commander when visiting dignitaries were invited to conferences under the NATO agreement. Typed and sent United States confidential and secret messages to various command centers throughout the world. Maintained confidential and secret files. Arranged government transportation requests for officers and enlisted personnel and their families.

Moreland Savings and Loan Banking Company, Moreland, TN
Secretary to the Loan Officer, 1987 - 1990
Typed loan applications, posted all lease payments, and quoted buyout figures.

Education

Waverly Secretarial School, Knoxville, TN
A.S. in Office Procedures, 1986
Courses included: Typing; Dictation; Computer Training Skills in Windows, Lotus 1-2-3, Word Processing, and Graphics.

Awards & Honors

- Valedictorian of the graduation class, Waverly Secretarial School, 1986
- Secretary of the month, June 1992, U.S. Naval Communication Station, Rhodes, Greece

Special Qualifications

Secret and Confidential clearance status issued by the United States Government.

References

Available upon request.

MARVIN MAHAFFEY

2144 Falconer Highway

Louisville, KY 40232

(502) 555-0496

SUMMARY OF QUALIFICATIONS

Expert, experienced technician trained in maintaining, servicing, and repairing radio equipment

PROFESSIONAL EXPERIENCE

1995–2003 United States Navy

Position: Electronics Technician First Class

Specialty: Radio equipment maintenance and repair

Responsibilities: Performed comprehensive services in installing, maintaining, and repairing radio equipment. Read and interpreted schematics. Used a variety of tools and equipment. Performed troubleshooting functions. Prepared preventive maintenance schedules. Maintained parts inventory. Provided other related duties.

EDUCATION/TRAINING

Graduate, Service School Command, San Diego, CA, 1996.

Completed Navy training courses in basic electronics, AC and DC circuits, electronic instrumentation, radio set maintenance, and related subjects.

REFERENCES

Reference information provided on request.

ANDREW G. MEUNIER

6300 BEASLEY ROAD
JACKSON, MISSISSIPPI 39225
601/555-7819

Personal Objective	Job with automotive repair or body shop
Experience	**Automotive Repair and Body Work** • Assisted with complete exterior repair of six cars • Assisted in engine repair and rebuild • Detail painting on two vans • Interior work on several vans **Home Maintenance** • Provided landscaping maintenance for apartment complex • Interior and exterior paining of two homes • Assisted with roofing of one new home and repair on another • Minor carpentry work for apartment complex
Work History	**Handyman, 2000–present** Delta Apartments 2400 Albermarle Road Jackson, MS 39213 Supervisor: Adrain Florio Duties: landscape maintenance, carpentry, general repair. **Custodian, 1999–2000** Alternative Junior High School 1900 N. State Street Jackson, MS 39202 Supervisor: Johnson Ableman Duties: basic janitorial work.
Skills & Activities	Sign language, drawing, and painting, member of Car Rally Club of Jackson, Boy Scouts of America (Eagle Scout).
Education	Wingfield Senior High School 1985 Scanlon Drive Jackson, MS Courses: auto mechanics, wood shop, Spanish
References	Available on request

CARLETTA A. WILLIAMS

2821 Crown Drive
Conway, South Carolina 29526
(803) 555-2833

SUMMARY OF EXPERIENCE

- Twelve years of experience in the United States Army.
- Progressed to rank of Warrant Officer.
- Specialized in maintaining and operating field artillery radars to provide target location.

TECHNICAL AREAS OF EXPERTISE

- Knowledge of effective practices in management and supervision.
- Knowledge of operational aspects of field artillery.
- Close familiarity with technical principles of equipment construction.
- Understanding of safety applications relevant to operations and maintenance.
- Solid understanding of basic electronics theory.

EMPLOYMENT HISTORY

U.S Army, 1990–2002.

Position: Target Acquisition Radar Technician

Served with distinction including postings at the following:

      Fort Knox, Kentucky

      Fort Sill, Oklahoma

      Operation Desert Storm (Persian Gulf)

      Fort Jackson, South Carolina

Rank: Warrant Officer

Awards: Received several medals and commendations. Listing and complete military record available on request.

EDUCATION

Associate Degree, Jefferson Community College, Louisville, Kentucky, 1993 (general studies). Graduate, Army Field Artillery School, 1994.

MEMBERSHIPS

Member, Women's Leadership Association

REFERENCES

Available on request.

COLLEEN QUINN
3104 Linden Court
Bradford, MA 01830
(508) 555-9576 home
(508) 555-0909 cellular
E-mail: cquinn@xxx.net

CAREER OBJECTIVE: A position in computer repair, installation, or service

PROFESSIONAL EXPERIENCE

- Served in U.S. Army, 1993–2003. Specialized in servicing and repairing computer systems supporting advanced communications equipment
- Performed a wide range of tasks in servicing, installing, and repairing computers and related equipment
- Installed computers and computer systems
- Diagnosed equipment problems and identified equipment malfunctions
- Installed printers and other peripheral devices
- Serviced and replaced components of computers and related equipment
- Transported computer equipment to and from repair locations, as well as performing work on-site
- Maintained up-to-date knowledge of advancements in computer technology

MILITARY SERVICE BACKGROUND

Reached rank of Sergeant

Earned excellent performance evaluations

EDUCATION

Successfully completed 1,036-hour training course in Automated Computer Systems Repair at Fort Gordon, Georgia

Completed 30 semester hours in computer technology, electronics, and related subjects at Aiken Technical College, Aiken, South Carolina, and Jefferson Community College, Lexington, Kentucky

Completed additional correspondence courses and other Army training courses

References, including complete military records, are available upon request.

Lisa Homedes

2870 Cross Line Road
Orangeburg, NY 14398
(914) 555-3740

Objective

To obtain a position as a sous chef.

Education

The Culinary School of Arts /Poughkeepsie, NY
Course of study included the preparation of appetizers, entrees, and desserts. Cooked foods of different cultures, mainly French, Italian, and Spanish. Educated on wine selections from around the world. Instruction on table settings for every occasion. Interpretation of recipes for increasing or decreasing ingredients proportionate to the quantity desired.
Diploma, 1999

Sparkill College/Sparkill, NY
A.S. in Business; Major: Accounting
Degree, 1990

Experience

The Gun Powder Cavern/Pomona, NY -- Internship, Summer 1999
Assisted chef in preparation of lunch and dinner menus. Responsibilities included keeping kitchen utensils in organizational readiness, all spices and herbs at near capacity level, and all menus updated to reflect the specials of the day.

Western Auto Hardware Store/Tappan, NY -- Bookkeeper, 1990 - 1994
Duties included accounts receivable and payable, assisting in payroll calculation, and maintaining files for payroll.

Palisades Diner/Tappan, NY -- Waitress, 1985 - 1990
Served lunch and dinner entrees.

Honors & Awards

Graduated top 5 percent of class, The Culinary School of Arts.
Dean's List, Sparkill College, 1988 - 1990

Memberships

Future Chefs of America (FCA), Poughkeepsie Chapter. Recording Secretary, 1998
National Accounting Fraternity, Sparkill College

References

Available upon request

ROBERT WILCOX

1805 Grayland Avenue
Price, UT 84501
(801) 555-1918 home phone
(801) 555-9089 cell phone

EMPLOYMENT OBJECTIVE

Position in the telephone, power, or cable industry

RELATED EXPERIENCE

Line Installer and Repairer, U.S. Navy, 1996–2002
Performed a variety of duties involved in installing, maintaining, and repairing electrical cables and communication lines, including:

- Utility pole erection
- Mechanical lift, plow, and other equipment operation
- Overhead communications and electrical cable installation between utility poles
- Installation of street lights and other lighting systems
- Splicing and sealing cables for watertightness
- Installation of voltage regulators, electrical transformers, and voltage regulators
- Related duties

EDUCATION

Completed special training including program in cable splicing and repair at Navy Construction Training Center, Port Hueneme, CA, 1996

REFERENCES AVAILABLE ON REQUEST

GREG GOLD
1661 Corn Row Drive
Cedar Rapids, IA 53309

319/555-2909 (Home)
319/555-8888 (Work)

JOB OBJECTIVE: Engineering Technician/Camera Operator

OVERVIEW: Experience with all camera operations for film and video. Skills include studio lighting, set design, film editing, dubbing, gaffing, audio-video switching, mixing, and technical troubleshooting.

EXPERIENCE: WCED-TV, Cedar Rapids, IA
Engineering Assistant, 7/99 - present

Drawbridge Productions, Des Moines, IA
Assistant Camera Operator, Summer 1998

WWOR Radio, Jackson, MS
Engineer, 9/97 - 6/98

EDUCATION: Jackson University, Jackson, MS
B.A. in Communication Arts, June 1999

REFERENCES: Available on request

Brian Hawkins

108-B North Madison
College Station, Texas 77843
(409) 555-1245

Employment Objective

Position as an air traffic controller or related position in aviation operation or management

Experience

- Fifteen years of experience with the U.S. Army (1986–2001), including twelve years of active service as an ATC operator
- Experienced with Visual Flight Rules (VFR), Special Visual Flight Rules (SVFR), and Instrument Flight Rules (IFR)
- Provided radar and nonradar air traffic control services
- Provided flight control for takeoffs, flight, and landings for military and civilian aircraft
- Performed with excellence and reliability

Education

Completed ATC training at Aviation Center, Fort Rucker, Alabama, 1989

Membership

Association of Air Traffic Controllers

References

References and additional background information, including transcripts, are available on request

Resumes for Social Service and Education Careers

ALICIA CARPENTIER
3890 West Arlington, Syracuse, NY 13201 (315) 555-3294

OBJECTIVE

A position as music department director at a public high school

OVERVIEW

- Ten years as a private instrumental, voice, and music theory teacher.
- Founder and director of *Santos*, a Renaissance choral and instrumental group.
- Coordinated fundraising for the Arts Council: established goals, formulated policies, organized efforts.

RELATED ACTIVITIES

1991 - present: Founded performance group focused on Renaissance music. Coordinated extensive research on early instrumentation, authenticity of performance. Act as director, arrange scores, and organize performances for the nonprofit chorus, *Santos*.

1996 and 1997:   Conductor of Student Orchestra, New York State Music Festival

1985 - 1991:   Member, Sacred Choir of Syracuse

1985 - 1991:   Member, Oberlin Conservatory Chorus; Member, A Cappella Choir

EDUCATION

M.A. in Renaissance Music History and Instrumentation, State University of New York, Syracuse, New York, 1987

B.A. in Musical Performance and Direction, Oberlin Conservatory of Music, Oberlin, Ohio, 1985

Page 1 of 2

EMPLOYMENT HISTORY

1995 - present   Director of Fundraising, Syracuse Community Arts Council, Syracuse, NY

Develop fundraising programs. Coordinate solicitation and disbursement of funds. Establish fundraising goals and policies for collecting contributions. Establish relationships with local, regional, and national organizations and coordinate events, support bases, and contacts.

1990 - 1995   Assistant Publicist, Syracuse Community Arts Council, Syracuse, NY

Wrote press releases, delivered presentations, and designed fliers and posters announcing competitions and events. Organized community events. Coordinated the 1994 Arts in the Park celebration in downtown Syracuse.

1985 - 1995   Private Music Instructor, Syracuse, NY

Taught voice, piano, and violin lessons on an individual basis. Instructed children and adults in basic music theory and technique.

References Provided Upon Request

Evelyn Moore
4366 South Street
Detroit, Michigan 48062
(616) 555-9698

Career Goal: To obtain a position as a secondary education instructor in the areas of
                    Science and Computer Science.

Education: September 1997 to present

                    Western Michigan University, Kalamazoo, Michigan
                    Secondary Education Curriculum
                    Biology Major, Computer Science Minor

                    September 1993 to June 1997

                    Littlefield Public School, Albert, Michigan
                    Graduated salutatorian, June 1997

Work Experience: February 1999 to present

                    McDonald's, 39 King Drive, Kalamazoo, Michigan
                    Phone (616) 555-5137
                    Swing Manager. Duties: cash audits, deposits, quality control of product,
                    customer relations, supervision of employees, inventory and ordering of
                    supplies, maintenance of restaurant appearance, register operations, and
                    associated paperwork.

                    May 2000 - Present

                    Computer Science Department, Western Michigan University, Kalamazoo,
                    Michigan
                    Phone (616) 555-4620
                    Computer Operator. Duties: software inventory and evaluation,
                    programming, entering and updating files, journal photocopying, and
                    article synopsis.

References: Available upon request

Liz Newson 3 Lee Road, Santa Barbara, CA 93101

NEWSON ASSOCIATES
Counseling & Alternative Medicine
Phone 805-555-8594
Hours Mon - Fri 8 - 4 & Evenings by Appointment

SERVICES

- Individual and group counseling for personal growth, academic progress, health and wellness, career decision making and advancement
- Hypnotherapy to resolve substance abuse, compulsive disorders, and other issues requiring behavioral modification
- Relaxation and stress management programs for groups and individuals (in my offices or on-site)
- Biofeedback for treatment of stress and sleep disorders
- Acupuncture and herbal treatment for stress management
- Assertiveness training seminars for women

CLIENTS

Consultant	UCLA Department of Psychology
Speaker/Consultant	Triton Wholistic Health Center
Therapist/Owner	Newson Associates

EDUCATION AND TRAINING

M.A. in Clinical Psychology, University of California
B.A. in Psychology, Augustana College
California Acupuncture License
State Certification in Hypnotherapy

MEMBERSHIPS

American Group Psychotherapy Association
California Mental Health Association

REFERENCES

Available

Alfred D. Landers

728 Bolero Court
Novato, CA 94945
(415) 555-2943

OBJECTIVE

To play an integral role on a pastoral care team in a hospital or mental health facility.

EDUCATION

Training Center for Spiritual Directors, Taos Benedictine Abbey, New Mexico, 1998. Intensive initiation into the art of spiritual direction.

Healing Ministries, Institute of Ministries, San Jose, CA, 1995 - 1997. Formation and advanced training, four semesters.

Clinical Pastoral Education, Mental Health, Western Coast Hospital, San Jose, CA, 1994 - 1996. Internship, four units.

PASTORAL EXPERIENCE

1997 - 1998   Community Member, Taos Benedictine Abbey
                Participated in counseling and prayer ministry with retreatants; participated in liturgies, retreats, and business office activities. Will complete training with an additional monthlong program next year.

1994 - 1997   Chaplain Intern, Western Coast Hospital
                Pastoral focus on mentally ill legal offenders. Provided Eucharist ministry to patients in medical, surgical, neurological, geriatric, and adult psychiatric units. Participated in liturgy and prayer services. Provided pastoral interviews and counseling for people of various religious denominations and for nondenominational people.

Alfred D. Landers - page 1 of 2

JOB HISTORY

1984 - present   Senior Commercial Lines Underwriter, Umbrella Insurance,
Group Department, San Rafael, CA
Handle Oil Jobbers program in commercial group department, a nation-wide program with heavy casualty, property, and inland marine coverage. Responsible for six states totaling in excess of $6 million annual premiums. Implemented company changes in underwriting practices and procedures. Developed 10-step program for profit. Audited current files.

1980 - 1988   Personal Lines Underwriting Supervisor, Umbrella Insurance, San Rafael, CA

1975 - 1980   Property and Casualty Underwriter, Umbrella Insurance, Newark, NJ

References upon request

JAMES COHEN
4987 West Avenue • Seattle, WA 98105
(206) 555-8765
ways32@xxx.com

OBJECTIVE

Entry-level position in a firm or agency focused on human rights and/or youth issues where I can put my strong multimedia and communication skills to work for the common good.

EDUCATION

Stanford University, School of Law, Palo Alto, CA
J.D. expected Spring '03

Antioch College, Yellow Springs, OH
Bachelor of Arts '00 in Video Communications and Women's Studies

---

EXPERIENCE

Intern, Power of Hope, Clinton, WA, Summer '00
- Coordinated travel and other logistics and facilitated workshops for arts-based youth empowerment camp. Managed database.
- Led plenary sessions of theater, activism, and sexuality.
- Supported youth in claiming their own voices.

Coordinating Assistant, Antioch College Admissions, March '98–April '00
- Telephoned and maintained database of prospective students.
- Served as resource and peer contact about college.
- Promoted in January '00 to reflect tenure, leadership development, and responsibility for training colleagues.

Organizing Intern, ACORN, St. Paul, MN, Summer '99
- Organized key neighborhood group, collaborated with coorganizer.
- Planned and executed campaigns.
- Produced promotional video from member interviews.
- Organized membership database, and performed the data entry needed to make database operational.
- Raised funds and became the leading organizer nationwide during final month on the job. Asked to return on permanent basis.

Member, BRIDGES, Antioch Sexual Offense Prevention Office, Summer '98
- Organized acting troupe into a full-time collective with an expanded mission.
- Spread message of sexual offense prevention and related sexuality issues through short pieces based on personal experiences of members.
- Worked on every facet of performance, including set, tech., and promotional materials.
- Performed at various campus and youth venues.
- Redeveloped troupe with new members for an Oberlin College conference in Spring '99.

Fellow, Wealth Gap Project, Northfield, MN, Spring '97
- Conducted research on behalf of welfare rights and wealth distribution campaigns.
- Worked in collaboration with local poor people's movement, developed alternative economic models, protested injustices.
- Project led to Minnesota enacting the toughest corporate welfare regulation in the nation.

Classroom Monitor, Carleton College, Northfield, MN, Spring '97
- Monitored class discussion for gender equality and other issues of participation.
- Met with professor to discuss findings and advise on improvement.

Actor, Skit Outreach Services, Hudson, WI, May '93–May '95
- Performed series of skits based on teen issues.
- Provided positive role model to junior high and high school youth.
- Developed new material, fulfilled responsibilities of contract, including remaining drug and alcohol-free.

VOLUNTEER EXPERIENCES AND ACTIVITIES

Mentor, Student Services, Stanford University, Fall '01–Present
- Assist incoming undergraduate students with first semester concerns.

Video Specialist, Turf Productions, Seattle, WA, October '00–August '01
- Provided expertise and equipment to assist youth multimedia troupe in reworking video used in performance.

Director, Theaterworks, Yellow Springs, OH, September '99–April '00
- Founded and organized youth theater troupe of local high school students for college senior project.

SKILLS

Digital editing, performance, Internet, oral Spanish proficiency, computer database systems, writing. Known for remarkable enthusiasm, improvisation, self-motivation, and compassion.

Arthur Lewis
789 Harborough Street
Boston, Massachusetts 02169
(617) 555-8962

Objective   to find employment in a human services field that offers new challenges and opportunities and utilizes the experience, skills, and knowledge from nearly 20 years of increasing responsibility in the education field

Specific Strengths

Creativity   ability to synthesize diverse ideas into coherent concepts, to think in new directions, and to assist others in more clearly stating their ideas and objectives

Tolerance   ability to work with a diverse population and enjoy the interaction and challenges of diversity; essentially team oriented and a "people" person

Assessment   ability to employ various standard and nonstandard assessment processes as well as mature insight in the evaluation of programs and proposals

Writing   ability to write informally and formally, imaginatively as well as in a scholarly, more research-directed style

Speaking   ability to present challenging concepts in formal oral presentations; strong small group skills and experience; significant teaching ability with diverse student population

Education

M.A.   Education, 1983, University of Massachusetts, Boston, MA

B.A.   African American Studies and American Literature, 1980, Boston University, Boston, MA

Employment History

Language Arts Department Head, Jamaica Plain High School, Jamaica Plain, MA. 1998 - present. Coordinate curriculum planning and implementation. Act as department liaison to school board and administration. Teach English, Creative Writing, Technical and Research Writing, American Literature, British Literature, and Multicultural Literature. Supervise the production and publication of a student literary magazine.

Arthur Lewis - page 1 of 2

Employment History (continued)

English and Writing Instructor, Jamaica Plain High School, Jamaica Plain, MA. 1990 - 1998. Taught English, Creative Writing, Technical and Research Writing, American Literature, British Literature, Multicultural Literature, and Speech to high school students. Tutored remedial and advanced students of Literature and Writing. Served as faculty sponsor of African American Student Union.

Language Arts Instructor, Franklin Junior High School, West Roxbury, MA. 1985 - 1990. Taught English, Reading, Speech, and Writing classes to 7th and 8th grade students. Faculty sponsor and advisor for the Student Drama Group.

Substitute Teacher, South Boston Districts, Boston, MA. 1983 - 1985. Taught Language Arts classes in junior and senior high schools in South Boston.

References Available on Request

EVELYN TICKEL
4987 Broadway, Boulder, Colorado 80304
303-555-3892

Objective

A position as a high school science or environmental studies teacher

Education

University of Colorado, Boulder, CO, Teaching Certification, grades 1 - 12, 1997

Colorado State University, Fort Collins, CO, Bachelor of Science, Zoology, 1972

Professional Experience

Instructor, Boulder County Environmental Education Center,
Boulder, CO

Instructed classes in zoology, environmental ecology, and plant and tree identification, using classroom and outdoor hands-on techniques. Supervised overnight trips for high school-aged students. Developed and wrote booklet on endangered Colorado wildlife for use as a textbook. Volunteer, part-time staff, 1995 - present.

Biological Assistant, University of Colorado Wildlife Department,
Boulder, CO

Participated in capture, tagging, and relocation of bighorn sheep in Colorado, and in dietary studies of large ungulates. Assisted in research of black-capped chickadees: made sonogram recordings, maintained 75 birds. Assisted in research of endangered fish species in Western Colorado rivers: collected fish, identified species, collected data, performed literature search, and compiled and condensed information. 1994 - 1995.

Consultant, Pokahu Ranch,
Maui, HI

Developed and wrote a conservation plan for the protection and restoration of the native ecosystem. Researched and evaluated the natural history, recovery plans, regulations, and recommendations of government officials. Performed species counts and determined the possibilities of rehabilitation of disturbed lands, eradication of pests, and reintroduction of endangered species. April - June 1995.

Page 1

Professional Experience (continued)

Scientific Technician, Washington State Department of Fisheries, Olympia, WA

Assisted in biological studies to assess the use of natural and artificial habitats by marine fish species for the purpose of developing criteria for habitat protection, mitigation, and enhancement. Collected and compiled data on salmons for habitat protection and harvest management protection purposes, including species identification, length, weight, scale sampling, sex, mark sampling, tagging, and red salmon spawning "nests" identification. Identified marine micro-invertebrates for fish stomach analysis. Performed herring and smelt spawn surveys, plankton tows, beach seines, and eelgrass samples. Interviewed sport and commercial fishers. Prepared data summaries, charts, illustrations, and graphs. Various departments, 1972 - 1994.

References provided upon request

Nancy Zimmerman

1275 Hadfield Road
Jackson, MS 80216
Pager: (803) 555-8300
Home: (803) 555-2771

Background

- More than 10 years of experience in public health nursing
- Committed to patient advocacy and social reform
- Experienced, effective mental health counselor

Employment

1995 - Present
Mental Health Counselor
Center Clinic, Jackson, MS

Counsel adolescent and adult women in one-on-one and group settings. Provide a safe and therapeutic environment for women confronting depression, low self-esteem, domestic violence, substance abuse, and other mental health issues. Chart patient progress daily and weekly. Develop long- and short-term therapeutic goals. Provide referral to other agencies and services as necessary. Serve on clinic board of directors.

1991 - 1995
Assistant Director
New Hope Women's Shelter, Ottawa, MS

Assisted director with all aspects of clinic management from fund-raising and long-term planning to daily operation of clinic. Recruited and trained volunteers, managed 24-hour telephone hotline, and assisted with counseling of residents. Admitted new residents and assessed their physical and mental state. Helped design and staff on-site child care program.

1988 - 1991
Public Health Nurse
Ottawa County, Ottawa, MS

Treated patients on-site and at two clinic locations. Assisted patients with home health needs: arranging for equipment, home health aids, or application for residential care. Diverse patient population and wide range of patient needs provided experience in everything from early childhood immunizations to hospice care.

Education

Augustana School of Nursing   RN   1988

University of Washington   BA   1986
Double major in Psychology and Sociology

Credentials

Mississippi RN license 856-121341
Red Cross CPR certification
Member, American Nurses Association

References Available

KARLI ROSE
8540 Los Robles Road
Fishers, Indiana 46038
(317) 555-8044

CAREER OBJECTIVE
An assistant principal position in an elementary school that will effectively utilize my creativity, enthusiasm, and organizational skills.

EDUCATION
INITIAL PRINCIPAL'S LICENSE, POSTGRADUATE STUDIES IN SCHOOL ADMINISTRATION, Butler University, Indianapolis, Indiana. Graduated December 1997 from the Experiential Program for Preparing School Principals (E.P.P.S.P.) MASTER OF SCIENCE IN ELEMENTARY EDUCATION, Butler University, Indianapolis, Indiana. August 1992. BACHELOR OF SCIENCE IN ELEMENTARY EDUCATION Butler University, Indianapolis, Indiana. May 1986.

EXPERIENCE

1994-Present	THIRD GRADE TEACHER, North Elementary, Noblesville Schools, Noblesville, Indiana. Utilized a variety of teaching strategies (cooperative learning, whole group instruction, 4MAT learning styles) to teach the core curriculum to multiability students in a self-contained classroom.
1991-1994	FIFTH GRADE TEACHER, North Elementary, Noblesville Schools, Noblesville, Indiana. Incorporated team teaching and computer literacy in teaching the core curriculum. Students were ability grouped as a grade level for math and reading.
1989-1991	FOURTH GRADE TEACHER, Clewiston Primary and Intermediate Schools, Henry County Schools, Clewiston, Florida. Created a peer tutoring system and individualized curriculum to meet the needs of multicultural, lowachieving students.
1987-1989	ADMINISTRATIVE SECRETARY AND VOLUNTEER TUTOR, New Hope of Indiana, Indianapolis, Indiana. Tutored Pike High School students in math and reading in this residential facility that serves the mentally/physically challenged.

KARLI ROSE, Page 1 of 2

1987   SECOND GRADE TEACHER, Crooked Creek School, Metropolitan School District of Washington Township. Contributed to the learning process in all elementary grade levels by administering the regular teacher's plans, grading papers, and giving feedback for follow-up.

PRESENTATIONS

LEARNING AND LIVING IN FUTURE EDUCATION (L.I.F.E.) CONFERENCE, Butler University, Indianapolis, Indiana, 1997. The presentation was entitled "Lifesaver-The Leader as a Visionary." Information was shared on attributes of an effective leader.

WHOLE GROUP INSTRUCTION IN READING, Noblesville, Indiana, 1997. Information was shared on group instruction, grading, and benefits to students.

REFERENCES

Furnished upon request.

JANE FITZGERALD
208 Prince George Street
Annapolis, MD 21401
(301) 555-1799

EDUCATION   George Washington University, Washington, D.C. M.A., Art Therapy, 1988. Stockton State College, Pomona, NJ. B.A., Art, Psychology minor, 1985.

EXPERIENCE   **Center for Children, Inc., La Plata, MD.** Individual and group therapist for victims of sexual abuse and their families. Initiated and supervised art therapy program for atonements with eating disorders. January 1996 - Present.

Anne Arundel County Department of Social Services, Anne Arundel, MD. Individual and group therapist for sexually and physically abused children. Facilitator for staff enrichment group. November 1991 - December 1995.

Charter Hospital, Charlottesville, VA. Provided art therapy to psychiatric patients in individual and group sessions. Served as treatment team member on the adult unit. Field supervisor for master level interns. Staff enrichment coordinator. March 1989 - September 1992.

Department of Human Services, Washington, D.C. Assisted social worker with cases involving abused and neglected children. Responsibilities included counseling, field and family visits, and preparing materials for court hearings. November 1988 - March 1989.

The Joseph P. Kennedy Institute, Washington, D.C. Art therapist intern for developmentally disabled students ages 5 - 12. George Washington University Medical Center Psychiatric Unit. Worked with hyperactive children, Alzheimer's patients, and anorectics. September 1986 - May 1988.

The Helmbold Education Center for the Mentally Handicapped, Ventnor, NJ. Psychology Intern. January 1984 - June 1986.

Department of Continuing Education, Stockton State College, Pomona, NJ. Adjunct Instructor of Art. June 1983 - May 1984.

Jane Fitzgerald,
page 1 of 2

PRESENTATIONS   "Abuse Prevention - for Children." U.S. Naval Academy, MD. February 1998.

"A Special Blend: The Role of Creative Arts and Expressive Therapy." Annual Meeting of the Associated Psychotherapists of Maryland. June 1996.

"Stress Management for Older Adults." Senior Citizen's Center, Anne Arundel, MD. December 1995.

PUBLICATIONS   *From My Heart to Yours.* Anticipated publication January 2000.

"Art Therapy and the Abused Child." *American Journal of Child and Adolescent Psychiatric Nursing.* August 1998.

"Art Therapy: An Effective Strategy in the Counseling of Alzheimer's Patients." *Arts in Psychotherapy Journal.* Fall 1995.

"Art Psychotherapy in the Treatment of the Chemically Dependent Patient." *Arts in Psychotherapy Journal.* Summer 1994.

AFFILIATIONS   The American Art Therapy Association: Credentialed Professional Member.

REFERENCES   Available Upon Request

KATRINA LEVOFSKY

18 Cavendish Drive
Madison, WI 53714
Klevofsky@xxx.com
(608) 555-3332

EDUCATION

Ph.D. Clinical Psychology, Marquette University, Milwaukee, WI, 1993
Dissertation topic: "The Analytic Attitude and Its Effect on Women."
B.S. Psychology, University of Toronto, Ontario, Canada, 1987

PROFILE

- Traveled extensively to study parenthood as a developmental phase in African and Asian cultures, 1997 - present.
- Book will be published by Harper and Row 2003.

EXPERIENCE

University of Wisconsin, Oshkosh, Wisconsin
- Sabbatical, 1997 - 1998
- Assistant Professor, Department of Psychology, 1993 - 1997
- Taught graduate courses in Abnormal and Developmental Psychology.
- Developed and taught undergraduate courses in Introductory Psychology.

PUBLICATIONS

(1994) *Parenthood as a Developmental Phase.* New York: International Universities Press.

(1995) "Mourning and the Birth of a Disabled Child." *Journal of American Psychoanalytic Association,* 8: 389-416.

(1996) "The Narcissistic Determinants of Professional Artists: A Portrait of Five Female Artists" *Psychiatry,* 33: 454-456.

PROFESSIONAL ASSOCIATIONS

- American Psychoanalytic Association
- The Freudian Society of Wisconsin
- Women in Science

REFERENCES

Available upon request

STANFORD UNIVERSITY
Career Planning and Placement Center
Stanford, California 94302

NAME: Ann M. Gisler

CAMPUS ADDRESS: 312 High Drive
                         Stanford, CA 97305
                         (415) 555-7802

PERMANENT ADDRESS: 4780 Green Street
                         Stanford, CA 94303
                         (415) 555-6234

OBJECTIVE: Position teaching reading in a reading lab of
                         a school corporation.

EDUCATION: Stanford University, Stanford, CA Reading
                         Specialist Degree, 1998

                         Purdue University, Lafayette, IN B.S.
                         Elementary Education

EXPERIENCE: Stanford University, Teaching Assistant Early
                         Childhood Laboratory School

                         Purdue University, Day Care Provider
                         Department of Childhood Education

REFERENCES: Contact the Career Planning and Placement
                         Center at 415-555-4499 for references and
                         transcripts.

Dori Kriler Davis • *1155 Ivy Lane* • *Indianapolis, Indiana 46220*

Education:

COLLEGE OF MOUNT ST. JOSEPH
> Bachelor of Arts, May 1985, 3.42 G.P.A.
> Major: Physical Education, Minor: Biology

MIAMI UNIVERSITY
> Master of Arts, August 1986
> Majors: Physical Education and Recreation Administration

I.U.P.U.I/BUTLER UNIVERSITY
> Teacher Certification, May 1998, 3.95 G.P.A.
> Area: Elementary Education

Relevant Experience:

BUTLER UNIVERSITY
Graduate Assistant, College of Education, 1997-present
> Team teach undergraduate preservice reading and language arts methods block and supervise afterschool tutoring practicum. Supervise innovative undergraduate elementary/early childhood preservice program.

Program Coordinator, Project Leadership-Service, July 1995-August 1997
> Provided training and supervision of two hundred students and teachers for youth empowerment through mentoring, community service, and leadership development.

BOYS AND GIRLS CLUB
Unit Director/Program Director, September 1990-July 1995
> Designed and coordinated all aspects of afterschool and summer programs for youth, ages six through eighteen. Involved in curriculum development and implementation, membership recruitment, retention, and rocognition, program publicity, community relations, and staff development.

NOBLESVILLE JUNIOR HIGH SCHOOL
Physical Education Teacher, February 1991-May 1991
Four-month contract to fill a maternity leave vacancy.

PRESTERA CENTER FOR MENTAL HEALTH SERVICES
Community Support Program Developer, October 1989-September 1990
Carried out a one-year grant for expansion of Community Support System for the chronically mentally ill in a four-county catchment area. Served as coordinator of employment and social adjustment education program.

REFERENCES AVAILABLE

Susan Ramos, MSN

986 Yates Street
Chicago, IL 60618
(312) 555-6978
Pager: (312) 555-3999
E-mail: ramos_sue@xxx.com

Work History

1/98 to Present, *Director of Education and Community Relations*
Bradley Medical Center

- Develop and implement all staff training, in-service programming, recertification programs.
- Supervise publication of in-house newsletter, press releases, and patient education literature.
- Design and direct marketing/community relations campaigns and special events.
- Serve as media contact/hospital spokesperson.

10/94 to 1/98, *Director*
Ridgeway Rehabilitation Center

- Directed daily operation of 50-bed residential substance abuse treatment center.
- Managed nursing and support staff.
- Assisted board of directors with long- and short-range budgets and planning.
- Directed fund-raising and community relations efforts.

8/92 to 10/94, *Assistant Professor*
St. Andrews College, BSN Program

- Taught public health nursing, pediatric nursing, and chemical dependency courses.
- Functioned as research assistant.
- Assumed responsibility for ongoing curriculum development.

6/90 to 8/92, *Level II RN*
Children's Hospital

- Served as pediatric staff RN for 250-bed hospital.
- Garnered a wide range of experience, including trauma, burn, and oncology cases.

Computer Proficiency
MS Word, Excel, Outlook
Netscape Navigator
Internet Explorer

Education
| MSN | University of Illinois | 1990 |
| BSN | University of Delaware | 1988 |

Credentials
Member, Illinois Nurses Association
Member, American Nurses Association
Illinois RN License #802-546931
Certified CPR instructor

References
On request

CARTER M. WINSLOW
555 AMSTERDAM AVENUE
NEW YORK, NY 10024
(212) 555-5727

PROFESSIONAL OBJECTIVE

To secure a position as a social worker with an agency that will enable me to apply my eight years of counseling and administrative experience.

EMPLOYMENT HISTORY

- **Institute for Behavior Resources. Washington, D.C.** March 1997 - present. Director of Youth Group Program for neglected and abused children. Responsible for staff of seven full-time caseworkers and six volunteers including screening and training of new staff members. Program's liaison with community and state agencies. Prepared grant proposals, which accounted for 70 percent of program's funding.

- **Institute for Behavior Resources. Washington, D.C.** October 1993 - March 1997. Youth Group Program social worker. Conducted psychosocial assessments and implemented appropriate counseling for neglected and abused children ages 7 - 12. Conducted workshops for educators and day care personnel on identifying signs of neglect and abuse and the proper procedure for reporting cases of suspected abuse. Served as consultant to State Child Welfare Department.

- **George Washington University Medical Center. Washington, D.C.** June 1992 - September 1993. Pediatric ward counselor. Led individual and group therapy sessions for children with physical injury related trauma. Counseled family members and designed and implemented support group for siblings of pediatric patients.

- **Family and Child Services. Washington, D.C.** June 1991 - May 1992. Social work intern. Collected statistical data on foster care placement of D.C. area children for annual report presented to the Mayor's Council.

- **Hope House. Washington, D.C.** November 1989 - May 1991. Volunteer counselor for children in safe house for battered women and their families.

EDUCATION

- George Washington University, Washington, D.C. M.S.W., 1991.

- University of Maryland, College Park, MD. B.A., Psychology, 1989.

REFERENCES

Available Upon Request

JESSICA NATHAN

87948 Fairview Place • Huntsville, Alabama 35804
Home: (205) 555-9856 • Pager: (205) 555-0014

OBJECTIVE   Psychiatric social work position in an adolescent treatment facility

RELATED EXPERIENCE

FOSTER PARENT

- Care for hard-to-place children. Accepted the extraordinary challenges of raising handicapped children and achieved dramatic improvements. Patiently and diligently encouraged independence and self-reliance with valuable results.
- Volunteered to participate in TEAM, a post-placement support group.
- Provided special classes, guidance, and psychological care for foster parents and children.
- Participated in training programs sponsored by the Huntsville Society for the Crippled and Disabled.

PSYCHIATRIC INSTITUTE OF HUNTSVILLE
1989-1998 Psychiatric Social Worker

- Developed individual and group counseling treatment programs for teens with a history of violent behavior
- Coordinated a teen drama program in conjunction with the Creative Arts Team
- Initiated a substance abuse program in coordination with NA and AA
- Coauthored six articles relating to adolescence, published variously in regional and national publications
- Planned supportive services to ease return to the community

EDUCATION

University of Knoxville, Knoxville, TN
M.S.W. 1988
B.A. Psychology 1986
C.S.W. 1980

References available on request

JAMIE C. DAY
6285 Barfield Road
Atlanta, GA 30328
(404) 555-9648

OBJECTIVE:
Seeking a teaching position in high school mathematics.

PERSONAL ATTRIBUTES:
- *Hardworking, with an excellent academic background and a dependable employment history.*
- *Takes pride in work, and eager to take on new responsibilities with the intention of seeing every project to a successful end.*

ACADEMIC QUALIFICATIONS:
Bachelor of Science in Mathematics
Minor in Education
Rose-Hulman Institute of Technology, Terre Haute, IN
May 1998
Rose-Hulman Scholarship Recipient

RELEVANT COURSEWORK:
Statistical Methods
Operations Research
Linear Algebra
Discrete & Combinatorial Algebra
FORTRAN
Numerical Analysis
Probability
Calculus
Differential Equations

EMPLOYMENT HISTORY:

1996-1997   **Summers State Farm, Indianapolis, IN**
Employed two summers as a farm worker. Gained experience and proficiency. Put in charge of checking the work of 20-25 employees and reporting to employer.

1995-1996   **Archer's Meat Packing, Fisher, IN**
Employed as clean-up person/meat packer. Assured sanitary conditions in the plant for each day's use.

1993-1995   **Tyner's Farm, Carmel, IN**
Employed two summers as farm worker. Involved in daily activities of farm production and maintenance.

1992   **Marion County Fair, Indianapolis, IN**
Employed as maintenance worker. Prepared display buildings, completed construction repairs, did general maintenance.

REFERENCES:

Available upon request.

PATRICIA WHITE

987 W. 44TH STREET • CHEYENNE, WY 82001 • (307) 555-9872

PROFESSIONAL OBJECTIVE

Opportunity to demonstrate superior teaching ability and administrative decision-making skills in an early childhood classroom.

SUMMARY OF QUALIFICATIONS

- Highly organized, motivated, and patient.
- Able to train and guide young children in their academic pursuits.
- Thorough knowledge of computers - IBM PC, Lotus 1-2-3, and WordPerfect.
- Notably skilled in speaking and writing French.
- Excellent rapport with all levels of employees.

EDUCATION

Fitchburg State College, Fitchburg, Massachusetts
Major: Elementary Education
December 1998

EXPERIENCE

Volunteer, Massachusetts Center for Early Childhood Education

REFERENCES

Excellent professional and personal references upon request.

JONATHAN K. SANDERS
6 WEYBRIDGE PLACE
CHAPEL HILL, NC 27514
(910) 555-3469

CAREER OBJECTIVE

To obtain a counseling position with a nonprofit organization that serves the needs of the homeless population.

EXPERIENCE

1998 - 2000 Job Development Counselor, Job Find, Chapel Hill, NC.

- Provided job counseling to homeless men in three area transitional housing programs.
- Increased community business participation in job placement program by 50 percent.
- Organized weekly employment workshops and quarterly job fairs.
- Increased revenue for job training 30 percent through community fundraising and 25 percent through federal grants.
- Wrote quarterly newsletter distributed to county businesses.
- Provided training seminars to shelter staffers throughout North Carolina regarding effective job counseling strategies.

1994 - 1998 Volunteer Hewlett Men's Shelter, Chapel Hill, NC.

- Responsible for overnight coverage of 12-bed facility two nights per week.
- Member of committee for volunteer recruitment.
- Chairperson fundraising committee.
- Provided information regarding social services programs.

EDUCATION

- B.A., Business, 1998, University of North Carolina
- Anticipated M.S.W., Spring 2001, Duke University

REFERENCES

Provided Upon Request

ROBERT MARTIN

2108 Rusk Street
Beaumont, TX 77701
(409) 555-8740

EXPERIENCE

1994 - present	**Houston Correctional Center, Houston, TX.** Correctional Specialist. Screen repeat juvenile offenders for potential placement in diversion programs. Assessment includes conducting interviews with offenders, reviewing police reports, interpreting psychological data, and conferring with other state-appointed personnel. Determine appropriate diversion placement and monitor progress through visitations, interviews, and follow-up case reporting.
1989 - 1993	**Long Lane Center, Liberty, TX.** Live-in Counselor. Provided overnight supervision for 16 adolescent boys with history of juvenile delinquency. Provided individual and group alcohol and substance abuse counseling. Initiated after-school work placement program and peer support groups. Worked in conjunction with Department of Children's Services and Houston Correctional Department.
1986 - 1993	**Center Stage Youth Hotline, Houston, TX.** Coordinator of Volunteers. Supervised 22 volunteers for 24-hour youth hotline. Initiated after school peer counseling program.
1984 - 1987	**Houston Police Department, Houston, TX.** Police Officer. Specialized in juvenile cases. Conducted seminars for educators and parents on issue of alcohol and substance abuse. Served as law enforcement liaison to Children's Court Appointed Advocacy Program.

EDUCATION

1989	B.A., Psychology, Texas State University
1985	Graduate of Houston Police Academy

REFERENCES

Available Upon Request

Melinda F. Jarviss
S. Inland Empire Way
Spokane, WA 99204
(509) 555-2641

Career Objective	To obtain a position in which I can combine my teaching experience with my concern for the environment.

Work Experience

1998 - present	**Environmental Education Group, Kettle Falls, WA.** Field Instructor. Provide environmental conservation education and appreciation to elementary school children. Lead school groups on nature hikes in and around Coulee Dam National Recreation Area. Prepare educational materials to supplement outdoor lessons. Visit local schools and prepare resource materials for classroom teachers.
1993 - 1998	**Hanover Elementary School, Hanover, PA.** Fourth and fifth grade science teacher. Responsible for all aspects of classroom management and instruction, including lesson planning, evaluation, and reporting. Initiated and supervised elementary science fair.
1992	**Frederick Elementary School, Abbotstown, PA.** Student teacher. Responsible for the instruction of four elementary science classes.
Education	1992, B.S., Biology, Gettysburg College
Certifications	Washington State Board of Education Elementary Certification Pennsylvania State Board of Education Master Educator, Elementary Certification
Memberships	Friends of Earth Mt. Spokane Conservation Group Spokane Recycling Committee American Association of Environmental Educators

References Available Upon Request

NICOLE M. FRANKLIN

8 Gaul Road North
Setauket, NY 11733
Home: (516) 555-9042
Work: (516) 555-1640

WORK EXPERIENCE

Adult Education Family Literacy Educator, Setaucket Board of Education, East Setaucket, NY. July 1998 - present

- Instructor for pilot program that combines GED tutoring with family and parenting skills training.

- Member of teaching committee that designed program, developed instructional materials, and submitted proposal for state funding.

- Confer with Department of Social Services caseworkers to ensure program participants receive full range of services.

- Currently serving as a consultant to two area adult education programs.

Instructional Assistant/Clerk for the Even Start Family Literacy Program, Setauket Board of Education, East Setaucket, NY. August 1997 - June 1998

- Tutored individuals, performed administrative tasks, initiated fundraising to provide computers for classroom instruction.

- Collected and computerized Even Start data for statistical reporting to State Board of Education.

Literacy Volunteer, Stoors, CT. December 1994 - July 1997

- Tutored adults in reading skills.

- Served on Volunteer Recruitment Committee.

- Trained new volunteers.

EDUCATION

B.A., Psychology, University of Connecticut, 1997

References furnished on request

GREG SIMON

947 W. Harwood Road
Lawrenceburg, IN 47025
(812) 555-5680

WORK EXPERIENCE

1998 - Present	**Lawrenceburg Police Department** Patrolman, Field Operations Division
1997	**Lawrenceburg High School** High School Liaison Officer, Investigation Division. Special Patrol, Juvenile and Criminal Investigations
1991 - 1997	**Indianapolis Police Department** Staff Aide, Criminalistics Division

EDUCATION

1991	**B.S., Law Enforcement Administration** Indiana Central University, Indianapolis, Indiana. Comprehensive Major Program combining Political Science, Sociology, and Psychology
	Police Training Institute South Bend, IN. Basic 10-week training, graduated #2 in class

PROFESSIONAL CERTIFICATIONS

Special Weapons and Tactics

Arson Investigation

Firearms Instructor

Narcotics Investigation

Evidence Technician

Breath Alcohol Testing

PROFESSIONAL MEMBERSHIPS

- Fraternal Order of Police
- Indiana Juvenile Officers

REFERENCES

Available Upon Request

JOHN J. ALLEN

Present Address
765 5th Street
Washington, D.C. 20016-8001
(202) 555-2213

Permanent Address
28 Octavia Trail
Carmel, IN 46032
(317) 555-6675

OBJECTIVE

Full-time teaching position in telecommunications research and development, particularly in optical fiber networks, satellite communications or antenna design.

EDUCATION

University of Washington
Currently pursuing Masters of Science in Electrical
Engineering with a concentration in telecommunications
and fiber optics.
Expected date of Graduation: January 2001

Whitman College
Bachelors of Science with Highest Distinction in
Electrical Engineering, May 1998

EXPERIENCE

University of Washington
Department of Electrical Engineering
TEACHING ASSISTANT, 1998-1999
Assisted with instruction in controls courses and the
Introduction to Electronics lab.

Amoco Incorporated, Washington, D.C.
SPECIAL TECHNICAL ASSISTANT, Summer 1999
Installed hardware and software for computer control of test equipment,
conducted stress tests on circuit boards, wrote software to capture and
plot oscilloscope waveforms.

Naylor Pipe Company, Chicago, IL
SENIOR STAFF TECHNOLOGIST, Summer 1998
  Conducted research on optical fiber communications systems. Primary research was on an experimental study of privacy and security issues in passive, fiber-to-the-home networks.

SKILLS
CAD tool experience
SPICE
MAGIC
IRISM
SUPREM

MEMBERSHIPS
Tau Beta Pi
Pi Tau Sigma

REFERENCES
On request

VELIO A. PANSERA

8415 Oketo Avenue
Niles, Illinois 60714
(708) 555-7102

CAREER OBJECTIVE

To obtain a position as a school psychologist.

EDUCATION

National-Louis University, Evanston, IL
Degree: Educational Specialist in School Psychology, 2000

Loyola University, Chicago, IL
Degree: Master of Arts,
Clinical Psychology, 1998

Illinois State University, Normal, IL
Degree: Bachelor of Arts, 1995
Sociology and Psychology

CERTIFICATION

Type 73 Illinois School Board of Education

WORK EXPERIENCE

8/99 - present
Glenview North High School, Glenview, IL
School Psychology Intern

• Administer and interpret psychological and educational diagnostic tests

• Lead group counseling sessions

• Conduct individual counseling sessions

• Teach social skills classes to special education students

• Coach Junior Girls' Softball

8/98 - 8/99
Martin Academy, Niles, IL
Therapist and Teacher Assistant

• Worked as a team member to develop appropriate levels of academic and behavioral assistance for students ages 10 to 19

• Participated in crisis intervention team

• Directed group therapy sessions

V. A. Pansera,
page one of two

WORK EXPERIENCE *continued*

1/98 - 6/98
Tauber Mental Health Center, Mundelein, IL
Psychology Intern

- Administered psychological tests
- Counseled chemically dependent adolescents
- Conducted individual and group therapy

Summer '97
Niles Park District, Niles, IL
Volleyball Day Camp Supervisor

- Taught basic fundamentals of volleyball to boys and girls ages 9 to 17
- Explained team strategies and instructed students on how to execute strategies

Fall 1995
St. Luke's Academy, Des Plaines, IL
Internship and Family Educator

- Served as a family educator for a home housing young women ages 6 to 17
- Worked with physically, emotionally, mentally, and sexually abused young women
- Assisted in the application of a behavior modification system

Fall 1994
Illinois State University, Normal, IL
Student Volunteer, Head Start Program

- Assisted in classroom activities
- Worked with children ages 3 to 5

MEMBERSHIPS

American Psychological Association
Illinois School Psychologists Association

References Available

Kerry H. Bourne

1732 Albana Drive • Indianapolis, IN 46200 • (317) 555-5570

Objective:

To obtain a teaching position in an elementary or middle school.

Teaching Experience:

Wishard Middle School, Taylor Mill, Kentucky
Mathematics/Language Arts Teacher   1999-2000

- Taught Algebra, English, and Creative Writing
- Advisor for Student Government
- Coached three cheerleading squads
- Planned and operated fund-raising projects

Northern University, Highland Heights, Kentucky
Social Studies Teacher   Summer 1999
- Developed enrichment program, "Travel the World"
- Taught gifted students, grades 4-8
- Taught geography, culture, language of foreign countries

Carthage Elementary School, Edges, Kentucky
Fifth Grade Teacher   1997-1999
- Taught all subject areas to fifth grade classes
- Coached cheerleading squad

Sullivan Learning Center, Edgewood, Kentucky
Math/Language Arts Tutor   1993-1997
- Instructed gifted and remedial students in areas of mathematics and reading

Education:

Mooreville College
B.A. Elementary Education, 1993
Summa Cum Laude

Bekridge University
Seeking Master's Degree
Elementary Education

References:

Furnished upon request

MICHAEL C. COOPER

87 Sherwood Court
Joliet, IL 34122
815/555-0967
mike_cooper@xxx.com

OBJECTIVE
Seeking a position as a director of a nonprofit organization with the primary role of a fund raiser.

SUMMARY OF ACHIEVEMENTS
- Organized a chapel fund drive for St. Francis' Children's Summer Camp. Donations in excess of $500,000.

- Coordinated a trust fund drive for the Senior Citizens' Retirement Home in Joliet. Contributions totaled $350,000.

- Planned week-long event for Papal visit during summer of 1993. Organized hotel accommodations for visiting dignitaries and scheduled the daily seminars and guest speakers' agendas.

EDUCATION
University of Notre Dame, South Bend, IN
M.D. in Theology, 1977
Curriculum included: Communications and Counseling, Scripture, Ecclesiology, History
Newman College, Baltimore, MD
B.A. in History, 1972

PROFESSIONAL EXPERIENCE
St. Francis Catholic Church, Joliet, IL
Pastor 1980 - 1994

Xavier High School for Boys, Chicago, IL
Instructor, Department of History, 1978 - 1980
Coach, Junior Varsity Baseball Team

ARTICLES PUBLISHED
"The Role of Religion in Today's High-Tech Environment"
"Integrating Religion in the Sports Arena"

SUMMARY OF QUALIFICATIONS
Well-rounded education.
Ability to communicate to large groups of people.
Trained to lead from consensus.

REFERENCES
Furnished upon request.

REBECCA BOSANGE

12 Delaney St. • Revere, MA 06125 • 617/555-8975
beckybosange@xxx.com

OBJECTIVE
To obtain the position of a nanny in a private residence.

EXPERIENCE
Nanny, Somerset, Bermuda, 1993 - 1998
Cared for two children from the ages of 18 months and 2 months in a private residence, for five years. Duties included monitoring their playtime activities, teaching them the French language, supervising dietary menus, and encouraging healthy outdoor activities with children of their own age.

Language Instructor, Marseilles, France, 1998 - 2000
Taught 3 children in one family ages 2, 3, and 5 years old the English language.

EDUCATION
Boston College, Newton, MA, 1990 - 1994
Major: Child Psychology
Graduated *summa cum laude*

Marseilles School of Cooking, Marseilles, France
Course of studies included canapes, entrees, and desserts.
Certificate awarded, 1996.

RELATED ACTIVITIES
Organized a program of outdoor summer activities for children ages 10 - 17 years old, at the Brookville Housing Development, Brookville, MA, 1992 - 1994.

Coordinated an annual Christmas party for young children at the Brookville Housing Development, Brookville, MA, 1991 - 1993.

ACHIEVEMENT
Coauthored *The Children's Book of Games*, published by Playtime Publishers of London, 1995.

HOBBIES
Writing, cooking, travel.

REFERENCES
Furnished upon request.

James S. Michalson, Ph.D.

3333 Elizabeth Street
Local, Indiana 47000

Home (317) 555-3364
Office: (317) 555-9274

Educational and Professional Training

Doctor of Philosophy, Educational Leadership
Miami University, Oxford, OH, 1994

Post-Graduate Studies, Guidance and Counseling
Xavier University, Cincinnati, OH 1987 - 1989

Master of Education, Public School Administration
Xavier University, Cincinnati, OH 1987

Bachelor of Science, Elementary Education
Miami University, Oxford, OH, 1985

Professional Experience

Superintend Local School Corporation
Local, Indiana, 1994 - Present
Provided overall leadership and direction for a growing suburban school district in Central Indiana. Specific accomplishments include revamping the overall K-12 curriculum, building two modern elementary schools, increasing teaching salaries by 17 percent, and successfully negotiating two labor contracts.

Teaching Fellow/Adjunct Faculty Member
Department of Educational Leadership
Miami University, Oxford, Ohio, 1992 - 1994
Taught undergraduate courses in the field of educational leadership, teacher education, and supervised student teachers in the area of elementary education. Served as an off-campus graduate instructor (Wilmington College) in the area of educational leadership.

Elementary Principal, North Union Local Schools
Richwood, Ohio, 1990-1992
Provided leadership for the overall operation of a multidimensional elementary school (K-6) with 500 students and 36 faculty members. Established a comprehensive microcomputer system for classroom usage. Developed longrange planning, budgeting, and student scheduling initiatives.

Assistant Elementary Principal, Fairfield City Schools
Farifield, Ohio 1988-1990
Assisted with all areas of staff development, faculty evaluation, student discipline, and curricular innovation for a (K-5) elementary building of 800 students and 49 staff members. Directed and implemented a series of community relations projects.

Classroom Teacher, Fairfield City Schools
Fairfield, Ohio 1985-1988
Introduced grade appropriate material (4-8) through oral presentations, visual demonstrations, and other innovative resources. Served as chairperson for numerous curricular design committees.

BOK CHUL LEE

475 Park Drive
Chicago, IL 60613
312-555-8645

OBJECTIVE

To pursue a career in a criminal or social service setting working for, and with, minors.

EDUCATION

M.A.
Northwestern University
The School of Social Work
Concentration, Clinical Social Work
Evanston, IL
June, 2000

B.A.
Northeastern Illinois University
Major, Criminal Justice; Minor, Social Work
High Honors List
Chicago, IL
December, 1997

A.A.
Malcom X College
Major, Liberal Studies
Chicago, IL
December, 1995

PROFESSIONAL EXPERIENCE

Cook County Services, Caseworker III
Chicago, IL
November 1999 - Present

Conduct investigations and submit intensive social studies involving private adoption placements and contested adoptions. In addition, responsibilities include investigating, by court order, the social conditions and residences of children whose parents are involved in divorce, paternity, and probate-related custody and visitation issues. Serve as an expert witness when subpoenaed.

PROFESSIONAL INTERNSHIPS

Board of Education, Chicago Public School System
Chicago, IL
September 1998 - June 1999

Provided individual, family, and group treatment to children and their families. Participated in child placements with a multi-discipline staff.

Office of the Public Guardian
Chicago, IL
January 1998 - September 1998

Interviewed children and adolescents to assess and document factual background of abuse and/or neglect prior to court hearings. Assessment concluded with in-home evaluation.

Circuit Court of Cook County/Juvenile Division
Chicago, IL
Spring 1997

Assisted probation officers with court duties on cases related to minor respondents, participated in field surveillance and home visits of minors, and completed and filed monthly and quarterly reports of minors' progress.

PROFESSIONAL MEMBERSHIPS

Illinois Social Work Council

National Association of Social Workers

References available on request

THERESA PORTER
2453 Cambridge Road
Kansas City, MO 64108
Cell Phone: 681/555-8976
Home Phone: 681/555-0654

JOB OBJECTIVE

A library science position that will utilize my management and materials acquisitions skills

CAPABILITIES

- Review purchasing materials and suggest acquisitions
- Develop budgets
- Act as community liaison
- Create publicity materials
- Study and report on the condition of special collections
- Handle reference calls and requests

ACHIEVEMENTS

- Developed community outreach program that increased library use
- Developed successful budget proposals
- Trained volunteers
- Supervised staff of six
- Updated and expanded reference library
- Developed specialized science collection

EMPLOYMENT

1996 - Present
Librarian
Kansas City Public Libraries
1991 - Present
Head Librarian
Wright High School, Kansas City, MO

EDUCATION

M.L.S.
Rosary College, River Forest, IL, Library Science, 1991
B.S.
State University of New York-Buffalo, Biology, 1989

REFERENCES AVAILABLE

Maria Patricia White

28 Octavia Terrace
Cincinnati, OH 45243
(513) 555-8673

Career Objective:

Elementary teaching position

Education:

Northwestern University, Evanston, IL
Graduation Date: May 1998
Bachelor of Science
Major: Elementary Education
G.P.A.: 4.0

Experience:

Student Teaching
Northview Elementary School, Carmel, IN
Fourth Grade, Open Concept

Professional Memberships:

International Reading Association, Ohio Council of IRA
Midwest Alliance for Excellence in Education

Special Skills:

Trained in TESA (Teacher Expectations and Student Achievement) and CEI
(Critical Elements of Instruction).

Activities and Honors:

Paul Douglas Scholarship (academic scholarship)
Dean's List
Outstanding Senior Award
Tau Beta Sigma Music Society
Kappa Delta Pi Honorary Society in Education

Certificates/Licenses:

Provisional Elementary License for Grades 1–6
Kindergarten Endorsement

References:

Available on request

TYRELL DAVIS

1811 Green Street
Cleveland, Ohio 44122
(216) 555-7837 - Work
(216) 555-3659 - Home

OBJECTIVE

Position in criminal corrections leading to supervisory/administrative work.

EDUCATION

Ohio State University, B.A. Degree, 1996

Major: Criminal Justice

Minors: Social Service and Political Science

Freshman Dorm Manager during senior year

EMPLOYMENT

Cleveland Youth Authority, Corrections Department, Parole Division

Position: Parole Officer (1996 - Present)

Supervisor: Walter Reed

DUTIES

- Supervise parole procedures for Cleveland Boys School and Ohio Youth Correctional Center.
- Prepare home evaluations, social histories, and interviews with inmates.
- Assess inmates' social problems; supervise juvenile offenders; counsel inmates and their families.
- Arrange residence, education, and employment for prospective parolees.
- Represent Cleveland Youth Authority at community functions and hearings; act as community liaison.
- Prosecute parole violators.

Reference available from current supervisor, Walter Reed, at (216) 555-7839.

Detailed references upon request.

Mark L. Longman

28 Limestone Drive
Springfield, Ohio 45501
937-555-4988

Career Objective:

To obtain a teaching position in elementary education, preferably in primary grades, and to use my skills in an effective professional manner.

Education:

Western State College, Gunnison, Colorado
Bachelor of Arts in Elementary Education, June 1998
Special Area: Kindergarten
G.P.A.: 3.5/4.0

Employment:

Kiddy-Land   1995–present
Responsibilities: Volunteer, inspire young children, assist in special arts and crafts projects, and assist with ongoing volunteer program in association with Lowell High School.

Gunnison Central Library   1993–1995
Responsibilities: Helped students with the use of microfiche and microfilm equipment. Assisted with updating on-line catalog. Trained students in use of Internet. Assisted with adult literacy program.

Computer Skills:

Knowledge of C and Pascal programming languages. Proficient in WordPerfect, Ventura Publisher, and Hotshot Graphics.

Activities/Honors:

National Merit Scholar
Biked and traveled across Europe during the summer of 1998. Active member of varsity swim team.

References:

Available on request.

ANGELA M. LORENZ

815 N. Campbell Avenue
Indianapolis, IN 46000
Home Phone: 317-555-4650
Work Phone: 317-555-5237

EDUCATIONAL PREPARATION

Initial Principal's Licence, Postgraduate Studies in School of Administration
Butler University, Indianapolis.
Graduation from Experiential Program for Preparing School Principals (EPPSP) will
take place in December of 1998.

Endorsement in Gifted Education,
Purdue University, Lafayette, Indiana, 1996.

M.S., Education, Indiana University/Purdue University
Indianapolis, Indiana, 1985.

B.A., Elementary Education
St. Mary-of-the-Wood, Terre Haute, Indiana, 1980.

PROFESSIONAL EXPERIENCE

Resource Teacher for Gifted/Talented Students in Grades 2 and 3
West Newton Elementary, Decatur Township, West Newton, IN, 1992-Present.

Educator for Grades 4 and 5, Lynwood Elementary
Decatur Township, Indianapolis, IN, 1990-1992.

Educator for Grades 5 and 6, St. Thomas Aquinas Grade School
Indianapolis, IN, 1985-1990.

Educator for Grades 4 and 5, St. Michael's Grade School
Greenfield, IN, 1980-1985.

Homebound Tutor for a severely handicapped student in Indianapolis School System
Indianapolis, IN, 1979-1980.

ADVANCE TRAINING AND SPECIAL ACTIVITIES

- Learning Styles/Gregoric Model, Indianapolis, Indiana.
- Cooperative Learning, Indianapolis, Indiana.
- TESA (Teacher Expectation/Student Achievement), Indianapolis, Indiana.
- Clinical Supervision Training, Curriculum and Instruction Department, Decatur Township.
- Critical Elements of Instruction (CEI - Madeline Hunter's Mastery Teaching Model).
- TESA/CEI link with Butler University. Coordinated Site Based Evaluation through Department of Education for Gifted and Talented Program in Decatur Township.
- Writing of Gifted and Talented Grand and Budget.
- Search Committee. Participated in selection process for an administrator for the School of Education at Butler University.
- Climate Audit, Sanders Elementary, Indianapolis, Indiana.
- Writing of Social Studies Curriculum and Policy Handbook.
- Outcome Based Education Committee.

PROFESSIONAL AFFILIATIONS

- Association for Supervision and Curriculum Development.
- Currently applying for membership in Phi Delta Kappa through Butler University.
- Currently applying for associate membership in Indiana Association of Elementary and Middle School Principals.
- Indiana Association for the Education of Gifted Children. Member of School Board for Holy Cross Central School.

REFERENCES

Available upon request.

Jessica Adams

121 Hawthorne Drive
Alameda, CA 94103
510-555-8520

Educational Background:	B.A. in English	Stanford University
	M.A. in English	Holy Names College

Additional Work:

St. Mary's College; California State University, Hayward
California State University, Chico
University of California, Santa Cruz
University of Hawaii, Honolulu

Credentials:

Standard Elementary
Standard Designated Subject Secondary
General Secondary
General Pupil Personnel Services
Administrative
Specialist: Reading
Specialist: Learning Handicapped

Teaching Experience:

Castilleja School, grades 1–12 (1 year)
American School in Japan, grade 4 (3 years)
Carlmont High School (6 years)
San Jose District Summer School (2 years)

Coordination:

Santa Clara Valley Unified School District, reading volunteers
   (1 year)
District Reading Committee (7 years)
District Special Education Committee (6 years)
Work Experience Coordinator, Carlmont High School
   (3 years)

Supervision:

Student aides, work experience (3 years)
CETA aide, career education, creation and formation of the
   Valley Youth Employment Center (1 year)
Work study program, district level (3 years)
Summer school student aides, 4 to 6 programs (2 years)
Teaching aide, Master Plan (3 years)
Additional program and aide (1 year)
Lead teacher, language arts, Carlmont High School
   (4 teachers in department)

FACULTY DATA SUMMARY SHEET

Risler, Margaret, Ph.D.
Associate Professor of Education
Graduate and Undergraduate Faculty

1. Academic Degrees

Ph.D.	Kansas State University	1988
M.S.	University of Indiana	1976
B.S.	Purdue University	1975

2. Professional Experience

1997 - present	University of Cincinnati, Associate Professor of Foundations of Education
1992 - 1997	Butler University, Associate Professor of Foundations of Education (on leave 1994–1996)
1994 - 1996	U.S. Department of Education, Office of Research, Director, Education and Society Division
1989 - 1992	University of South Carolina, Assistant Professor of Education
1985 - 1989	Ohio Wesleyan University, Graduate Teaching Assistant
1983 - 1985	United States Armed Forces Institute, Education Research Specialist
1976 - 1983	Indianapolis Public Schools, Social Studies Teacher

3. Faculty and Administrative Load

Fall Semester 2001

EDUC 208	The School and the Community	3 semester credits
EDFN 408	Introduction to Reading	3 semester credits

Spring Semester 2002

EDUC 202	Introduction to Instructional Methods	3 semester credits
EDFN 748	The School in Modern Society	3 semester credits

Summer Semester 2002

EDFN 408	Introduction to Reading	3 semester credits
EDFN 748	The School in Modern Society	3 semester credits

Risler, Margaret
Data Sheet, page 1 of 3

Other Collegiate Assigments 2001 - 2002
Tenure and Promotion Study Committee (Departmental)
SACS Committee (Departmental)
Committee on Higher Order Thinking (College)
Families, Communities, and Children's Learning Center Committee (University)
Advising: six doctoral committees (major professor on two)

4. Current Professional and Academic Association Memberships
American Educational Research Association
American Educational Studies Association
Associates for Research on Private Education
Conference on Faith and History
History of Education Society
Midwest History of Education Society
National Council on Religion and Public Education
Southern History of Education Society

5. Current Professional Assigments and Activities
President Elect, Associates for Research on Private Education AERA/SIG
Program Chair, Religion and Education AERA/SIG
Guest Editor, *Private School Monitor*
Reviewer, *Educational Foundations*
Member, Editorial Board of Review for Religion and Public Education
Proposal Reviewer, AERA/SIG Associates for Research on Private Education
Proposal Reviewer, AERA/SIG Religion and Education
Consultant, U.S. Department of Education, Office of Research

6. Publications
BOOKS
Risler, Margaret M. *Getting Ready for School*, Educational Press, 2001
Risler, Margaret M. *Ready for Kindergarten*, Educational Press, 2000
Risler, Margaret M. *Vocabulary for the Primary Grades*, Educational Press, 1998
Risler, Margaret M. *Considering Private Schools*, McKinny Press, 1997

ARTICLES
Indianapolis News
June 16, 1999, "Why Parents Should Read to Their Children"
Cincinnati Enquirer
September 8, 1998, "Getting into College"
Free Time
June 1997, "Books to Read This Summer"

7. Research Interests
How Television Hurts Children's Ability to Read
Home Schooling

ALEXANDER HO

986 Parker Lane   **Business (415) 555-2939**
Walnut Creek, CA 94595   **Home   (415) 555-9875**

CAREER OBJECTIVE

Teach jounalism at the high school level and advise yearbook and newspaper productions.

EDUCATION

University of California at Berkeley
Bachelor of Arts in Journalism, May 1998
Cumulative G.P.A.: 3.5/4.0

Courses

Newswriting and Reporting   Public Relations Methods
Mass Communication Law   News Editing
Advanced Advertising Copywriting   Reporting Public Affairs
News Photography   Graphics and Typography

LICENSE

Licensed to teach jounalism to grades 9–12 in California, May 1998

TEACHING EXPERIENCE

Student Teacher at Archer Technical High School
Berkeley California, Spring 1997
Taught grades 9–12

Student Teacher at Benjamin Davis High School
Berkeley, California, Fall 1996
Taught grades 10–12

WORK EXPERIENCE

Student Assistant, Berkeley Library
September 1995 to May 1996
Circulated library materials to students, helped students with the use of microfiche and micro-film equipment, updated on-line card catalog, processed research works for professional bindery, opened and closed library.

Receptionist/Switchboard Operator, Duke Associates, Chicago, IL
Summer 1996
Operated 14-line switchboard and directed incoming calls, greeted executive clients and performed customer relations, assisted with clerical duties.

AWARDS

Nominated for Browne & Smithe Journalism Award, 1997
Keitzer Scholarship, 1997-1998

REFERENCES

Recommendations are available upon request.
A credentials packet is available from:
University of California at Berkeley
588 Sunset Road
Berkeley, CA 94720

MARGARET CHANG

1483 Kathleen Court, Westport, CT 06880; Phone: 203-555-4523

Psychiatric Social Worker

Summary

Trained psychiatric social worker comfortable in a variety of settings, experienced in dealing with diverse client population, seeking new opportunities to assist clients with social and psychiatric adjustment needs.

WORK HISTORY

Home Health Caseworker
Lutheran Social Services of New England, 1994 to Present

Provide comprehensive discharge planning for patients leaving Lutheran Community Hospital. Referral to appropriate community services and programs for nursing, child care, housekeeping, counseling, and other ongoing needs.

Intake Counselor
Wheeler Psychiatric Institute, 1990 - 1994

Conducted initial interviews with patients and family members. Explained the Institute's programs and fees, patient's rights and responsibilities. Assisted patients and family members with decision to admit. Referred patients to appropriate community services.

Counselor
Westport Women's Center, 1988 - 1990

Provided private counseling for area women related to personal and career goals. Developed support groups for women dealing with issues of substance abuse and incest survival.

Margaret Chang - page 1 of 2

EDUCATION

M.S.W
Columbia School of Social Work

B.A.
Boston College/Major: Psychology

SKILLS

Computer literate
Fluent in Spanish and French
Knowledge of Sign Language

REFERENCES

Available upon request

Elizabeth Sherrill

238 Sunset Drive
Kalamazoo, Michigan 49718
613-555-5553

Employment History:

1995–Present **Substitute teacher** for Lakeview Public Schools and Comstock Public Schools for more than 100 days, all levels, K–12 including shop, home economics, reading, band, art, and drafting.

1989–1995 Woodlawn Nursery School, Kalamazoo, Michigan. **Teacher of three- and four-year-old children.** Responsibilities included development and execution of art, music, language skills, small and large motor activities, discipline, classroom management, orientation, open house, special programs, curriculum, parent conferences, and evaluation and report cards for each student.

1977–1981 Comstock Public Schools, Kalamazoo, Michigan. **Sixth grade teacher** at Comstock Middle School. Supervisor of student teacher. Team teaching. Developed science curriculum. P.T.A. representative.

1971–1977 Michigan Bell Telephone Company, Kalamazoo, Michigan. **Long distance telephone operator.**

Education:

1989–1992 Western Michigan University, Kalamazoo, Michigan. Competed 18 hours of graduate work toward master's degree in elementary education.

1977–1981 Western Michigan University, Kalamazoo, Michigan. Completed 20 hours of graduate credit for elementary certification.

1973–1977 Western Michigan University, Kalamazoo, Michigan. B.S. degree in secondary education. Earth science and history majors.

Education (continued)

1969–1973   St. Augustine High School, Kalamazoo, Michigan.
               Diploma, 1973.

Community Service:

1986–Present   Girl Scout leader, five years. Webelos leader, one year. P.T.A., nine
               years. Hot lunch volunteer, three years. Room mother, nine years.

References:

Available upon request

GLORIA PRICE

17 Dayton Street
Tempe, Arizona 85281
602-555-8057

Overview
Secondary school principal and former teacher with 12 years of experience. Extensive background in budgets, community relations, teacher contract negotiations

Capabilities
- Administration of large public and private high schools. Principal of 1,500-student suburban public high school, former principal of 1,200-student private academy.

- Supervision of teachers and school staff. Supervised 80 unionized public high school teachers. Directed staff of 65 teachers and other personnel at private academy.

- Preparation and management of $1 - $6 million school budgets.

- Successful fundraising drives and grant proposals to fund new construction and repair of existing facilities.

- Curriculum design for new computer literacy program for high school district.

- District representative for teacher contract negotiations.

- Four years' experience as high school English instructor.

Experience
Principal, Maine County High School, Tempe, AZ
8/94 to Present

Principal, St. Vincent's Academy, Yuma, AZ
1/89 to 5/94

English Instructor, Alamar High School, Houston, TX
9/85 to 1/89

Education
B.A., English
Southern Methodist University
Dallas, Texas

M.S., Public School Administration
Arizona State University
Tempe, Arizona

Publications
"Computer Literacy and Facilities Design," *Curriculum Review*,
vol. 81, March 2000

"The Multicultural Classroom," *Instructor*, vol. 21, number 2,
January 2001

Personal
Desire to relocate to Chicago area. Willing to travel to Chicago for
personal interview.

Available Fall 2002.

References
Excellent professional references available upon request.

Harry D. Lorton
196 Cambridge Drive • St. Paul, MN 55631
(612) 555-1213

Objective:
To obtain a teaching position in either elementary education or with children who have a special need in reading.

Education:
University of Minnesota, Minneapolis, MN
Currently completing master's program in reading

Syracuse University, Syracuse, NY
Bachelor in Science May 1995
Major: Elementary Education
Minor: Reading

Experience:
Brentwood Elementary School: Minneapolis, MN
June - March 2002
Marge Needham, Cooperating Teacher, Grade 5
Student teaching responsibilities: all teaching duties, attending staff and parent-teacher organization meetings, participating in textbook adoption sessions for social studies, attending Teacher In-Service Day to evaluate performance-based accreditation.

Waterfront Director/Lifeguard: Minnesota DNR, Saint Croix State Park, Stillwater, MN Summers 1996 - 1999

Public Relations Intern: KFYI-TV Channel 2, Minneapolis, MN
January - May 1999
Researched and wrote history of the station and assisted in public relations.

Literary Magazine Editor: University of Minnesota, Minneapolis, MN
Fall 1997 - present
Conduct staff meetings, select materials for publication, and design the final layout.

Honors:
Sigma Tau Delta English Honorary
John Newcombe Wright English Award

References:
Available on request

FRANK MADDEN
8053 WINDSOR DRIVE
CINCINNATI, OH 45242
(513) 555-4380

OWNER Madden Translation and Interpretation Services

> Established 1994. Professional translation and interpretation service for health care, legal, and other professionals. Staff of six. Languages include German, Spanish, French, Russian, and Korean.

PARTIAL CLIENT LIST

- Cincinnati General Hospital
  Translate documents and act as interpreter for health care staff.

- Kepler Associates, Ltd.
  Assist attorneys in taking depositions, translate documents, interpret during courtroom proceedings.

- Catholic Charities, Adoption Services Division
  Translation of documents and interpretation services pertaining to international adoptions.

EDUCATION

> B.A., Modern Languages
> University of California
> Berkeley, California

SKILLS

> Extensive international travel
> Knowledge of Microsoft Word

COMMUNITY SERVICE

> Advisor to International Students at Xavier College
> ESL Tutor, Cincinnati Public Library

REFERENCES AVAILABLE ON REQUEST

Holly Smith
14 Randall Road
Atlanta, GA 30315
404-555-9463

Job Objective

Camp counselor position for the summer of 2000

Education

University of Alabama, B.S. degree in progress
Expected graduation date: June 2001
Major: Psychology/Child Development
Minor: Recreation and Leisure

Certifications

Red Cross trained and certified swimming instructor
CPR certified

Employment

Summer 2001
<u>Counselor</u>, Junior Adventure Camp, Atlanta
Supervised, with 3 other counselors, a group of 50 children, ages 7 to 10, at park district day camp. Led games, explained craft projects, supervised field trips and weekly visits to the local water park.

2000 - 2001
<u>Day Care Worker,</u> Kids' Place, Tuscaloosa
Worked 15 hours per week during sophomore year at local day care center. Responsible for playground supervision, recreational activities, and routine care of children aged 6 months to 5 years.

Summer 2000
<u>Swimming Instructor</u>, Water World, Atlanta
Swimming instructor in Red Cross-approved swimming program for ages 4 to 10. Planned and conducted swimming lessons, evaluated students for proper class assignment, acted as lifeguard.

References

Furnished Upon Request

Rachel Allen Douglas

8695 Maple Drive
Indianapolis, IN 46032
(317) 555-1876

Career Objective:

I am seeking a position as a high school Spanish teacher. I hope to become part of a school that has a positive and progressive environment that will allow me to grow as an educator. I am also interested in coaching track and field.

Education:

B.A. in Spanish, May 1998
Western Illinois University, Macomb, Illinois

Honors:

Dean's List, Western Illinois University
Phi Delta Kappa, National Honorary in Education
Phi Beta Kappa
Recognition for Excellence in Teaching

Professional Affiliations:

Midwest College Placement Association
Professional Development Committee
Newsletter Task Force
Liberal Arts Steering Committee
Kappa Delta Pi

Experience:

I have worked at the university learning center. I tutored students in Spanish and language arts. During my summer vacations, I worked at Oakland Community College, Bloomfield Hills, Michigan, as a clerk-typist. I was required to perform various clerical duties such as typing and operating various office machines.

References are available upon request.

Martha Cameron Smith

68 Miller Road
Minneapolis, MN 55401
(612) 555-9876

Objective
To obtain a position as an elementary classroom teacher.

Certification
Michigan Provisional Certificate
K-5 Classroom
6-8 Science and Health

Education
Bachelor of Science, April 1997
Michigan State Unversity
Minors: Elementary Education, Science and Health (currently enrolled in Math minor classes)

Instructional Theory into Practice: ITIP Training, KVISD (June 1998)

Related Experience
Substitute Teaching
Plainwell Community Schools, Plainwell, MI
June 1997 to Present
Independently supervise up to thirty students in grades K-5.

Directed Teaching
Indian Prairie Elementary School, Kalamazoo, MI
January to April 1997
First grade classroom. Managed class independently on a regular basis. Organized and presented unit plans in all subject areas and extended lessons with appropriate activities.

Participation
Gull Road Elementary, Comstock, MI
September to December 1996
Second grade classroom. Directed whole group instruction as well as individual small group work in math and science areas.

Teacher's Aide
Northeastern Elementary School, Kalamazoo, MI
January to June 1996
First grade classroom. Organized and presented units in math, science, and reading skills. Developed enrichment activities to supplement lessons.

Other Experience

Certified Blood Pressure Screener
University Wellness Center
Kalamazoo, MI
February 1995

Medical Secretary
Kalamazoo Clinic
Kalamazoo, MI
Summer 1994

References

Available from:
Michigan State University Placement Services
East Lansing, Michigan 48823

RENU PATEL
45 Washington Street
Rochester, New York 14611
Phone 716-555-8945

EMPLOYMENT

1992 - Present (Currently on Leave)
Assistant Professor of English, University of Richmond
Richmond, Virginia
Specialist in Victorian literature. Conduct literature and writing classes. Faculty advisor. Extensive committee work. Published scholar.

1991 - 1992
Composition Instructor, University of Iowa
Iowa City, Iowa
Taught first-year composition students. Conducted composition courses, administered writing competency exams to first-year students, tutored at writing lab.

EDUCATION

Ph.D., English
University of Chicago

B.A., English
Kenyon College

PUBLICATIONS (PARTIAL LIST)

"The Forgotten Bronte: Anne Bronte and the Gondal Saga," *Victorian Studies Quarterly*, vol. xxii, April 1999.

"Literary Merit and the Multicultural Syllabus," *Journal of College English*, Spring 1998.

Editor, *Shakespeare's Sisters: Essays on Women Writers*. New York: University Press, 1997.

DETAILED C.V. & REFERENCES AVAILABLE

Patricia Young

66 Chambers Rd.
Hartford, CT 00112
(860) 555-6843

Objective	High School Teacher
Education	Hartford College, Hartford, CT B.A. in Secondary Education, 1998 Minor in Spanish
Coursework	Principles of Education Principles of Secondary Education American Literature Spanish Career Counseling Secondary Administration Special Education Comparative Literature Spanish Literature
Student Teaching	Central High School, Hartford, CT Taught Spanish I, 1997, 1998 Supervised discussion section of Spanish Literature, 1998
Activities	Secretary, Associated Student Government President, Spanish Club Tennis Team

References submitted upon request.

BRYCE T. STEWART

Permanent Address:
8664 Clay Center Road
Carmel, IN 46032

Campus Address:
626 E. Seminary Street
Greencastle, IN 46135

OBJECTIVE
An elementary teaching position, grades 1-5.

EDUCATION

DePauw University, Greencastle, IN
  Bachelor of Arts, Degree in Elementary Education, December 2000
  Minor in American History
  GPA 3.52/4.0
  Karl Marx University, Budapest, Hungary (December 1997)
  Austro-American Institute, Vienna, Austria (Fall 1997)

EXPERIENCE

Student Teacher
  Supervised learning activities for 34 fifth grade students:
  • developed and implemented leaning centers and resource areas
  • designed problem solving environment for mathematics
  • executed disciplinary procedures and held conferences with parents
  • provided social studies instruction for 25 sixth grade and 27 fourth grade students
Central Elementary School, Greencastle, IN (Fall 1998)

Teaching Intern
  Observed and aided activities for 24 fourth grade students:
  • provided individual instruction in developmental math for 15 students
  • taught computer keyboard
  • directed drama presentation
Orchard Park Elementary School, Carmel, IN (January 1998)

Teaching Intern
  Aided fifth grade classroom of 18 gifted/talented students:
  • taught German language
  • provided motivational strategies for independent learning
  • monitored progress of student-designed reading curriculums
  • implemented Bloom's taxonomy in social studies activities
Hinckle Creek Elementary School, Gifted and Talented Program,
Noblesville, IN (January 1997)

Camp Counselor
  Served as head counselor:
  • supervised 18 boys (ages 7-11)
  • delegated responsibility to four counselors
  • corresponded frequently with parents
  • coordinated small and large group instruction in sailing, soccer, swimming, riding, and lacrosse
Camp Lincoln for Boys, Lake Hubert, MN (Summers 1996-1998)

ACTIVITIES

Delta Upsilon: Executive Board, 1999
                     Chapter Secretary, 1999
                     Social Chairperson, 1998
                     Philanthropy Chairperson, 1996

Ambassador Club: Steering Committee, 1997-1998

DePauw Admissions Office: Tour Guide, 1997-Present
                            Orientation Leader, 1998

Intramural Sports: Team Captain, 1996

HONORS

Dean's List, 1997-Present
Mortar Board (senior scholastic society)
Kappa Delta Pi (education honor society)

REFERENCES AVAILABLE UPON REQUEST

PATRICIA KELLY

17 Woods Road
Frederick, MD 21702
301-555-3495 (Office); 301-555-3859 (Home)

BACKGROUND

Experienced academic administrator with demonstrated ability in key areas of financial management, teacher supervision, curriculum development, and community relations.

ADMINISTRATIVE EXPERIENCE

School Superintendant
Frederick, MD
January 1995 to Present

Supervise faculty of 700 teachers. Manage budget of $75 million. Accomplishments include construction of two new elementary schools, implementation of successful bus safety program adopted by other cities, best student/teacher ratio in the state, student test scores in the top 5 percent of national ratings, ongoing teacher enrichment programs.

Principal
Wakefield Academy
Baltimore, MD
September 1991 to December 1994

Participated in staff hiring, training, and evaluation. Financial management of school, including direction of fund-raising efforts. Oversaw curriculum development and textbook adoptions. Interacted with school board, PTA, and community groups. Supervised marketing campaign that increased school enrollment by 7 percent. Designed inservice programs for teaching staff.

Patricia Kelly
page 1 of 2

COUNSELING EXPERIENCE

Guidance Counselor
Bethesda High School
Bethesda, MD
September 1988 to June 1991

Provided personal and academic counseling to high school students. As college admissions advisor, arranged college fair that allowed seniors to meet with admissions representatives from 15 colleges. Seventy-five percent of counselees attended first-choice college. Managed work/study program. Designed and implemented Graduation First, a program of personal/academic counseling, flexible scheduling, and work/study options to assist at-risk students and lower the dropout rate.

TEACHING EXPERIENCE

Reading Instructor
North Ridge High School
Bethesda, MD
August 1986 to June 1988

Substitute Teacher
Clarke County School District
Clarke County, MD
August 1985 to June 1986

EDUCATION

M.Ed.
School Administration
University of Virginia

B.A.
Education
Penn State University

REFERENCES

Detailed references will be furnished upon request.

Grace Miller
615 Robin Lane
Toledo, Ohio 55431
419-555-4803

Objective: Position as a music therapist

Background: Talented, degreed professional with eight years' experience. Excellent singer, pianist, guitarist. Comfortable with clients/students of all ages and backgrounds. Resourceful and compassionate care and instruction.

Employment: Teaching, counseling, and music therapy positions.

9 - 89 to Present
Rockdale Nursing Center/Toledo, Ohio
Music Therapist

- Direct recreational and therapeutic music activities at this 500-bed, long-term care facility

- Assess patients' needs

- Conduct group music activities

- Perform for patients and staff

- Arrange for musical presentations by local choirs, school groups, and professional musicians

6 - 89 to 9 - 89
Toledo Summer Arts/Toledo, Ohio
Assistant Music Director

- Assisted music director at this summer camp for young musicians

- Provided information and tours for prospective students and their families

- Designed and supervised group musical activities

Grace Miller - page 1 of 2

9 - 92 to 6 - 94
Shultz Junior High School
Music Teacher
- Taught music education classes
- Directed choir
- Produced, directed, and publicized large-scale holiday performance each year
- Vocal coach for annual variety show

Education
B.A., Kenyon College
Major: Music
Minor: Psychology

M.A., Ohio State University
Major: Music Therapy

References: Will be provided upon request

KRISTI CULLOM
2345 N. State Avenue
Indianapolis, IN 46345
(317) 555-5867

EDUCATION

Initial Principals, License, Post-Graduate Studies in School Administration, Butler University, Indianapolis, Indiana. Graduated December 1997 from the Experiential Program for Preparing School Principals (EPPSP).

Master of Education, Guidance and Counseling, Indiana University, Indianapolis, Indiana, 1991

Bachelor of Science, Elementary Education, Ball State University, Muncie, Indiana, 1987

PROFESSIONAL
EXPERIENCE

1992 to Date   ELEMENTARY SCHOOL COUNSELOR, Avon
Community School Corporation, Indianapolis, Indiana
Develop and implement the Elementary Guidance Program in three schools. Provide consultation to classroom teachers concerning behavioral, social, academic, and personal problems of students. Develop classroom and individual discipline plans. Present classroom lessons. Facilitate group counseling. Participate in staffing and case conferences. Participate on Teacher Assistance Team. Handles child abuse cases. Serve as liaison between child protective services and school. Organize fifth grade Life Positive (Just Say No) program in three buildings. Serve as acting principal in principal's absence. Summer school experience with grades three and four. Provide inservices for teachers. Facilitate six-week parenting workshop.

1991-1992   TEACHER GRADE 6, Brownsburg Community
School Corporation, White Lick School,
Brownsburg, Indiana

1989-1991   TEACHER GRADE 5, Seton Catholic School,
Richmond, Indiana

1987-1989   TEACHER GRADE 4, Mississinawa, Valley
Middle School, Union City, Ohio

WORKSHOPS/
PRESENTATIONS

"Parenting Skills Workshop," Parents a Avon Elementary Schools, Indianapolis, Indiana, 1996-1997

"Team Building," Life Conference, Butler University, 1997

"Effective Guidance Program for the Elementary School," EPSP Cohort Group, Butler University, 1997

"Alternative Schools," EPPSP Cohort Group, Butler University, 1996

"School for the 21st Century," EPPSP Cohort Group, Butler University, 1996

"Multicultural Education Curriculum in the Schools," EPPSP Cohort Group, Butler University, 1996

"Goal Setting," While Oak and Maple Staff, Avon Elementary Schools, Indianapolis, Indiana, 1996

AFFILIATIONS
Association for Supervision and Curriculum Development
Phi Delta Kappa

REFERENCES
Available Upon Request

Marvin A. Marcato
101 Eagle Drive • Boulder, CO 80233 • (303) 555-9877

Objective
To obtain an administrative position at the secondary level.

Education
University of Colorado, Boulder, CO
Experiential Program for Preparing School Principals
(EPPSP), December 1997
Major: School Principalship

University of Denver, Denver, CO
Master of Music, May 1995
Major: Music Education

Fresno Pacific College, Fresno, CA
Bachelor of Music Education, 1989
Major: Instrumental Music
Minor: Jazz Studies

Administrative Experience
1996-Present   Metropolitan School District of Taylor Township, Boulder, CO
Director of Secondary Summer School
Duties: Entire organization and implementation of secondary summer school,
grades seven through twelve, including curriculum development, teacher hiring and
evaluation, student discipline, ISTEP testing coordination, and general building
operations.

Teaching Experience
8/93-Present   Metropolitan School District of Taylor Township, Boulder, CO
Director of Bands
Duties: Instrumental music director grades nine through twelve; including concert,
jazz, marching, and pep bands. Music theory instructor.

7/92-8/93   **Denver Community Schools, Denver, CO**
Band Director
Duties: Assist entire instrumental program, grades six through twelve, high school band director, and general music grades six and seven.

8/91-7/92   **University of Denver, Denver, CO**
Graduate Assistant/Music Director
Duties: Responsible for organization and implementation of University Lab School.

6/89-8/91   **Tri-County Area Schools, Fresno, CA**
Director of Bands
Duties: Entire instrumental music program, grades six through twelve, and high school choir.

Professional Memberships

Association for Supervision and Curriculum Development (ASCD)
Indiana Bandmasters Association (State Officer)
Indiana State School Music Association

Chapter 10

Resumes for Finance, Sales, and Law Careers

ELI LEVINSON
908 Jefferson Heights, #6B
Minneapolis, MN 55404
(612) 555-1298 home
(651) 555-3764 cell

OBJECTIVE

To secure a midlevel management position in finance that will utilize my analytical, managerial, and training skills.

SUMMARY

A proven self-starter with exceptional communication and interpersonal skills. Extensive management experience in diverse fields including financial services, data processing, field operations, and manufacturing.

ACCOMPLISHMENTS

Coordinated data processing operations for the 2000 census in the Minneapolis office, included training supervisors and staff members.

Served as technical advisor on operational activities of the data processing and field departments during the 2000 census.

Coordinated field activities of over 800 employees in conducting a complete enumeration of population and housing in the state; included managing the preparation, check-in, and review of census materials.

Managed departmental budget.

Developed compliance, financial, and operations procedures for full-service brokerage house.

Reconciled conversion of customer accounts between clearing firms.

Taught securities training classes to prospective stock brokers.

Implemented financial procedures for securities firm for reconciliations and financial reporting.

Streamlined commission accounting procedures.

Eli Levinson, page one of two

CAREER HISTORY

U.S. DEPARTMENT OF COMMERCE—BUREAU OF THE CENSUS
Minneapolis, MN
1997–2000
Manager, Field and EDP Operations

VENTURE CAPITAL CORPORATION
Baltimore, MD
1995–1997
Vice President, Chief Financial Officer, Chief Compliance Officer

KEN FOX AND ASSOCIATES
Madison, WI
1994–1995
Chief Financial Officer

MIDWESTERN CAPITAL SECURITIES, INC.
Madison, WI
1992–1994
Securities Analyst

NORTHERN FINANCIAL SERVICES
Pittsburgh, PA
1990–1992
Supervisor of Compliance, Supervisor of Operations

NEW YORK STOCK EXCHANGE
New York, NY
1987–1989
Lead Clerk, Options Department

PROFESSIONAL LICENSES

Foreign Currency Options Principal, 1995
Debt Registered Options Principal, 1995
Financial and Operations Principal, 1992
Municipal Securities Principal, 1992
Registered Options Principal, 1990

EDUCATION

University of Pennsylvania, B.A., 1987

Mary Macarty

12 Oak Dr.
Jackson, TN 44559
(607) 555-2345
macartym@xxx.net

Education:

University of Tennessee
> Candidate for Juris Doctor (expected spring 2001)
> Honors: Executive Editorial Board, Business Manager of the
> *Business Journal*
> Member of the Moot Court Society

Vanderbilt University
> Bachelor of Arts, 1997, Major in English
> City of Munich Extension Study Abroad, Interdisciplinary

Publications:

Business Developments Journal, December 2000
> Authored article titled "Recent Developments in Business Development
> Law, Legal Implications of Tax Deferred Financing."

Activities:

- Law School - LITP Program participant
- Student Legal Services
- Tax preparer for Social Responsibility Program
- Member Law Society
- Student advisor to incoming law students

Legal Experience:

District Attorney's Office, Holbrook County, TN
Legal Internship, fall semester 2000

- Active involvement in all aspects of the prosecutor's office pursuant to
  Tennessee Third Year Practice Act.
- Courtroom experience and involvement in plea negotiations and drafting
  of indictments and trial briefs.

Jillian & Smoot
Summer Associate, 2000

- Researched and wrote legal briefs.
- Filed motion papers and memoranda in real estate, labor, employment discrimination, and negligence cases.
- Assisted in closings, digested depositions, and attended pretrial conferences.

Chief Judge Allan Nothings, United States Federal Court of Appeal
Judicial Clerkship, spring semester 1999

- Researched and drafted opinions on bankruptcy cases and proceedings.
- Acted as courtroom deputy and observed adversary proceedings, motion practices, and key meetings.

NORTON W. WALTERS

10563 S.E. Powell Blvd., Tulsa, Oklahoma 75135 (918) 555-4436

PERSONAL FOCUS

Financial analysis and strategic marketing management

PROFESSIONAL EXPERIENCE

Financial

Financial analysis, cash flow analysis, securities analysis, business and economic forecasting and feasibility studies.

Marketing

Market analysis and testing, strategic planning and administration, market research, opinion polling and analysis, coordinating and facilitating focus groups.

Management

Program and project management, staff supervision, budget preparation and administration, MIS reviews and management audits, public relations, staff development, personnel recruitment and selection, union contract interpretation and administration, Affirmative Action and EEO compliance planning and administration.

Communication

Team building, employee relations counseling, dispute resolution and mediation, public speaking, report writing, group facilitation.

CAREER PATH

President and CEO, Step One Enterprises, 1994 - present

Began and manage trading and brokerage corporation with affiliations in China, Hong Kong, Taiwan, and the Philippines. Sold business after achieving personal and professional goals.

Consultant, Various corporate and public sector clients, 1991 - 1994

Provided business consulting services in market analysis, marketing strategy and planning, public relations, budgeting and financial analysis.

CAREER PATH CONTINUED

Division Manager, State of Oklahoma, Employment and Human Services,
1980 - 1990

Managed job development and placement with staff of 24. Conducted program evaluation and planning. Developed public relations program and hired personnel. Served as liaison to Governor's office for employment issues.

EDUCATION

Master of Business Administration, Finance and Management

University of California, Berkeley, 1990

Bachelor of Arts, Philosophy

University of Colorado, Boulder, 1966

References furnished upon request

ALAN JACKSONELLI
34 Tufts Lane • New Orleans, LA 56778
806-555-2234 • jacksa@xxx.net

Education:

Tulane University School of Law
  Candidate for J.D., 2002

Washington University
  B.A. in Political Science & Sociology, 1994

Activities:

Law school:
  Moot Court Special Teams, Finalist Fall Moot Court Competition, International Law Society.

College:
  Campus representative, Washington Center for Learning Alternatives; treasurer, South Forty Programming Board; member, Pre-Law Society; member, co-ed football and softball teams.

Legal Experience:

Tulane University, *Research Assistant*, 2001–present
  Update and research information on plea bargaining. Examine guidelines for judicial discretion to determine acceptance or rejection of plea bargains.

William Gardner P.C., *Paralegal*, 2000–2001
  Prepared court documents and interrogatories; worked with clients through informal interviews and discussions. Researched personal injury and workers' compensation claims. Organized cases and case files.

James Laughlan Esq., *Summer Intern*, 2000
  Prepared briefs, documents of custody, and client insurance forms; investigated personal injury, property damage, and medical malpractice claims through trials.

Other Experience:

Special Committee on Aging, *Intern*, fall semester 2002

  Attended congressional hearings in areas of interest to the committee. Wrote memoranda. Analyzed medical and scientific literature. Researched data from the Library of Congress. Interviewed and prepared witnesses for hearings.

Manpower Inc., *Sales Representative*, 1994–1998
  Acted as a liaison between temporary workers, client corporations, and employers; interviewed temporaries. Updated and improved local agency's website.

SHEILA RYAN
73 Wisconsin Street
Portland, OR 97219
Phone 503-555-3958

Objective: A responsible position as a political aide

Key Skills

• Fund-raising
• Public Speaking
• Speech Writing
• Office Management
• Research

Job Experience

Office of Congresswoman Mary Martin/Office Manager/1998 to Present

• Compile statistics and write weekly status reports
• Attend staff meetings
• Supervise office staff, including training, scheduling, and evaluation
• Draft responses to constituents' letters
• Assist with fund-raising efforts
• Write and present speeches on congresswoman's policies to women's and community groups

Office of Assemblyman Walter Smith/Office Assistant/1995 - 1998

• Responded to constituents' concerns
• Heavy telephone and correspondence duties
• Wrote campaign brochure and press releases

Volunteer Work

League of Women Voters/Assistant to Educational Director/1994 - 1995
Amnesty International/Active Member/1994 - Present

Education

B.S.
University of Wisconsin/Madison
Political Science Major

References on Request

BARBARA A. MACOM

600 China Point Drive   Virginia Beach, VA 23455   Telephone: (757) 555-5884

OBJECTIVE:

To obtain a responsible position in the legal field that will utilize my past business and management experiences and allow me to apply my legal education.

EDUCATION:

JD—Regent University School of Law, 2001
CPA Certificate—Virginia Board of Accountancy, 1991
BSB Accounting—University of Minnesota, 1985

EXPERIENCE:

1993 - Present
COOPER, INC./FASHION LEATHERGOODS, Ames, VA
Controller/Vice President of Finance

Responsible for all financial reporting, preparation for and coordination of audits, and budgeting activities. Perform analysis of actual results compared to budget and prior periods. Identify areas for cost reduction. Evaluate profitability of proposed projects using pro forma financial analysis. Determine requirements for and acquire foreign currency contracts, maximizing value on exchange rates. Supervise activities of accounts payable department. Monitor inventory adjustments, and organize annual physical inventory. Assist with corporate tax returns, and prepare and file various types of tax returns. Responsible for correspondence with tax authorities, lenders, and suppliers. Involved in establishment of systems to increase efficiency and effectiveness of various administrative processes.

1992
AXEL/RHODES COMPANY, Santa Maria, CA
Controller

Responsible for financial reporting, payroll, job cost, and budgeting for this public works contractor. Researched and implemented employee benefit plan. Verified state trade rates to ensure compliance with Davis-Bacon Act and other regulatory requirements. Successfully negotiated with lender to increase line of credit, resulting in equipment purchases for company expansion. Improved receipts by developing proposals, preparing timely progress payment reports, and negotiating with city officials.

page one of two

1991
BUDGET RENT-A-CAR OF SOUTHERN CALIFORNIA, Santa Monica, CA
Accounting Manager

1987 - 1990
HEALY ENTERPRISES, Virginia Beach, VA
Staff/Reimbursement Accountant

1985 - 1987
DIAMOND, INC, Virginia Beach, VA
Staff Accountant

REFERENCES:

Available upon request.

Sandra L. Gardiner

81 Huntington Lane • Buffalo, NY 11456 • Cellular: 716-555-7849

Objective

To secure a challenging position in sales and sales management.

Work Experience

The GAP Clothing Store, Erieview Mall, Erie, PA
   Manager: 1995 - 1998
   Duties: Supervised 8 full-time and 3 part-time employees.
   Interviewed and hired sales employees. Conducted training seminars for sales force.

Kaufman's Department Store, Erie, PA
   Sales Clerk: 1994 - 1995
   Duties: Sold merchandise, assisted buyer on trips to purchase stock.

Qualifications & Awards

- Extensive knowledge of sales techniques and the ability to train staff employees to utilize these techniques effectively.
- Received Sales Person of the Month award for nine consecutive months while employed at Kaufman's.
- Awarded Top Manager status for highest sales revenue for a GAP store in the eastern division in 1998.

Related Experience

- Contributed written articles on sales techniques for the *Sales Review Quarterly*.
- Codirected a five-day intensive sales seminar for retail sales training offered annually at the GAP training school in Philadelphia.

Professional Membership

Association of Retail Managers, Erie, PA
   Office held: President, 1996 - 1998

Additional

Willing to travel. References furnished upon request.

LINDA S. WOODS
3302 Harbor Drive South
#4554
Ft. Lauderdale, FL 33020
305/555-8903
305/555-9000
swoods@xxx.com

WORK EXPERIENCE

South Florida Boat Co., Miami, FL

District Sales Manager, 1994 - present
Planned successful strategies to identify and develop new accounts. Increased sales by at least 20 percent each year (45 percent in 1996). Researched and analyzed market conditions to seek out new customers. Developed weekly and monthly sales strategies. Supervised seven sales representatives.

Miami Freight, Inc., Miami, FL

Account Executive, 1992 - 1994
Handled sales accounts for southern Florida area. Expanded customer base by 25 percent during my tenure. Conducted field visits to solve customer complaints. Maintained daily contact with customers by telephone to ensure good customer/company relations. Wrote product information flyers and distributed them through a direct-mail plan.

Harrison Pandy, Inc., Denver, CO

Sales Representative, 1991 - 1992
Sold and serviced office copiers to businesses and schools in the greater Denver area. Maintained good customer relations through frequent contact. Identified potential customers for management.

EDUCATION

University of Colorado, Boulder, CO

B.A., 1991
Major: Economics
Minor: Music
G.P.A. 3.3/4.0

PROFESSIONAL MEMBERSHIPS

South Florida Sales Association, Treasurer, 1996 - 1998
Miami Chamber of Commerce, 1994 - present

REFERENCES

Available on request

KAREN XIROU

565 Winwood Lane
New Port, Florida 33589
(813) 555-0906
xirouk@xxx.com

EDUCATION

Stetson University College of Law, Saint Petersburg, Florida
Juris Doctor degree expected May 2002
Class Rank: Top 10 percent
Honors and Activities:
Stetson Law Forum
Honor Roll, Spring and Fall 2001
Research Assistant
International Law Society
Trial Advocacy Society
Intramural Sports

University of South Florida, Tampa, Florida
Master of Business Administration, May 1998
GPA: 3.34/4.0
Honors and Activities:
Vice President, Chi Omega Sorority
Dean's List, 5 of 12 semesters
Varsity Soccer Team
Presidential Academic Scholarship

University of Florida, Gainesville, Florida
Bachelor of Arts in Business Administration
GPA: 3.26/4.0
Honors and Activities:
Outstanding Freshman Award
Varsity Cheerleader
Dean's List
Resident Hall, Dorm President

EXPERIENCE

Federal Judicial Intern, Honorable Alexander L. Paskay, Chief Judge, Fall 2000
United States Bankruptcy Court, Middle District of Florida
Researched bankruptcy issues
Observed bankruptcy proceedings
Composed legal memoranda
Wrote preliminary orders

page one of two

Customer Service Representative, Jennings Service Corporation, 1999
Orlando, Florida
- Managed more than 100 customer accounts valued at over $100,000
- Handled customer complaints

Sales Representative, J.C. Penney Corporation, 1996 - 1998
Clearwater, Florida

REFERENCES

Professor Richard Sykes
Stetson University College of Law
1401 61st Street South
Saint Petersburg, Florida 33707
(813) 555-1121, ext. 889

Rialda K. Inger
Padilla & Associates
209 Ellis Drive
Dunedin, Florida 34598
(813) 555-0097

Professor Mark Thomas
Stetson University College of Law
1401 61st Street South
Saint Petersburg, Florida 33707
(813) 555-1121, ext. 448

MARY AZUL-AKIM

234 Oak Dr.
Edmonton, KS 77654
(607) 555-2345

EDUCATION:

University of Kansas
Candidate for Juris Doctor

University of Pennsylvania
Bachelor of Arts, Major in English

City of London Extension
Study Abroad, Art History Program

HONORS:

Executive Editorial Board
Business Manager of the *Bankruptcy Developments Journal*
Member of the Phi Beta Kappa Society

PUBLICATIONS:

Bankruptcy Developments Journal: Authored article titled "Recent Developments in Bankruptcy Law—Appointments, Rights, and Remedies of a Trustee"

ACTIVITIES:

- Law School Mentor Program
- Student Legal Services
- Tax preparer for community outreach program
- Member of Women and the Law Society
- Student advisor to incoming law students

LEGAL EXPERIENCE:

Carlton County Attorney's Office
Legal Intern
- Active involvement in all aspects of the prosecutor's office pursuant to the Kansas Third Year Practice Act
- Courtroom experience and involvement in negotiations, indictments and trial briefs

page one of two

Jackson & Barnes
Summer Associate
• Researched and wrote briefs and memoranda
• Filed motion papers and memoranda in labor and employment discrimination cases
• Attended pretrial conferences

Chief Judge Alice Young, United States Bankruptcy Court
Judicial Clerkship
• Researched and drafted opinions on a number of cases and proceedings
• Acted as courtroom deputy and observed adversary proceedings, motion practices, and pretrial meetings

References and transcripts available upon request

Regina Ford

1532 Walnut Street
Sacramento, CA 95819
(916) 555-3663 home
(916) 555-3474 cellular

OBJECTIVE

A supervisory position that utilizes my experience and skills to generate staff effectiveness, enhance productivity, and meet organizational goals.

SUMMARY OF QUALIFICATIONS

- Sixteen years of experience in retail banking and five years in operations.
- Skilled at team building, creative problem solving, and technical training.
- Communicate well with senior management, staff, and customers.

ANALYSIS OF EXPERIENCE

Supervision

- Monitored daily workload.
- Hired and trained staff.
- Established policies for handling customer complaints to promote quality service and quick resolution.
- Prepared monthly management reports.
- Developed employee incentive program.
- Introduced ideas that reduced expenses by 25 percent.

Customer Service

- Directed staff of 10 customer service representatives.
- Settled payment disputes.
- Answered almost 300 calls and letters daily.
- Redesigned job functions to improve quality control standards.
- Cross-trained staff in several positions to cover for vacations and absences.

Accounting

- Reconciled outstanding items on bank statements.
- Cleared and reconciled bank advances.
- Established new depository account procedures.

page one of two

WORK EXPERIENCE

Customer Service Supervisor
First National Bank
Sacramento, CA
1996–2001

Branch Service Manager
Wells Fargo
Modesto, CA
1990–1996

Operations Supervisor
Wells Fargo
Stockton, CA
1984–1990

EDUCATION

California State University, Sacramento
Business Management degree, 1984
Several American Institute of Banking courses

PERSONAL INTERESTS

Bowling, hiking, softball, and reading

WARREN DEVEROE

118 W. 86th Street, #3C
New York, NY 10024
(212) 555-4960 home
(212) 555-7635 cellular

SPECIALIZATION

Nonprofit fundraising and marketing consultant

CAPABILITIES

- Experienced in all aspects of direct mail campaigns
- Design, write, and produce informational and fundraising letters and brochures
- Manage telemarketing campaigns
- Conduct market research
- Write press releases for radio, TV, newspapers, and magazines
- Degrees in business and marketing
- Eight years as successful business consultant

CLIENTS

- National Public Radio
- World Wildlife Federation
- Special Olympics
- Mothers Against Drunk Driving
- Cancer Federation
- Americans for International Aid

EDUCATION

Queens College
B.S./Business Marketing

Villanova University
M.B.A./Financial Management

REFERENCES

Will be furnished upon request

DELORES A. GRIFFITH

3215 HIGHLAND AVE.
MANHATTAN, KS 66500
CELL: 316-555-6767

OBJECTIVE
Seeking a position as a sales representative within the retail industry.

EDUCATION
Manhattan Community College, Manhattan, KS
A.S. in Business Administration - 1987
Major: Retail Merchandising; GPA: 3.7

Williamson High School
Williamson, KS; Diploma - 1985
Senior Class President
Student Council Vice President

EMPLOYMENT
Kaufman's Department Store, Kansas City, KS
Retail Sales Clerk, Women's Apparel Department
Top 10 percent of retail clerks in revenue sales, 1996 - 1999.

Sallie's Gift and Boutique Shop, Manhattan, KS
Sales Clerk - Responsible for opening the shop each day and performed all sales transactions, 1991 - 1996.

Rite-Aid Drug Store, Manhattan, KS
Sales/Stock Clerk - Stocked shelves with merchandise, assisted with inventory control, made sales transactions, delivered prescriptions for pharmacy, 1987 - 1991.

PART-TIME EMPLOYMENT
Avon Company, New York, NY
Sales Representative/Team Leader, Eastern Kansas
Have been successful sales/team leader since 1995 and have maintained a sales staff of approximately 30 part-time team members. Sales revenue for this division has consistently been in the top 10 percent of total sales revenue estimated annually for central Midwest localities.

ACTIVITIES
- Coordinated Chinese Auction Charity Bazaar for the Senior Citizen Community Center of Manhattan, KS.
- Organized the annual "Toys for Tots" campaign with donations from local merchants during holiday season in Manhattan, KS, since 2000.

REFERENCES
Furnished upon request.

HECTOR METCALF
1099 Vista Drive
Clearwater, Florida 34525
(813) 555-8834

EDUCATION

STETSON UNIVERSITY COLLEGE OF LAW, St. Petersburg, Florida

J.D. to be conferred: July 2002
Honors: *Stetson Law Review*, Staff; Federal Taxation of Business, Highest Grade; Law I and II Academic Scholarships; Honor Roll, Spring 2001.
Activities: American Bar Association/Law Student Division; Computers in the Law Association, Vice President; Phi Delta Phi, Vice Justice; Research Assistant, Professor Deter Lave.
Competitions: National Client Counseling Competition, Second Place; Aguire, Moorhis & Bells Moot Court Competition, Quarter Finalist.

UNIVERSITY OF WISCONSIN, Madison, Wisconsin

B.A. in Journalism, May 1998
Honors: Dean's List, 8 out of 12 semesters
Activities: Sports editor of school newspaper

EXPERIENCE

PUBLIC DEFENDER'S OFFICE, THIRTEENTH JUDICIAL CIRCUIT, Clearwater, Florida

Fall 2001 Semester
Clinical Internship
Duties: Assisted assistant public defender with all aspects of indigent criminal defense, including active participation in actual motion hearings, depositions, and criminal trials.

GREEN, HANCOCK AND WILLIAMS, P.A., Tampa, Florida

May 2000 - February 2001
Law Clerk
Duties: Researched a wide variety of legal issues, drafted legal documents, and assisted with depositions.

THE ST. PETERSBURG TIMES, St. Petersburg, Florida

June 1998 - April 2000
Staff Writer, City Section
Duties: Wrote copy for city section on local political scene.

References available

Pilar Maria Espinosa
77 Norse Avenue • La Crosse, WI 53949 • (608) 555-3116

_____

Objective:
*Position in dynamic urban legal practice where I can continue to research
case law precedent and provide strong counsel.*

Experience:
Associate
Ackworth & Thomas
2001–Present

Law Clerk
Fynde & Lostee
Summer 2000

Medical Law Research Assistant
Lockland, Strong and Campbell
1997–1998

Education:
University of Wisconsin, Madison
J.D., 2000

Madrid Law Program
1999

University of Wisconsin, River Falls
B.A. History, 1997

Other Experience:
Peace Corps Volunteer, Dominican Republic
1997–1999

Special Skills:
Website design and maintenance
Fluent in Spanish, both written and spoken
Conversational in American Sign Language

HAROLD C. JONES
Bobb Hall
6 W. Allis Drive
Room 34
Pittsburgh, PA 28920
404/555-2384
bearcub@xxx.com

OBJECTIVE:

Position in sales management.

EDUCATION:

University of Pittsburgh, Pittsburgh, PA

Bachelor of Arts in Economics
Expected June 2001

HONORS:

Pitt Honorary Scholar
Pennsylvania Honor Society
Freshman Economics Scholarship, 1999

ACTIVITIES:

Student Government
Freshman Advisor
Homecoming Planning Committee
Basketball Team

WORK EXPERIENCE:

Nabisco, Inc., Philadelphia, PA

Sales Intern, 2000
Assisted sales staff in research, demographics, sales forecasts, identifying new customers, and promotion.

University of Pittsburgh, Pittsburgh, PA

General Office, Registrar, 1998
Processed transcript requests. Entered registrations on the computer. Provided information to students.

SPECIAL SKILLS:

Able to translate Spanish. Experience using Microsoft Word, Excel, and Access software programs.

REFERENCES:

Available on request.

ROBIN J. LAWFORD

68 Lake Street
Ann Arbor, MI 48109
(313) 555-7426 home
(313) 555-2242 cell

OBJECTIVE

Position in investment banking.

PROFESSIONAL EXPERIENCE

Summer 2000
Associate—Investment Banking, Morgan Stanley, Chicago, IL

- Analyzed debt, equity, and derivative products for telecommunications clients.

- Worked on merger and acquisition presentation for a European client.

- Assisted in due diligence for a major industrial company's IPO.

1996–1999
Analyst—Planning and Analysis, Cygnet Insurance Company, Paris, France

- Drafted annual business plans and revenue and profit projections.

- Analyzed variances from fiscal plan.

- Prepared monthly financial statements for internal use.

- Improved outdated MIS mainframe application.

EDUCATION

University of Michigan School of Business
M.B.A., Finance and Communications, 2001
Member of the International Business Club and the Women in Banking Association

Dartmouth University
B.A., English, 1996

The Sorbonne, Paris, France
Exchange Program, 1994

ADDITIONAL INFORMATION

Fluent in French and German
Traveled extensively in Europe
Enjoy painting, water polo, and tennis

Rob Halo
23 Access Blvd.   Houston, TX 44587   (504) 555-7623   halor@xxx.com

Houston Bancorp
2000 - Present
Associate Corporate Counsel

- Responsible for the legal functions relating to corporate practice, governance, and insurance.

- Particular emphasis on antitakeover, 16b, and Corporate Code of Conduct issues. Designed and executed revisions of the director/officer liability and indemnification policy.

- Organized and executed a compliance review of all company-owned real estate with sale and lease-back requirements, including title insurance and surveys.

- Designed and wrote three nonqualified management incentive plans with related deferred funds and three nonqualified performance unit plans.

- Sole in-house counsel on numerous pension, stock option, 401(K), ESOP, Supplemental Executive, and welfare benefit plans.

- Extensive experience in negotiation of performance plan design and administration, drafting, and substantive review of outside counsels' drafts for consistency and accuracy.

- Monitored and directed litigation involving potential contingent liability of $100 million.

- Developed, executed, and maintained all legal documentation pertaining to the CIRRUS electronic banking network.

- Negotiated and wrote financing, banking, and fund transfer agreements for the treasurer's office, as well as term and revolving credit agreements; letters of credit documentation; loan participations; guaranties; and equipment lease pricing of state-of-the-art equipment purchase contracts for corporate banking, corporate finance, international, and corporate services.

- Responsible for regulatory analysis on financial services issues, including investment services, electronic banking, and securities product development.

- Negotiated and wrote computer equipment contracts, software licenses, and computer service agreement for the company.

Education

University of Houston
J.D., 2000
Editor of *Banking & Legal Issues Review*

University of Texas
B.A. Sociology, 1997

Admitted to the Texas and Oklahoma Bar.

References available on request.

tami rogers

1226 Tate Rd.
Lincoln, MA 09887
(617) 555-9866
rogerstt@xxx.net

education:

University of Boston
J.D., 2000
GPA: 85.31/100
Rank: 24/131
Laws Review
Note and Comment Editor
Dean's List

University of Massachusetts
B.A. Sociology, 1997
Dean's List
Senator-Student Association
VP–Residential Group Council

publications:

"The Corporate Opportunity Doctrine: An Examination of Precedents
and Opportunities." *American Journal of Contract Law*, September 2001

professional experience:

Lacy & Lacy
Associate
2001 to Present

The Honorable Jackson Lant
Massachusetts Court of Appeals, Eastern District
Law Clerk
2000 to 2001

Brown, Jones & Givens
Law Clerk
1998 to 1999

References available upon request.

VAJID L. SINGH

P.O. Box 1296
Stanford, CA 94309
(415) 555-0701

EDUCATION   *Master of Business Administration, June 1999*
                  Stanford University, Stanford, CA

                  Bachelor of Technology, Civil Engineering, July 1993
                  Institute of Technology, New Delhi, India

EMPLOYMENT

August 1993   *Field Engineer*
to July 1997   Nardini Co., Ltd. (subsidiary of Ferguson Construction,
                  Inc., United Kingdom)
                  New Delhi, India

                  • Managed construction sites as independent profit
                    centers consistently achieving target margins.

                  • Supervised and directed work of four supervisors and
                    25 skilled workers.

                  • Prepared cost estimates and quantity surveys for
                    contract bids and analyzed project proposals.

                  • Collected, analyzed, and interpreted data pertaining to
                    financial and production performance of site as well
                    as wrote reports to facilitate control.

                  • Negotiated and liaisoned on a regular basis with labor
                    unions and clients.

September 1997   *Graduate Teaching Assistant*
to June 1999   Stanford University
                  Stanford, CA

                  • Graded, tutored, and advised students enrolled in
                    Operations Management class.

page 1 of 2

Vajid L. Singh
page 2 of 2

EMPLOYMENT (cont.)

September 1997   *Microcomputer Laboratory Monitor*
to June 1999   Stanford University
                  Stanford, CA

- Guided and assisted students and faculty in the productive use of analytical, graphics, and word-processing PC software.

- Served more than 100 users during peak laboratory usage.

COMPUTER   Proficient in use of following PC programs, operating
BACKGROUND systems, and languages: RBase for DOS, Statgraphics, SPSS-PC+, Lotus 1-2-3, Quattro Pro, Excel, Harvard Graphics, MS-DOS, Netware, Pascal, BASIC, FORTRAN.

AWARDS &   Awarded $5,000 fellowship in 1997 by Education Trust
HONORS   to pursue study in the U.S.
                Member - Beta Gamma Sigma (national honor society for business students)

REFERENCES Supplied on request

Grace Delaney
1000 Chestnut Street
San Francisco, CA 94117
(415) 555-9080 home
(415) 555-5687 cell

OBJECTIVE

Financial management position with personal and professional growth potential.

PROFESSIONAL EXPERIENCE

Coopers & Lybrand (1995 to present)

I have been employed by Coopers & Lybrand for over five years. As an audit supervisor, I am responsible for all facets of audit and non-audit engagements including planning, budgeting, report preparation, and supervision of senior and staff accountants. I have client service responsibilities for public and privately held companies in the retail food service, construction, and manufacturing industries.

Specific experience and achievements with Coopers & Lybrand include:

Involvement in the initial public stock offerings for five clients which included discussions with and reporting to the Securities and Exchange Commission.

Supervision of services for a developmental stage steel mill which entailed becoming familiar with complex financing arrangements.

Experience in the use of microcomputers and the input and output data from all sizes of EDP shops.

Performance of special litigation support procedures.

Consultation in the sale of client business which included contacting potential buyers.

PROFESSIONAL ORGANIZATIONS

American Institute of Certified Public Accountants, California
Association of Certified Public Accountants

EDUCATION

Bachelor of Science in Business Administration
Major in Accounting
University of San Francisco, 1995

REFERENCES

Furnished upon request.

Thelma Delbello

87 Ridge Rd.
Carlson, CA 98443
(304) 555-8963 cellular/voice mail
delbello@xxx.net

Areas of Legal Expertise

Marketing and Public Relations:

- Presented numerous seminars to lenders, title insurers, and attorneys on the legal aspects of originating mortgages that conform to the secondary mortgage market.

- Originated and participated in our company's legal/marketing team and obtained an increased market share in California through aggressive proactive business development and customer service efforts.

Negotiations and Legal Representation:

- Negotiated changes for approval of legal documentation in two developments, which created large, unique retirement/recreational communities in California, making $50 million in investments available to our company.

- Negotiated changes in complex legal documentation on-site at a cooperative housing development in Los Angeles, making available $2 million in new investments.

Employment Experience

Federal National Mortgage Association
1998–Present
Senior Counsel

Education

UCLA, School of Law, J.D., 1998
Editorial Staff, *Journal of Public Law*

UCLA, AB Liberal Arts, History Major, 1995

Also completed partial credits for MBA in finance and international business at UCLA.

LISA ERDMAN

398 Berger Street
Medford, OR 97501
(503) 555-8007

OBJECTIVE

Position in payroll or other related business operations

MILITARY WORK EXPERIENCE

United States Navy, 1996–2002

Rating: Disbursing Clerk First Class (E-6)

Duties included the following:
- Maintained personnel financial records, including payroll
- Processed travel allowances and reimbursements
- Prepared correspondence and reports
- Processed vouchers for receipt and expenditure of funds
- Applied Navy regulations in computation of pay
- Prepared payroll checks
- Trained and supervised less experienced personnel
- Coordinated office work flow

TRAINING/EDUCATION

Successfully completed courses in the following:
- Keyboarding
- Office procedures
- Automatic data processing
- Payroll accounting
- Office administration
- Internal auditing
- Principles of supervision

REFERENCES AVAILABLE ON REQUEST

TIM RASTA
1208 Laster Lane
Dallas, Texas 67533
(503) 555-3546 home
(503) 555-8956 cellular

University of Texas, School of Law
Candidate for combined Juris Doctor and Master in Business Administration degrees.

HONORS:
- Selected for inclusion in the 23rd edition of *Who's Who Among American Law Students.*
- Member of the Editorial Board, Business Manager, and a Recent Developments Editor: *Bankruptcy Developments Journal.*

ACTIVITIES:
- Member, Association for Business Professionalism
- Member, JD/MBA Society
- Member, Student Bar Association
- Member, Legal Association of Law Students
- Head Judge, Intercollegiate Business Games Organization

Texas A&M, School of Business
Bachelor of Science in Business Administration 1992
Majors: Finance and Economics; GPA 3.72/4.0

EXPERIENCE:
Summer Associate, 1992
Texas Southern Bank
- Assisted several branch banks in preparing for an important audit by the United States Banking Service.
- Wrote Texas Southern's annual proxy statement and Form IO-K in compliance with federal securities laws.
- Wrote the bank's new employee stock option plan.
- Assisted outside counsel in meeting Internal Revenue Code requirements for qualifying the bank's amended retirement plan.

Trader
1992 - 1995
Goldman Brothers
- Answered client inquiries about financial implications of investment operations.
- Advised clients of their rights and alternatives in mergers or tender offers.
- Supervised stock transfer for the brokerage clients of over 20 affiliated banks.
- Rule 144 stock and stock for estates, trusts, corporations, and partnerships.

References available upon request.

WAYNE SUSSMAN

24 Toad Fond Road   Utica, New York 45009   (897) 555-5894   sussman@xxx.net

EDUCATION:

University of New York - Utica
Candidate for J.D., 2002
Class rank: 24/106

University of Utica, 1998
B.A. Economics
GPA: 3.7/4.0

HONORS & ACTIVITIES:

Law School:
- Dean's Advisory Committee
- Managing Editor, *Utica Law Journal*
- Dean's List
- Three-quarter tuition merit scholarship

Undergraduate:
- University Task Force on Greek Housing
- Student Alumni Association
- Campus Judicial Board
- Honors College
- William Randolph Hearst Foundation Scholarship Recipient
- Gamma Beta Phi Honor Society
- Alpha Lambda Delta Honor Society

EXPERIENCE:

Marpan, Kraven & Stagey, 2001
Summer Associate
- Worked exclusively in the real estate practice area.
- Drafted briefs and legal memoranda.

Randall & Connors, 2000
Summer Associate
- Worked in the trust and real estate practice areas.
- Conducted legal research and drafted a variety of briefs and legal memoranda.

Kent, Jameson & Thorn, 1999
Summer Associate
- Worked in the litigation, corporate, and real estate practice areas.
- Prepared legal memoranda and loan agreement modifications.
- Reviewed proposed contract provisions between lenders and clients.

MARIA CARVELLE
167 East Flamingo Road • Las Vegas, Nevada 88675 • (702) 555-4433

EXPERIENCE

- Researched, reviewed, and verified rent invoices for office leases
- Monitored lease renewals, terminations, and option dates
- Compiled data for Administrative Space Requisitions
- Arranged and managed commercial real estate closings
- Organized and administered title closings
- Summarized leases and revised rent rolls of commercial properties for financial analysis package
- Formed corporate entities and drafted certificates of incorporation
- Updated records, prepared by-laws, and drafted special resolutions
- Managed ten midsize strip centers that included maintenance, tenant relations, and rent collection
- Developed an advertising campaign to lease vacant space in strip centers, resulting in all available space being rented
- Assisted in producing the 1999 International Shopping Convention

EMPLOYMENT HISTORY

- Real Estate Administrator 2/98 - 4/99, Sprint International Inc., New York, NY
- Legal Administrative Assistant 9/97 - 2/98, Marchall, Tulley, and Jones, New York, NY
- Legal Assistant 9/93 - 8/97, Kiwi Management, Inc., Bogota, NJ
- Assistant Director of Property Management 11/88 - 9/93, The Hill Group, New York, NY
- Legal Assistant 2/86 - 11/88, Hal T. Rose, P.C., New York, NY

EDUCATION

N.Y.U. Real Estate Institute 1987 - 1993
Courses in real estate sales, transactions, syndication, and tax laws
Brooklyn College, City University of New York -- B.A. History, 1983

LICENSES/SKILLS

Broker's license, Notary Public
Microsoft Word, Acces, Excel, and PowerPoint

References available on request

WOODROW ARTHUR TONEY

76 N. Washington Blvd.
Houston, TX 72009
714/555-4890

OBJECTIVE:

A management trainee position in the manufacturing industry.

WORK EXPERIENCE:

R&G Sugar, Inc., Houston, TX

Salesman, 1995 - 1999
Sold refined sugar products to retail businesses. Named top salesman of 1996. Maintained good customer relations by identifying customer needs. Trained new sales representatives and advised them on effective selling techniques.

Popson Camera Co., Milwaukee, WI

Salesman, 1990 - 1995
Sold cameras to retail outfits in the south suburban Milwaukee area. Increased territory sales by 85 percent in five years. Demonstrated and planned specific uses for products in various offices. Maintained constant contact with accounts.

EDUCATION:

Popson Sales Training Course, Milwaukee, WI

Summer 1990

Cobert Technical High School, West Allis, WI

Graduated 1989

Football Team, Cocaptain

REFERENCES:

Available upon request.

NOAH RICHTMAN

3440 South Aldrich Avenue • Minneapolis, MN 55405 • (612) 555-7986

EDUCATION

University of Minnesota Law School, Minneapolis, MN
J.D., May 1998, cum laude

University of Wisconsin - Madison, WI
B.A., May 1992, with distinction

HONORS

Maynard Pirsig Moot Court Best Brief Finalist
Maynard Pirsig Moot Court Invitational Oral Argument Tournament Participant

PROFESSIONAL AFFILIATIONS

Minnesota State and Federal Bars
Western District of Wisconsin Federal Bar

LEGAL WORK EXPERIENCE

Commercial Associate Attorney (November 2000 - present)
Haas, Helfman, and Tate, Minneapolis, MN

- Negotiate and draft purchase agreements and related documents for clients in asset and stock purchases.
- Negotiate and draft workout agreements, credit agreements, and commercial leases.
- Advise corporate clients and draft documents in the areas of corporate formation, governance, finance, securities, franchising, licensing, and trademark law.

Commercial Associate Attorney (September 1998 - November 2000)
Kato & Associates, Minneapolis, MN

- Negotiated and drafted purchase agreements and related documents in asset and stock purchases.
- Negotiated and drafted commercial leases and finance and security agreements.
- Advised corporate and start-up clients and drafted documents in the areas of corporate formation, governance, finance, securities, franchising, licensing, and trademark law.
- Filed and administered Chapter 11 bankruptcies, and drafted pleadings and argued motions in same.
- Negotiated and drafted plans of reorganization and all creditor settlement agreements.
- Drafted all pleadings, conducted motion practice and depositions, and negotiated and drafted settlement agreements in commercial, trademark, and bankruptcy matters; drafted and argued appellate briefs.

Law Clerk (June 1997 - July 1998)
Harolds, Wickman and Kane, Minneapolis, MN
Drafted research memos, pleadings, and all litigation documents for tort law practice.

Legal Research Assistant (October 1996 - April 1998)
Institute for Health Services Research, School of Public Health, Minneapolis, MN
Researched all changes in Medicaid laws and rules. Trained other research assistants in research methods.

Law Clerk (May 1996 - September 1996)
Misfeldt, Stark, Richie & Wickstrom, Eau Claire, WI
Drafted research memos and all litigation documents for broad commercial litigation practice.

REFERENCES

Available upon request.

Laura C. Rudolph

68 East 29th Avenue, #18C
Philadelphia, PA 19104
(215) 555-7504
lcrudolph@xxx.net

Education

Wharton School of Business, Philadelphia, PA
M.B.A., Finance, May 2001
Investment Club, Real Estate Club, Admissions Interviewer

University of Pennsylvania, Philadelphia, PA
B.A., Economics, May 1987
Phi Beta Kappa, Dean's list, golf team

Experience

Office of Kobe Sato, H.O.R., Tokyo, Japan
Legislative Assistant, Summer 2001

Provided research and translation services to a member of the Liberal Democratic Party.

Cushman and Wakefield, Philadelphia, PA
Sales Intern, Summer 2000

Cold-called potential clients. Prepared sales presentations for brokers. Responsible for the Philadelphia metropolitan area.

Leisure Developments, Honolulu, HI
Assistant Project Manager, 1995–1998

Managed construction, finance, and design of three hotels. Prepared financial analyses and budgets. Handled design and construction problems.

Personal

Proficient in Japanese.
Volunteer tutor for inner-city youths.
Drummer and singer.

Dorothy Samuels

#3 Rose Drive
Tettley, TN 22334
(608) 555-9833 home phone
(608) 555-9876 cellular phone

Summary:

Highly competent researcher and expert in tax and other financial compliance areas. Energetic and enthusiastic.

- Experienced at working with a diverse group of clients and judges.
- Able to relate effectively and efficiently to colleagues and senior-level managers.
- Detail-oriented and reliable.

Experience:

Tennessee Mogul, 1987 to Present

1997 to Present:

Senior Staff Attorney

- Responsible for the efficient legal representation of over 350 cases.
- Assisted in the conversion of the legal administration system process from a manual approach to a computerized system.
- Increased levels of customer satisfaction based on annual client surveys of the legal process.
- Organized and implemented an annual symposium on legal issues facing the industry. Attracted over 123 attorneys representing industry groups, corporations, and law firms. Received positive feedback on the event from senior management as an effective tool for increasing awareness of the company among a variety of constituents.

1987 to 1997

Staff Attorney

- Provided legal support to the Vice President of Legal Affairs for the corporation.
- Coordinated support staff and conducted research on all tax, compliance, and regulatory issues.
- Handled daily court appearances and routine legal matters.
- Served as the company facilitator for industry round tables.

Education:

University of Mechlenberg
J.D., Cum Laude, 1987
Assistant Editor, *Mechlenberg Law Review*

University of Tennessee
B.A. Philosophy, 1984

References provided upon request.

Westin Cartwright III
125 Lovel Drive
Oakton, CT 06457
754-555-0987
cartwrig@xxx.com

Education

Yale University

School of Law, Candidate for Juris Doctor degree, June 2002
Honors: Moot Court Semifinalist
Activities: Moot Court Participant, Volunteer for Student Legal Services, member International Law Society
Internship: Department of Health and Human Services

- Responsibilities include researching topics on health, exclusion, and rescission of adjustment status.
- Authored memoranda regarding programs involving developmental needs and immediate relative status.
- Prepared briefs submitted to the board of appeals.
- Attended court held before the Subcommittee on Aging.

University of Chicago

Bachelor of Arts degree in History and Political Science, 1998
Honors: Selected for law internship, Dean's List
Activities: Student Pre-Law Committee, Political Science and History Academies

California International University

Intensive summer Greek language program
Activities included seminars in Cyprus and other travel

Legal Employment

Research Assistant, **Yale University School of Law, fall semester 2001**

- Researched and wrote weekly quizzes for Professor Jane Jacobs's Law and Society course.
- Extensive use of law library, LEXIS, and Westlaw systems.
- Enhanced research and writing skills.

page one of two

Paralegal, **Mark Canton, Counselor at Law**
- Followed trade legislation, antidumping, and countervailing cases.
- Gained insight into the workings of international trade, government agencies, and congressional offices.
- Assisted with preparation of briefs submitted to federal agencies.
- Researched areas of barter, countertrade, and Generalized System of Preferences.

Law Clerk, **Karen Summers, Esq.**
- Assisted with research regarding tax sales and personal injuries.
- Prepared memoranda, attended client interviews, and assisted legal team in gathering information.
- Gained exposure to small private practice.

References available upon request.

ERIC COLLIER

8354 South Dixie Drive
North Miami Beach, Florida 33160
E-mail: ecollier@xxx.com
(305) 555-7658

OBJECTIVE

A position as tax attorney in a firm located in North Miami

EDUCATION

Yale Law School, Ph.D. Law 1957
Yale University, B.S. History 1954

SIGNIFICANT ACHIEVEMENTS

Worked with Mario Cuomo to establish the United Nations fund
for Latin American Children.

Developed and chaired the Matthew McAustin Foundation for the Arts.

Represented Nancy Carnegie in her opposition to development of Newberland Wand
in Georgia. A 1983 legal decision preserved the area under the National Park Service.

Legal advisor to the New York Mets, 1970 - 1989

Negotiated the acquisition of two textbook concerns: Rinehart and Company and John
C. Winston, 1959

Became a partner in the Wall Street firm of Wilson, Carter and Mills in 1958. Continued with this firm until 1990.

VOLUNTEER EXPERIENCE

International Executive Service Corps, Stamford, Connecticut

Served as consultant to developing international businesses in Iran, South Korea,
Columbia, and Peru.

REFERENCES ARE AVAILABLE UPON REQUEST.

Alex Santiago

2378 Mill Way
Milwaukee, WI 53704
(262) 555-6433

Barton Brewing Companies

2000 - Present
Staff Attorney

- Organized annual negotiation agreements for labor contracts that totaled $125 million annually and resulted in $5 million annual savings against budget.
- Coordinated centralized material distribution to 10 breweries.
- Restructured $10 million in corporate lease agreements for high-speed packaging equipment.
- Supervised two lawyers and recruited four additional interns from local area law schools.
- Managed a variety of corporate programs totaling $60 million annually.
- Negotiated Sparrow Snacks loan requirement, annual copacker contracts, and premiums.
- Personally achieved annual company savings of $200,000.

Cleanease Corporation

1989 - 2000
Chief Counsel

- Responsible for all legal activities, including regulatory compliance and contracts.

Johnston & Steel

1983 - 1989
Staff Attorney

- Served clients in the real estate and petroleum industries.

Military:

Corporal. United States Army Signal Corps, 1976 - 1980

Education:

University of Wisconsin, Madison
J.D., 1983

University of Wisconsin, Whitewater
B.A., Political Science, 1970

References available upon request.

ARTHUR PAUL EVERETT
72 Lighthouse Lane
Coral Gables, FL
(305) 555-4132

EDUCATION

University of South Florida, Tampa, FL
Bachelor of Science in Biology
Graduate May 2001

Summer Study: University of South Florida Marine Lab, Tampa, FL
Biological Oceanography, Summer 2000

EXPERIENCE

Financial Intern - Bank of Miami, Miami, FL, Summer 2001

Solved individual account problems for clients. Processed transfer of new stock for over one thousand client accounts after bank acquisition of Marine Banks. Standardized management reports for customer service department.

Environmental Law Intern - Mitchell & Keller Law Firm, Summer 1999

Assisted in the preparation of pretrial files for clients in the environmental section.

Counselor - Oceanlife Camp, Summer 1998

Instructed campers in scuba diving, snorkeling, lifesaving, and marine wildlife. Responsible for all campers between the ages of 13 and 18. Organized and coordinated group activities.

SKILLS AND ACTIVITIES

Marine Explorers Club
University of South Florida Diving and Swim Club
Proficient in library research, writing, and editing
Experienced with Microsoft Word, Microsoft Excel, website design

RAMON PARK

16 Port St.
Providence, RI 00727
401/555-9020

CAREER OBJECTIVE:

Credit Manager.

SKILLS & ACCOMPLISHMENTS:

- Conducted studies of clients' financial statements and past credit records.
- Established credit and collection systems.
- Worked with the sales force to develop credit policies.
- Oversaw all credit requests.
- Supervised and reduced delinquent accounts.
- Interviewed applicants for credit and gathered the necessary information for granting credit.
- Simplified credit processing system.
- Maintained good customer relations.
- Reduced turnover in personnel.

EMPLOYMENT HISTORY:

1997 - present	Haring & Andrews, Inc., Providence, RI
	Credit Manager
1993 - 1997	National Credit, Inc., Boston, MA
	Assistant Collections Manager
1991 - 1993	Marshall Field's, Chicago, IL
	Credit Assistant

EDUCATION:

1991	University of Colorado, Boulder, CO
	B.A. in Accounting
	Summa Cum Laude, Dean's List
1995	Providence College, Providence, RI
	Financial Analysis Seminar
2001	Providence College, Providence, RI
	Financial Management Training

MARIAH T. MORIARTY

3407 Archview Lane
St. Louis, MO 63137
E-mail: moriarty@xxx.org
(314) 555-9879 home

QUALIFICATIONS SUMMARY:

Excellent litigator with a record of winning a high percentage of trial cases. Areas of practice include:

- Criminal law
- Contract law
- Wrongful death
- Risk management
- Labor and industry claims
- Civil trial law
- Medical negligence and malpractice
- Employment claims
- Workers' compensation

EDUCATION/CERTIFICATIONS:

1985 Washington University Law School, St. Louis, MO
Juris Doctorate

1982 Mills College, Oakland, CA
Bachelor of Science in Political Science

CONTINUING EDUCATION:

Postgraduate course work in civil and criminal proceedings, contract law, trial law, jury selection, and litigation

Certification:
Member, Missouri State Bar

Professional Associations/Honors:
American Trial Lawyers Association
Missouri State Trial Lawyers Association
Missouri Bar Association

page one of two

PROFESSIONAL EXPERIENCE:

1995 to Present
Hane, Slueter & Jensen, P.S., St. Louis, MO
Trial Attorney

- Tried criminal cases involving murder, rape, theft, and embezzlement.
- Gained civil trial experience in contract disputes, EEO, labor and industry, and workers' compensation.
- Provided defense work for clients with medical negligence and malpractice litigation.
- Prepared appellate briefs.
- Appeared in District and Superior Court of Appeals.
- Won over 70 percent of trial cases.
- Settled more than 400 cases out of court.

1992 to 1995
Able and Able, P.S., St. Louis, MO
Trial Attorney

- Provided defense work for clients charged with murder, assault, rape, burglary, and fraud.
- Litigated civil trials involving insurance claims, risk management claims, and labor and industry claims.
- Maintained files on over 350 cases at a time.
- Personally represented over 10,000 clients.
- Settled a high percentage of cases out of court.

1987 to 1995
St. Mary's Medical Center, St. Louis, MO
Consulting Attorney (concurrent position)

- Advised administrators of 2,200-staff hospital on legal issues.
- Served as primary legal advisor to CEO and board of directors.
- Chaired and served on risk management committee.
- Implemented new risk management policies and protocols.
- Saved hundreds of thousands of dollars in potential litigation costs by settling cases out of court.
- Handled all federal tort claims.
- Represented hospital at trial.
- Was honored at banquet for employees who "Go the Extra Mile."

References are available and will be furnished upon request.

LARRY MCGRATH

12 Half Moon Drive
Portland, OR 34221
(607) 555-6677
E-mail: mcgrath7@xxx.com

EXPERIENCE:

1998 - Present
Legal Services of Portland
Attorney

- Interview, counsel, and correspond with clients, primarily in consumer areas, including truth in lending, fraud, and buyer transactions.
- Conduct extensive research.
- Represent mental patients in civil and administrative disputes.

1997 - 1998
Compton Legal Services
Attorney

- Drafted motions and pleadings.
- Researched memos for supervising attorney.
- Represented several clients at informal hearings.
- Cases involved housing and bankruptcy.

1990 - 1994
United States Army
Ft. Hood, Texas
Training Resource Manager

- Provided training to the SAFF offices of the 23rd Signal Brigade, a unit of 2,200 personnel. Forecasted, allotted, and scheduled land and training resource requirements.
- Designed and organized an in-house records system.
- Wrote several sections of an army "how-to" manual.
- Awarded army commendation medal.

EDUCATION:

University of Portland, School of Law
J.D., 1997

Southwest Missouri State University
B.S., Accounting, 1988
Captain, ROTC

Latimer Schwartz

67 Cleveland Rd.
New York, NY 10221
(212) 555-7843

Experience

Corporate Counsel
1994 to Present
Insurance Systems of the United States

- Responsible for all corporate and regulatory legal work for start-up Internet subsidiary.
- Responsible for negotiating major computer software licenses and contracts with corporate customers.
- Hired by the firm as a result of legal and business advice rendered while at Queen & Knokic.
- Awarded sales incentive trip as result of assistance in closing new business in first six months on the job.

Attorney
1990 - 1994
Queen & Knokic

- Hired as walk-on at premier New York law firm.
- Designed innovative capital structure for $8.76 million private placement used to start new ventures.

Education

University of New York, School of Law
J.D., 1988

SUNY - Buffalo
B.A. English, 1982

References available upon request.

ANGELINA BROWNE

418 BRADLEY STREET
BAY CITY, MI 48706
517-555-5967
angiebrowne@xxx.com

OVERVIEW

Licensed RN and labor relations specialist with diverse experience in health education. Interested in challenging in-house position with nursing association or union.

WORK HISTORY

1996 - Present
Labor Relations Specialist

Self-employed labor relations specialist. Participate in contract negotiations as the collective bargaining representative for RNs. Successfully negotiated four labor agreements during the past year, all including an increase in hourly wages.

1992 - 1996
President
Michigan Nurses Association

Directed professional nursing organization with 5,500 members and an annual budget of $250,000. Recruited members, supervised publication of monthly newsletter, directed daily operation of office, and coordinated continuing education efforts and special events.

1988 - 1992
Educational Director
Lutheran General Hospital

Managed all educational programs. Developed orientation materials and in-service programming. Monitored staff certification and provided recertification programs in-house and off-site. Supervised production of in-house newsletter and patient education literature.

WORK HISTORY (CONT.)

1986 - 1988
Part-time Lecturer
Saginaw College BSN Program

Taught maternal and child care courses in accredited BSN program. Responsible for two sections and up to 40 students per semester. Received excellent student and peer reviews.

QUALIFICATIONS

MSN   Wayne State University   1986
BSN   Central Michigan University   1984
Michigan Nursing License   411-608542
National Labor Relations Board Certification
Member, American Nurses Association
Member and Past President, Michigan Nurses Association

REFERENCES

Susan Riley
President
Michigan Nurses Association
517-555-1629 Office
517-555-8990 Cellular

Karen LoBianco
Director of Nursing
Lutheran General Hospital
517-555-6100 Office

CAROL SCHMIDT

12 Overlook Drive
Denver, Colorado 88021
Pager: (303) 555-4467
cschmidt@xxx.com

OBJECTIVE

To seek a position as a travel consultant within a travel facility with opportunities for advancement.

PROFESSIONAL EXPERIENCE

Lufthansa German Airlines
Los Angeles, California
Reservation Sales, 1995 - 1999
Provided travel arrangement reservations for passengers. Computed international fares and taxes; secured hotel and car reservations; arranged sale of ticket with credit card, travel agency, or airline ticket office. Working knowledge of the Siemans and Amadeus computer program system. Training course successfully completed in Germany: Advanced Reservations, Psychology in Sales, and Quality in Daily Work.

South African Airways
San Francisco, California
Customer Service Reservation Sales, 1992 - 1995
Booked international reservations using the Safari computer program system, with passengers, tour operators, wholesale consolidators, and travel agents. Courses successfully completed: Effective Sales Techniques in Reservations, Johannesburg, South Africa. International Fare Calculation, New York City.

Premier Travel Agency
Denver, Colorado
Travel Agent, 1989 - 1992
Booked vacation and corporate travel reservations for clients on the phone and in person including hotel, car, cruise ship, and rail reservations.

EDUCATION

Atlantic Travel Agents School, Kansas City, Kansas
Certification, 1989
Comprehensive training in all phases of air, land, and sea reservation-booking transactions. Manual and computer fare calculation, ticket issue, agency accounting systems, and general office duties.

SUMMARY OF QUALIFICATIONS

- Ability to work well under pressure and to get the job done sucessfully.
- Well-traveled and knowledgeable of the mores and customs of various cultures.
- Able to work on a variety of projects simultaneously to successful completion of tasks.
- Proficient in five airline computer systems.

HONORS & AWARDS

- Top sales revenue agent at Lufthansa, Los Angeles, 2001
- Highest score in Fare Calculation course, New York City, 1994
- Travel Agent of the Year Award, Denver, 1991

REFERENCES

Furnished upon request

ROBERT LOUIS OSBORNE
47 Tyler Way
Phoenix, AZ 87932
(602) 555-3339

CAREER OBJECTIVE

To be an active member of a dedicated team, providing management, accounting, personnel administration and/or training services to a quality-oriented company or organization.

PROFESSIONAL EXPERIENCE

Contracted Business Administrative Services
Maintain office at residence, 1996 - present.

Provide full charge accounting services through to balance sheet. Offer financial consulting services for local organizations and individuals on a limited contract basis. Services include staff training, development of computer skills, preparation and filing of government and state tax returns and payroll documents.

Utilize 486-DX-66, CD-ROM technology with ACCPAC, QUATTRO PRO, MICROSOFT WORD, LOTUS 1-2-3, WORDSTAR (Advanced), MEDTEC (HEALTH TECH.), MICROSOFT PUBLISHER, MICROSOFT ACCESS, MICROSOFT POWERPOINT, POWER UP, INSTANT ARTIST, CALENDAR CREATOR

1993 - 1996
Phoenix General Hospital, Phoenix, Arizona
Medical Office Management Director

Responsibility and accountability for a staff of nine full-time and four part-time employees.

1986 - 1993
Lancet Consulting Service, Orlando, Florida
Manager

Provided financial and personnel management services to local businesses including clients in medical practices, home furnishings, automobile companies, and service organizations.

1964 - 1986
U.S. Government
Administrative Specialist

Conducted extensive administrative, management, and personnel services to commands with up to 2,500 personnel. Personally accountable and responsible for department budget up to $150,000.

EDUCATION

University of Delaware, Wilmington, Delaware
B.S. in Economics, Diploma 1963
Major: Economics, GPA 3.7
Minor: Accounting

SPECIALIZED TRAINING

Management by Objective (MBO), 1993
Trained in business plan development; subject addressed specific tasks, completion dates, personnel requirements, and cost factors. Goal setting for the work place, division or firm, all meeting overall objectives of management.

Equal Opportunity Employment, 1990
Workshop skills in dealing with personnel from varied backgrounds and ethnic groups. Trained for the evaluation of specific job requirements, to ensure all personnel are treated equally in the employment/promotion process.

Affirmative Action and Human Relations, 1989
Trained to ensure goals are equal for all within the work place environment.

COMMUNITY ACTIVITIES

- Editor and publisher of Tyler Way News, a monthly newsletter advising residents of local events and to unify the Neighborhood Watch Association.
- Homeowners Association, President, 1998
- Big Brothers Association, 1994 - present

REFERENCES

Furnished upon request.

Jane M. Michaels

12 Harvard Avenue, Apt. G
Reno, NV 72367
702-555-9956
J_Michaels@xxx.com

Objective
An assistant accounting position with opportunities for advancement.

Education
Brighton College, Blairsville, NV 1986 - 1990
Major: Business

Work Experience
Sam's Club department store, Blairsville, NV
Accounting Assistant: 1995 - 1999
Duties: Maintained accounts payable and receivable records. Executed a modified version of the existing accounts payable filing system that increased efficiency by 15 percent. Developed a charge card system for employee purchases that eliminated a business transaction by deducting the payment from the employee's paycheck.

Bell's Landscaping Service, Tartan, NV
Accounting Clerk: 1991 - 1995
Duties: Maintained accounts payable and receivable files. Responsible for the monthly payroll ledger and twice-weekly bank deposits.

Summary of Qualifications
- Excellent interpersonal and communication skills.
- Proficient in handling a variety of tasks concurrently.
- Easily adapt to new procedures and concepts.

Computer Skills
Excel, Lotus 1-2-3, Windows, Solomon General Ledger

References
Furnished upon request.

ANN MORI
32 Kapalua Way
Honolulu, HI 96822
(808) 555-4316
E-mail address: annmori@xxx.com

SUMMARY

An experienced professional with strong analytical and administrative skills. Proven performer across organizational lines.

PROFESSIONAL EXPERIENCE

Pacific Bank - Honolulu, HI, 1996–present.

Commercial Loan Officer, 2000–present.
- Responsible for developing new commercial business loans and servicing existing customers.
- Wrote credit reports and recommended appropriate action.
- Supervised lobby staff, loan clerks, and account representatives.

Assistant Personnel Manager, 1996–2000.
- Responsible for staffing and policy guidelines.
- Coordinated policy changes.
- Directed payroll and benefits functions.
- Assisted in the integration of employee benefits, payroll, and related functions.

EDUCATION AND TRAINING

Courses at Hilo Community College and Hawaii Pacific College
- Analysis of Financial Statements
- Business Communication
- Business Accounting
- Real Estate Principles
- Computer Science

Professional Courses
- Credit Analysis I and II
- Commercial Loan Documentation
- Website Design and Management

CARL JONES

123 Wilson Ave. • Chicago, IL 60698 • 312-555-7654

NATIONAL LAUNDRIES CORPORATION
1997 TO PRESENT
ASSISTANT TAX MANAGER

Supervisory responsibility for preparation and review of consolidated federal, state, local, pension, and partnership returns for over 150 companies.

Coordinated federal and state partnership and pension tax audits, fielding questions from agents or auditors and responding in a timely manner.

LAXTER COMMUNICATIONS
1990 TO 1997
SENIOR TAX ANALYST

Responsible for preparation of federal, state, and local returns on consolidated and separate return basis for over 200 companies.

Researched tax questions on acquisitions, reorganizations, mergers, liquidations, and dispositions.

TWENTIETH CENTURY MOVING CORPORATION
1985 TO 1990
TAX ANALYST

Conducted tax compliance and research projects for consolidated groups of companies.

Coordinated federal tax audits, sourcing units and responding to IRS audit information requests.

EDUCATION:

University of Illinois, College of Law
J.D. 1985

Depaul University, School of Business
B.S., Accounting 1982

PROFESSIONAL AFFILIATIONS:

Member of the Illinois State Bar and various federal courts
American Bar Association
Illinois State Bar Association
Illinois County Lawyers Association
National Association of Accountants

Arlene Kingston
45 Rivermont Way
Dallas, TX 77230
204/555-8294

Background Summary:

Over 20 years of experience as a corporate attorney with a number of leading financial organizations. Managed a wide variety of legal matters involving real estate financing and development, litigation and dispute management, contracts, government regulation, and insurance. Responsible for promoting the company to prospective customers. Received a number of recognitions for outstanding service.

Accomplishments:

- Implemented procedures to control outside billing, saving $150,000 annually.
- Awarded performance incentive award for writing a unique mortgage purchase commitment contract.
- Helped create a new system for marketing financial services to families with young children. Received performance award for these efforts.
- Developed and implemented legal guidelines for the approval for purchase of mortgages secured by leasehold estates and property subject to recreation leases resulting in keeping this market open.
- Supervised the defense of a $1.5 million securities fraud case to an agreed settlement.
- Managed the legal aspects of three fraud investigations and supervised resulting litigation against two Texas lenders, saving $500,000.
- Supervised major multistate litigation against corporate defendants for recovery of more than $5 million in losses over a two-year period.

Jackson Manufacturing

Staff Legal Advisor
1992 - Present

Education:

University of Texas, School of Law, J.D., 1982
University of Maine, B.A. Law and Society, 1979

BARNEY SCHINEBLUME
23 Ross Way
Dayton, OH 67554
(703) 555-9834
schine@xxx.net

Chief
Office of the Judge Advocate
1986 - Present

- Coordinated with local U.S. attorney's office on claims resulting in litigation. Drafted litigation reports detailing facts, law, recommendations, and required pleadings.

- Advised for the installation of medical and dental staff on preventive law issues relating to malpractice and premises liability.

- Pursued claims against liable third parties for damage and/or injury to Army property or personnel.

- Served concurrently as installation magistrate deciding on propriety of search, seizure, or confinement of soldiers and searches of property on the installation.

Trial Defense Counsel
U.S. Army Trial Defense
1990 - 1996

- Represented military defendants at over 75 felony and misdemeanor trials before juries or military judge. Achieved 14 acquittals.

- Negotiated numerous pretrial agreements favorable to clients.

- Obtained pretrial dismissal of charges in over 55 cases.

- Represented dozens of soldiers before separation tribunals and advised hundreds of clients facing nonjudicial punishment action.

- Selected from defense counsel Army-wide for six-month deployment to Korea for duty with multinational peacekeeping force.

Education

Yale University, School of Law
J.D. Cum Laude, 1990

Boston University
B.A. History, 1987

ABDUL ST. NORTUNG

189 Hinson St.
Pittsburgh, PA 15241
(412) 555-6464

EDUCATION:

Clarkston College, School of Law
J.D., cum laude, 1990

Cleveland University
B.A. History, 1997
ROTC Commander
Order of the Lambs

CHIEF, OFFICE OF THE CHIEF ADVOCATE
1996 - PRESENT

- Assisted the installation magistrate in deciding on propriety of specific legal actions against soldiers. Coordinated legal efforts with civilian agencies.
- Pursued claims against individuals for misuse or illegal use of property or personnel.
- Coordinated with local attorney generals on legal claims by individuals. Drafted reports outlining legal alternatives and recommendations.

DEFENSE COUNSEL
1990 - 1996

- Selected from a candidate group of 150 officers to participate in an 18-month deployment to Russia for duty with multinational legal team.
- Represented 123 U.S. servicemen and women before legal tribunals and consulted with more than 500 clients facing reprimands or other legal actions.
- Represented military defendants at hundreds of felony and misdemeanor trials before juries or military judge.

References available upon request.

Resumes for Newcomers and Recent Graduates

JASMINE PARKER
4223 Kilauea Avenue
P.O. Box 2214
Honolulu, Hawaii 96819
Phone: 818-555-2294

OBJECTIVE

To obtain a position in fisheries and wildlife management administration that will utilize my skills in scientific research, analysis, and communication.

EDUCATION

Honolulu Community College, Honolulu.
Enrolled in summer open enrollment programs, 1997 and 1998.
Earned 3.6 G.P.A. in science courses.

Kaimuki High School, Honolulu.
Graduate 1998. Science G.P.A.: 4.0. Cumulative G.P.A.: 3.56

SCIENCE BACKGROUND

Designed and conducted research project on underwater testing procedures
Assisted with research project designed to decrease mercury toxicity
Completed two years of general biology, including one college-level course
Completed two semesters of marine biology, including one college-level course
Completed one college-level course in scientific research methods
Completed one college-level course in fisheries science

COMMUNICATIONS BACKGROUND

Wrote report on fisheries management problems in Hawaii, presented at Science '97.
Completed four years of writing, including college-level course in technical writing.
Member, Kaimuki High School Forensics Club; presented several prepared speeches.
Winner, Honolulu Toastmasters Honorable Mention for presentation
on science careers for women.

REFERENCES AVAILABLE

Stephanie Brown

Present Address:	Permanent Address:
P.O. Box 5041	7893 Virginian Lane
Baton Rouge, LA 70802	Ashland, KY 41101
(504) 555-2398	(606) 555-1365

Education:

Grantham College of Engineering - 9/98 to present
Expected to graduate in 6/02 with Bachelor's degree in Computer Engineering.

Experience:

Summer Intern   6/01 - 9/01
Tandem Computers, Slidell, LA
- Worked with Mechanical Design Group
- Managed the receiving and shipping of prototype parts
- Assembled and evaluated prototype parts and systems
- Redesigned problem parts
- Edited and prepared graphic design for departmental handbook

Part-Time Intern   4/00 - 9/00
Pillar Corporation, Ashland, KY
- Learned the inside workings of a small design consulting firm
- Researched current products to focus design of new concepts
- Designed ideas for new dinnerware sets

Summer Intern   6/99 - 9/99
Praxis Design Inc., Ashland, KY
- Used visual editors to alter program resources
- Edited program code
- Designed program icons and screens

Current Activities:

Member, Kappa Kappa Gamma Sorority

Hobbies:

Skiing, biking, camping, hiking, running, and playing the violin

References:

Available upon request

Maria Black

1419 Cedar Drive
Dayton, OH 45226
(513) 555-8754

Qualifications:	Bachelor of Science in Pharmacy, 1999
School of Pharmacy:	Dayton University
Special Award:	Merrell Dow Dayton School of Pharmacy's Annual Award for Excellence, 1999

Previous Experience:

	Hooks Pharmacy Dayton, OH	Summer Student 10 weeks, 1999
	Royal Hospital Dayton, OH	Summer Student 8 weeks, 1998
	Ohio Drug Dayton, OH	Saturday Staff 9/94 - 1/99

Present Position:	Pharmacy Graduate Intern Program Dayton Community Hospital Dayton, OH
Interests:	My main interest is in clinical pharmacy.
	During my intern year, I have attended Dayton University evening classes on clinical pharmacy and an Ohio State University course in ambulance first aid.
References:	Available on request.

CHRISTIANNA M. NELSON

900 Bear Valley Drive   Escanaba, MI 49829   (906) 555-2380

IMMEDIATE OBJECTIVE

To obtain a position as a physical therapist aide enabling me to work with physically disabled individuals while I attend college. I would prefer employment with a company that would be able to place me in a permanent physical therapist position once I have graduated from college.

LONG-TERM OBJECTIVE

To become a physical therapist.

EDUCATION

Escanaba High School in Escanaba, MI - 1999
GPA 3.9/4.0

My educational plans are to attend Calvin College in Grand Rapids, MI. I plan to major in education of the physically handicapped.

ACADEMIC ACTIVITIES

I was a member of the high school Interact Club (a community service organization) for four years. I was president of the club my senior year.

EMPLOYMENT HISTORY

Summers 1998, 1999   BAY DE NOC CAMP, Madison, WI

Camp Counselor for developmentally disabled teenagers and adults.

Academic years 1997, 1998, 1999
ESCANABA HIGH SCHOOL, Escanaba, MI

Volunteer Aide to Special Education teacher.

REFERENCES AVAILABLE UPON REQUEST.

RUTH M. DAVID

572 FIRST STREET
BROOKLYN, NY 11215
(212) 555-6328
ruthie@xxx.edu

Education

Princeton University, Princeton, NJ

Degree expected: M.B.A., June 2000
Class Rank: Top 25 Percent
Honors: Associate Editor, Business Journal

University of Wisconsin, Madison, WI

B.A. in Political Science, May 1998
Honors: Dean's List
Marching Band Drill Instructor, Section Leader
Residence Hall Council President

Business Experience

International Business Machines, White Plains, NY

Intern/Sales, 6/99 - 9/99
Assisted in PC Sales Division. Worked to promote distribution to retail outlets. Helped to coordinate product demonstration program used throughout the country.

Other Experience

Citizen Action Group, New York, NY

Field Manager, 6/98 - 9/98
Promoted citizen awareness of state legislative process and issues of toxic waste, utility control, and consumer legislation. Demonstrated effective fund-raising and communication methods to the canvas employees. Developed and sustained employee motivation and productivity.

University of Wisconsin, Madison, WI

Resident Assistant, Office of Residential Life, 8/96 - 5/98
Administered all aspects of student affairs in university residence halls, including program planning, discipline, and individual group counseling. Directed achievement of student goals through guidance of the residence hall council. Developed and implemented university policies.

University of Wisconsin, Madison, WI

Staff Training Lecturer, 8/97 - 11/98
Conducted workshops for residence hall staff on counseling and effective communication.

References available on request.

David T. Sanchez
10001 W. Edina Ave.
Edina, MN 53989
612/555-5453

STRENGTHS:

- Excellent communication and people skills

- Strong photographic and processing skills

- Academic and hands-on training in commercial art

- Computer literate, with working knowledge of QuarkXPress and PageMaker

EDUCATION:

University of Minnesota, St. Paul, MN
B.A. in Commercial Art, expected May 2000

WORK EXPERIENCE:

Minneapolis Magazine, Minneapolis, MN
Commercial Artist, Summers 1997 - present

University of Minnesota, St. Paul, MN
Designer, University Publications, 1999

University of Minnesota, St. Paul, MN
Photographer, Student Gazette, 1998 - 1999

WORKSHOPS:

Website Design Seminar, University of Minnesota, 1999
Illustration Workshop, Art Institute of Chicago, 1998
Midwest Design Seminar, Northern Illinois University, 1997

REFERENCES AVAILABLE

Toby Waterson

200 South Third Avenue
Arcadia, California 91006
213-555-9226

Objective	A position with the technical department of a manufacturing company.
Experience	Technical Design
	• Designed and built solar-powered car (one-person).
	• Designed multi-media computer-directed light and sound presentation.
	• Developed model for automated, solar-powered home.
	• Completed two years of design and technology program.
	Engine Mechanics
	• Built motor for solar-powered car.
	• Assisted with engine rebuilding on two Volkswagens.
	• Assisted in engine repair on riding and other lawn mowers.
Work History	Grounds Crew/Maintenance, June 1997-present
	Riverview Apartments
	Arcadia, California
	• Duties: landscape maintenance, some plumbing, carpentry, general repair.
	Library Assistant, 1996-1997
	Foothills Junior High School
	Arcadia California
	• Duties: audio-visual equipment repair, office work, reshelving, data entry.
Education	Arcadia Senior High School, Class of 1998
	Major: Design and Technology
References	Available on request

Norman L. Potter
4322 Clares Street
Butler, PA 16003
(412) 555-6897

OBJECTIVE

To obtain a part-time position with an architectural firm that will enable me to gain experience in the field of architecture. The position should provide the possibility for advancement with the completion of my scholastic studies.

EDUCATION

Butler High School, Butler, PA, 1999
Graduated in the top 20 percent of the class
GPA: 3.2/4.0
Next year, I will attend Butler County Community College where I plan to major in drafting.

WORK EXPERIENCE

Food Service Worker   June 1999 to August 1999

McDonald's Restaurant, Butler, PA
Responsible for taking and preparing food orders, operating the cash register, preparing food, cleaning lobby and food area, and stocking supplies.

General Worker   Prior to June 1999

Miscellaneous Jobs
Performed baby-sitting and gardening tasks.

OTHER EXPERIENCE

Completion of Drafting 1 and 2 courses in high school
Proficient in computer-assisted design

References available upon request.

Burke Anderson

260 E. North Avenue
Baltimore, Maryland 21202
301/555-4458

Objective

A career in technology design and development that will utilize my skills in technology innovation and traditional and computer-aided drafting.

Education

Baltimore City High School, Baltimore, Maryland
Major area of study: science and technology
G.P.A. in major: 6.0 (scale of six); cumulative G.P.A.: 4.85

Accomplishments

Tied for Best of Show in regional competition, Technology Challenge '00, held at Massachusetts Institute of Technology, for the design and construction of a hovercraft.

Qualified for competition in Technology Challenge '99 with the design and construction of a solar-powered remote-controlled sailboat.

Completed the following course work, maintaining a 6.0 grade point average:

Drafting 1-4	Metal Technology
Electricity/Electronics	Wood Technology
Computer-Aided Drafting	Design and Technology 1-2
Career Mechanics	

Participated in Cooperative Work Experience projects in drafting and career mechanics.

Work Experience

Drafting Intern, Cardell Associates, Baltimore, Maryland, Summer 2000. Duties: Checked blueprints of CAD-drafted plans for parts and equipment manufactured by Cardell. Drafted initial drawings of existing parts that required changes to fit new machinery.

Mechanics Intern, East Baltimore Auto, Baltimore, Maryland, Summer 1999. Duties: Worked as assistant mechanic for import cars. Learned diagnostics procedures and equipment operation.

Activities

Techies, BCHS technology club
Young Sailors of Baltimore
Radio Club

References and portfolio of drafting projects available on request.

JANIS DARIEN

345 W. 3rd St. #42
Boston, MA 02210
Telephone: 617/555-3291
E-mail: janis@xxx.com
Website: www.xxx.com

JOB OBJECTIVE: To obtain a position as a Marketing Management Trainee.

EDUCATION:

Boston University, Boston, MA
    B.A. degree in Economics, 1999
    Dean's List four quarters
    3.45 GPA in major field
    3.21 GPA overall
    Homecoming Planning Committee

Pursuing graduate studies toward a Master's degree in Marketing at Boston University, Evening Division.

Central High School, Evansville, IN
    Graduated 1995
    Top 10 percent of class
    Business manager and coordinator of student newspaper
    Vice President of senior class
    Student Council
    Pep Club

WORK EXPERIENCE:

Lewis Advertising Agency, Boston, MA
Marketing Assistant, Summer 1998

    Assisted Marketing Manager in promotion, product development, and demographic analysis.

Paterno Marketing, Boston, MA
Telephone Interviewer, Summer 1996 - 1997

White Hen Pantry, Evansville, IN
Cashier, Summer 1995

SPECIAL SKILLS: Fluent in French. Familiar with PC hardware and software.

REFERENCES: Available on request.

DEBBIE R. NEWELL
2986 Middle Avenue
Rapid City, SC 57701
(605) 555-1307

OBJECTIVE:

Full-time employment as a secretary while
I attend night classes.

PARTICULARS:

- Typing - 75 wpm
- WordPerfect, Word
- Lotus, PowerPoint, Quicken

EDUCATION:

Rapid City High School, Rapid City, SC
Degree: 2000 General Studies

I will attend Western Dakota Vocational Technical
Institute for 2 years beginning in the fall of 2000.

WORK EXPERIENCE:

Kmart
Clerk - women's clothing department
Cash Register Operator
9/98 to present
Full-time during the summer
Part-time during the academic year

EXTRACURRICULAR:

- Member of the high school choir and jazz choir.
- Participated in Girl Scout activities for 3 years.
- Served as a camp counselor for Brownies
  and Pixies at the City Park.

REFERENCES:

Available upon your request.

KARIN BOWLES
2050 CROWN BOULEVARD, APT. C • DENVER, CO 80204 • (303) 555-2280

GOAL

A career in business administration.

EXPERIENCE

LEADERSHIP

As a member of the finance committee for the Associated Students of Kennedy High School, I was responsible for supervising the planning and execution of school-wide fund-raising projects such as candy sales and the student carnival. I also set meeting dates and presided over meetings, reported to student council, and worked with the student government advisor on budgeting.

COMMUNICATION

Worked on the publicity committees for several student events and election campaigns. Wrote text for fliers and signs and assisted with speech writing. Each campaign ended in election victory for my candidate.

Completed two semesters of business communications courses. Also completed three years of honors-level English composition and three years of French. Have working knowledge of spoken and written French.

ORGANIZATION

Served as assistant librarian, a position usually held by a paid professional, during the semester prior to graduation. Directed a research methods seminar for freshman students. Answered questions about library reference materials and on-line research sources. Supervised student workers in shelving books. Updated computerized database.

EDUCATION

Kennedy High School
2855 S. Lamar Street
Denver, CO 80227
9/96-6/00
Final G.P.A.: 3.75

Pertinent Courses: Business Law, Accounting, Computer Applications in Business, Office Procedures, Word Processing, Business, Management

REFERENCES

Available on request

Timothy J. Davison

1286 West Shore Road, Apt. 5
Warwick, Rhode Island 02889
Telephone: 402-555-2117

Objective

A position as chef's assistant at a restaurant featuring specialty or gourmet cuisine.

Education

The Culinary Institute
New York, NY
Video correspondence course, to be completed December 2000.

Taft Senior High School
Warwick, RI
Class standing: Junior

Special Skills

Worked with International Student Club to plan and prepare a meal for 250 parents and students. Involved with menu planning and food preparation for dishes from all over the world.

Catered a dinner party for six people as part of a donation of services to fund-raise for local Boys and Girls Club. Prepared and helped serve five-course dinner.

Completed one year of culinary video correspondence course that involved preparation of primarily French cuisine. Although not required by course, I have followed a procedure of preparing the lesson plan menu for a group of four to six people who provide a written evaluation of the meal and its presentation.

Completed two years of high school food preparation courses, including experience with food decoration.

Work Experience

Kitchen Prep Staff, June 1999-present
Warwick Towers Restaurant
Warwick, RI

References are available on request.

DAN LUI

17 Dinge Road
Terre Haute, IN 52211
317/555-1331 (Home)
317/555-2339 (Office)

OBJECTIVE:	A position in the field of Electrical Engineering with an emphasis on aviation electronic systems.
EDUCATION:	B.S. in Electrical Engineering, May 1999 Rose-Hulman Institute of Technology, Terre Haute, IN G.P.A. 3.75 Graduated with Honors
WORK EXPERIENCE:	*C & S Industrial Design Consultants, Richardson, TX* Summer Intern, 1998 Assisted in research and development department of aviation electronics firm. Input data, typed performance specifications reports, calibrated lasers, and maintained test equipment. *Rose-Hulman Institute of Technology, Terre Haute, IN* Assistant to the Director, Financial Aid, 1997 - 1998 Processed applications. Handled general office duties.
ACTIVITIES:	President of Student Chapter of Institute of Electrical and Electronics Engineers Peer Advisor, Engineering Department
REFERENCES:	Available upon request

JOHN UMIAK
P.O. Box 1648
Palmer, Alaska 99645
Message phone: 907-555-8406

OBJECTIVE   Career in fisheries and wildlife.

EDUCATION   Sustina Valley Junior-Senior High School
                 Graduation date: May 1998. G.P.A. 3.6.

                 Courses were primarily in biological sciences, with an
                 emphasis in special projects on salmonid fishes.

                 Matanuska-Sustina College

                 Enrolled in 1998 summer program, took courses in general
                 biology and marine biology.

EXPERIENCE   Matanuska Fisheries
                 June 1998-present

                 Work on fishing boat crew, fishing for salmon, halibut,
                 crab. Maintain fishing equipment, check fishing nets daily
                 for damage and repair them as needed.

                 Independent project
                 1997-1998

                 Coordinated research project on salmon runs in local
                 stream. Working with my high school biology teacher, I
                 designed research procedures, collected data, and discovered
                 a 20% decrease in salmon populations between 1991
                 and 1992 spring Chinook runs.

REFERENCES   Available on request.

AMANDA MARTIN

1076 North 27th
Phoenix, Arizona 85028
(602) 555-3874

GOAL:	A career in the computer industry.
EDUCATION:	Shadow Mountain High School, 1996-2000
	Cumulative G.P.A.: 3.75
	Relevant Courses:
	Computer Science
	Computer Applications
	Computer Programming (BASIC, PASCAL)
	Algebra
	Geometry
	Trigonometry
	Precalculus
ACHIEVEMENTS:	Worked on five-member team to develop new computer software for grading multiple-choice tests, recording grades, and providing bell curves and other averages that could be used for assigning letter grades.
	Customized programming software for use by students with visual impairments.
	Won annual district prize for best computer programming solution.
REFERENCES:	Available upon request.

NAME: Carla Grant

ADDRESS: 2976 Lucky Lane
                   Cleveland, TN 37320

TELEPHONE: (615) 555-1745

OBJECTIVE: Full-time position in a clothing store as a sales clerk.

EDUCATION: Knoxville High School, 2000
                   Knoxville, TN
                   GPA 3.0/4.0

                   My educational plans are to attend Cleveland State Community
                   College part-time. I will major in marketing and sales.

EXPERIENCE: JCPenney
                   May 2000 to present
                     Cash register operator

                   The Emporium
                   January 1998 to November 1999
                     Sales clerk

EXTRACURRICULAR:
                   • Junior Achievement, 1999, 2000
                   • Member of Zenith Group (a public speaking club), 2000
                   • Sophomore Magazine Sales - Class Coordinator, 1998

QUALIFICATIONS:
                   I am a committed, hardworking, and punctual employee who
                   interacts skillfully with customers.

REFERENCES: Kay Dietze, Junior Achievement Sponsor (615) 555-2778
                   Linda Nealis, JCPenney (615) 555-4410

MARYLOU BADEMACHER

1414 N. Montebello Drive
Berkeley, CA 98028
415/555-4930

EDUCATION: University of California at Berkeley

Bachelor of Science in Business

Expected June 2001

HONORS: Beta Gamma Upsilon Honorary Society

Dean's List

Manley Writing Award, 1999

ACTIVITIES: Treasurer, Gamma Gamma Gamma Sorority

Freshman Advisor

Homecoming Planning Committee

Alumni Welcoming Committee

WORK EXPERIENCE: AT&T, New York, NY
Marketing Intern, 2000

Assisted marketing staff in the areas of research, demographics, sales forecasts, identifying new customers, and Internet promotion.

University of California at Berkeley
Office Assistant, Journalism School, 1998 - 2000

Assisted with registrations, filing, and typing. Arranged application materials. Assembled course packs.

SPECIAL SKILLS: Fluent in German. Hands-on computer experience using Microsoft Office 2000.

REFERENCES: Available on request.

ELIZABETH ENGLE

2316 King Street
Richardson, TX 75080
972/555-2552

GOAL

Petroleum engineering position with small, independent oil exploration and production company.

EDUCATION

University of Texas at Dallas
B.S. in Petroleum Engineering, expected May 2000

COURSEWORK

Petroleum Engineering Design
Rocks and Fluids
Reservoir Modeling
Reservoir Engineering
Secondary Recovery
Drilling Design & Production

WORK EXPERIENCE

UNIVERSITY OF TEXAS AT DALLAS
Lab Assistant/Physics Dept., 1998 - 2000

Assisted professors in the Physics Department with lab experiments and general office work.

MEMBERSHIPS

Society of Petroleum Engineers
Engineering Club

SPECIAL SKILLS

Working knowledge of Lotus 1-2-3 and Wordstar

REFERENCES AVAILABLE

Michael Han

435 S. Monaco Parkway • Denver, Colorado 80204 • (303) 555-4481

Education

West High School
951 Elati Street, Denver, 1997-2001. Diploma. G.P.A.: 3.86.

Aachen Gymnasium
Bonn, West Germany, 1999-2000 (Exchange Student).

Skills & Achievements

- Trained in basic bookkeeping, invoicing, inventory, and payroll procedures.
- Speak fluent Chinese and German; working knowledge of French.
- Experienced with various computer software and hardware, including MS DOS, Macintosh, and CP/M operating platforms; WordPerfect, Microsoft Word, and MacWrite word processing; Lotus 1-2-3 and Works spreadsheet; and dBase and Filemaker Pro Database software, among others.
- Experienced with providing customer service in small retail sales outlet for computer equipment.
- Excellent writing and communications skills.
- Effective leadership skills; served as president of senior class, vice-president of junior class, student senator during first and second years.
- Selected by American Field Service (AFS) as exchange student to Aachen, West Germany.

Employment History

Summer Sales Intern
Computer Express
Denver, Winter 2000-2001.
Duties: Provided information and assistance to clients in small computer hardware and software dealership that handled both IBM and compatibles and Macintosh computers. Self-trained in a wide range of software in order to better match appropriate software and hardware systems to clients' needs.

REFERENCES AVAILABLE

Mary Jo Baptiste

2240 N.W. Nebraska Avenue
Washington, D.C. 20016
202-555-7465

Objective
To obtain a training position as a preschool guide in a Montessori preschool.

Experience
Parks & Recreation Day Camp Leader, Washington, D.C., Summer 1999 and 2000.
Planned programs for children 4-8 years old. Built rapport and communications with parents. Provided supervision of children on play structures during breaks. Taught teamwork skills through problem solving in groups of six children. Taught crafts, songs, and dances. Led storytelling for children aged 10-14.

Outdoor School Counselor and Instructor, D.C. School District, 1998-2000.
Counseled, supervised, and instructed sixth-grade students from various Washington elementary schools during one-week program each spring. Assumed responsibility for twelve girls. Served as live-in counselor three years, one year as instructor emphasizing environmental education.

Other part-time employment: Waitress, housekeeper, clerical assistant.

Educational Background
Coolidge High School, Washington, D.C.
Graduation Date: June 2001

Relevant Courses: Human Development, Childhood Education, Psychology, Sociology, Social Science, Speech and Communications.

Honors: Who's Who Among American High School Students, Future Teachers of America, Volunteer Student Activist of the Year (all-school nomination), District of Columbia Youth of the Month (President's Council on Youth), Quill and Scroll (journalism honor society).

Special Skills and Interests
Reporter on the high school newspaper staff for two years. Published an article in the City Paper, Washington, D.C., February 2001. Knowledge of Native American culture, including traditional songs, dances, and crafts.

References are available upon request.

Dale Crivello

275 Huntington Drive
Middlebury, VT 05753
(802) 555-4294

Objective: Part-time position as a chef or assistant chef providing the opportunity of advancement upon my graduation from college.

Education: Middlebury High School
- Expected graduation date: 2000
- GPA: 3.5/4.0
- Relevant course work:
      Mathematics through Geometry
      Home Economics 1 and 2
      Nutrition
      2 years of French
- I will attend New England Culinary Institute in Montpelier, VT, in the fall. I will major in food production, management, and services.

Work Experience:

2/99 - 8/99   **Denny's Restaurant**
                     I was the preparation cook.

6/98 - 8/98   **Swensen's Ice Cream Factory**
                     I dipped cones and decorated various ice-cream products.

Other Experience:

- Varsity football team, 4 years, MVP senior year
- Soccer league, 4 years
- Ski club, 4 years

References: Available on request.

SAMUEL JUN-LAN CHEN

2110 Cottage Grove Avenue • Chicago Heights, IL 60411 • 847-555-2645

OBJECTIVE	To obtain a laboratory research assistant position in a scientific lab.
EDUCATION	Bloom High School, Chicago Heights, Illinois Graduated with highest honors, 1998. Cumulative G.P.A.: 3.96

RELEVANT COURSES TAKEN:
- Biology (two years)
- General Chemistry (one year)
- Organic Chemistry (one year)
- Physics (one year)
- Botany (one semester)
- Math (algebra, trigonometry, calculus)

EXPERIENCE

Laboratory Assistant, Bloom High School,
Chemistry Section, 1997-1998
- Assisted teacher with laboratory preparation and set-up
- Answered student questions about laboratory experiments
- Graded lab worksheets and recorded grades for chemistry teacher
- Maintained chemical stockroom and kept track of supplies

Laboratory Assistant, Bloom High School,
Biology Section, 1996-1997
- Assisted with laboratory preparation and clean-up
- Worked with students on dissection projects (frog, fetal pig heart)
- Graded student lab worksheets
- Installed and tested new computer software for simulated dissection
- Directed students in use of computer software

ACTIVITIES
- Member, Future Scientists of America
- Secretary, Bloom High Science Club
- Coordinated visitation day for seven scientists from Chicago-area research institutions and manufacturing companies
- Served as general science assistant for science teachers

REFERENCES   Available on request.

STEWART SULLIVAN

OBJECTIVE

To secure a position on the production staff of a printing company where I can utilize my skills with graphic design and layout.

EXPERIENCE

Graphic Artist, Student Yearbook Staff, 1996-1998

Assumed responsibility for overall design concepts in 212-page hardbound yearbook.

Provided design assistance to editorial staff. Developed graphic elements for pages needing artwork.

Designed page layouts.

Mastered computer page-layout technology and desktop publishing software.

Prepared photographs for publication (cropped, sized).

Supervised staff of production assistants.

Production Assistant, *Borah Gazette*, 1995-1997

Prepared layout for student newspaper.

Cropped, sized, and positioned photographs.

Designed graphics to accent advertisement section.

EDUCATION

Borah Senior High School, Boise, Idaho
    Class of 1999. Grade point average in art: 4.0.
    Areas of study: journalism, photojournalism, graphic design, art (painting, drawing, watercolor, ceramics).

REFERENCES

Available on request.

1220 North Cole Road • Boise, Idaho 83709 • 208-555-2477

LAURA KIRSTEN HUMMEL

529 Paul Revere Drive
Longmeadow, MA 01160
(413) 555-3093

OBJECTIVE:	**A part-time job that will allow me to support myself while attending culinary school.**
EDUCATION:	**2000 Graduate of Longmeadow High School** **My scholastic GPA was 3.1/4.0.**
FUTURE PLANS:	**I will attend Bay Path College and study food preparation and other culinary skills. I then plan to attend a university and major in restaurant management.**
EXPERIENCE:	**The past three summers I have worked at *Charlie's Deli Cafe* in Longmeadow, MA. My duties included taking food orders, checking stock, preparing food, and operating the cash register.**
PERSONAL:	**I was a two-year member of Longmeadow High's German Club.** **I was a cheerleader at Longmeadow High for four years.** **I am hardworking and dedicated.**
TRANSPORTATION:	**I own a 1990 Mazda truck that can be used for transportation and work if necessary.**
REFERENCES:	**Jay Johnson, Teacher, Longmeadow High School, (413) 555-0711.** **Mary Hicks, Coach, Longmeadow High School, (413) 555-0711.**

MICHAEL SHEPPARD

1056 King Street Extension

Huntington, IN 46750

(219) 555-8465 home phone

(219) 555-3657 cellular phone

PROFESSIONAL EXPERIENCE

Seven years' experience in the United States Army (1996 - 2003), specializing as a parachute rigger

JOB DUTIES

- Packed both aircraft cargo and personnel parachutes
- Fabricated, assembled, and rigged airdrop equipment
- Loaded, positioned, and secured cargo for airdrop
- Inspected and inventoried airdrop equipment
- Provided technical guidance to less experienced personnel
- Tested ripcord and canopy release assemblies
- Conducted inspections of airdrop equipment

EDUCATION

Graduate, Quartermaster School, Ft. Lee, VA (396-hour course in advanced parachute rigging), 1997

Graduate, Jefferson High School, Huntington, IN, 1996

REFERENCES

Available on request

Parker Adams

226 N. Fifth Street, Apt. 42
Fairbury, Illinois 61739
Telephone: 815-555-1154

Position Desired:

Full-time summer employment that makes use of my background as a lab assistant and agricultural worker. My long-term career goal is to become a biomedical engineer.

Education and Training:

Prairie Central High School, Fairbury, Illinois.
Graduation anticipated: June 2001

My major area of emphasis has been science. During the past three years, I have completed all of the science courses offered at PCHS, including Biology, Chemistry, Anatomy and Physiology, Physics, Earth Science, Field Biology, Horticulture, and Advanced Chemistry. I have participated in extra-credit research projects in most of these courses. Science grade point average: 3.68.

Experience:

Organization: As a lab assistant in the science program, I have organized labs, maintained inventory of supplies, entered data into the computer, and assisted students with class assignments.

Equipment: I have operated microscopes, digital meters, and oscilloscopes. I also drive a tractor when working on my grandfather's seed farm.

Efficiency: During my junior year, I worked as a laborer on the family farm approximately 20 hours per week. I was concurrently working on a special honors science project which required several hours each week of after-school study. I was able to manage my time efficiently and maintain a 3.9 grade point average for the year.

Honors:

First Place Project Award, Science VII, Regional Skills Conference, 2000
Honorable Mention, Science VI, Regional Skills Conference, 1999

References are available upon request.

STANLEY TRUMBULL
3 S. Sioux Trail
Ottawa, Ontario, Canada K1P 5N2
613/555-1782

OBJECTIVE: A career in the field of anthropology

EDUCATION: UNIVERSITY OF OTTAWA, Ontario, Canada
                    B.A. in Anthropology, expected June 2000

HONORS: Dean's List, 1999
                    Phillips Anthropology Award, 1999

EMPLOYMENT
HISTORY: OTTAWA UNIVERSITY, Ontario, Canada
                    Department of Animal Behavior
                    Research Assistant, 9/99 - Present
                    Input data for animal behavior studies.
                    Maintain lab equipment.
                    Monitor animals and recorded data.

                    OTTAWA UNIVERSITY, Ontario, Canada
                    Admissions Office
                    Student Assistant, 9/98 - 4/99
                    Conducted campus tours.
                    Processed applications.
                    Assisted in student recruitment and general
                    public relations.

                    PARKER & PARKER, Detroit, MI
                    Office Assistant, 6/98 - 9/98
                    Handled data entry, processed orders, phones.

ACTIVITIES: Anthropology Club, 1998 - Present
                    Student Government Representative, Fall 1998

                    References Available

Allison Barnes

2880 West Braddock Road
Alexandria, Virginia 22302
Telephone: 703-555-1283

Career Objective

To obtain a position with a small theater company where my background in theater will allow me to make contributions in a variety of areas.

Experience

- Directed production of Arthur Miller's *Death of a Salesman*. Took play to state drama competition and received honorable mention.
- Played Lisl in Community Theatre production of *The Sound of Music*.
- Won the part from among 84 auditioners.
- Designed sets and costumes, and worked on costume and set building crews, for a production of Shakespeare's *Twelfth Night*.
- Sang the lead in *Oklahoma*.
- Played a walk-on part in *Our Town*. Served backstage as key grip.
- Assisted with design and production of lighting for *Faculty Follies*, an entirely student-directed production starring teachers, counselors, and administrators from throughout the high school.
- Operated video cameras during dress rehearsals for *Our Town* and *Twelfth Night*.
- Wrote reviews of local theater (non-school) productions for student newspaper. One review was published in the weekend edition of the *Alexandria Gazette*.

Education

Williams Senior High School, Alexandria, Virginia, Class of 1999

Courses: Drama, Advanced Drama, Play Writing, Special Projects: Theater, Shakespeare, Creative Writing, Advanced Composition, and Journalism

Work History

Waitress, New Morning Cafe, Alexandria
January 1996-present

References available on request.

JOHN NOWARK

217 Arthur Avenue
Omaha, NE 68103
(402) 555-5003

Career Goal: To secure a position as an assistant greenskeeper.

Education: **Dundee High School** Graduate, 2000
General Education
GPA 3.00/4.00 overall, 3.50/4.00 science
Science Classes:

	Horticulture	2 semesters
	Biology	2 semesters

Art Courses:

	Ceramics	1 semester
	Basic Art, Drawing	1 semester

Mathematics:

	Algebra	2 semesters
	Geometry	2 semesters

Experience: Summers 1998 to 2000
Sugar Hill Nursery
453 Eureka Lane, Omaha, NE 69337

Nursery Assistant - Prepared nursery beds for planting; watered, weeded, and sprayed trees, shrubs, and plants; and filled orders.

Summers 1996 to 2000
4-H Camp
1500 Eureka Lane, Omaha, NE 69337

Counselor - Responsible for 20 children each year for one week in the month of July.

References: Available upon request.

McHale Newport

2200 River Road, No. 126 • Annapolis, Maryland 21401

301/555-8461

Professional Goal

To obtain an entry-level position in the news department of a daily newspaper where I can utilize my journalistic skills and professionalism.

Education

Broadneck Senior High School
1265 Green Holly Drive, Annapolis, Maryland
Class of 1999

Writing Experience

Student Reporter, The BSHS Times, Broadneck High School, 1995-present

Wrote articles on student government, administrative decisions, school board meetings, student activities, sports events, and profiles of student leaders and teachers. Entered copy on computer word processing software. Served one semester as interim editor, determined story assignments for student reporters, worked with advisor on writing editorials, and edited news copy submitted by student reporters. Served as staff photographer on several occasions.

Freelance Writer, 1997 to present

Published two articles in the "Teen Beat" section of the Capitol (Annapolis daily newspaper). Published one personality profile of the high school principal in American Teen magazine. Submitted several query letters and manuscripts to a variety of magazines for publication.

Activities

Junior Press Club of Annapolis (a local high school division of the Maryland Press Club) The Lancer, Broadneck SHS student annual (helped with photography, layout, editing) Aperture (photography club)

References and portfolio of writing and photography are available on request.

Mary Alice Simpson

1280 Delaware Avenue, Apt 116
Buffalo, New York 24214
716-555-8482

Objective

I am seeking an internship with a business enterprise where my skills in writing and communication may contribute to the effectiveness of the organization.

Education

Holy Angels Academy, 24 Shoshane Street, Buffalo, New York 14214
Class of 2001
Cumulative Grade Point Average: 3.38

Course of Study

My high school curriculum has offered me a broad background in liberal studies and business in preparation for attending college. In addition to course work in business, management, and accounting, I participated in the college preparatory honors program, which offered intensive courses in U.S. and European History, English Composition, Research Methods, and Social Studies.

Achievements and Activities

Selected to serve as senior monitor for academic testing programs.

Served on student government committee for finance. Conducted several successful campaigns to raise funds for school programs.

Participated in the a capella choir, madrigal singers, and concert choir.

Assisted with parent night preparations and planning.

Member of the *Quill* staff, which published a school literary magazine.

Published three poems in *Quill*.

References are available on request

R o b i n   W e i s s

2250 Second Avenue
Akron, Ohio 44313
Telephone: 216-555-9941

JOB SOUGHT   Salesclerk with sporting goods or department store.

EDUCATION   Firestone High School, Akron, Ohio
                     Class of 2000

EXPERIENCE   **Salesclerk, Firestone Student Store, 9/00-present.**
                     Operated student store sales. Handled cash
                     exchanges and credit account charges. Balanced
                     daily receipts.

                     Referee, Summit County Soccer Clubs, 1998-2000.
                     Served as referee for elementary and junior high
                     school-level soccer games.

SPECIAL SKILLS   Trained in CPR and advanced lifesaving.

                     Knowledgeable about a wide variety of outdoor sports.

ACTIVITIES   Recreational Water Sports Club
                     Outdoor School Counselor
                     Explorers Club

REFERENCES   Available on request

LORETTA M. ALSTON

305 Doris Avenue
Baldwin City, KS 66006
(913) 555-0211

OBJECTIVE

To obtain a position in which my secretarial skills, ability to organize, and willingness to assume responsibility can be employed.

EDUCATION

Baker University; Baldwin City, KS, 2000
Major: English Literature

EXPERIENCE
Summers
1998 - 1999

REINHARDT & ASSOCIATES LAW CORPORATION
Baldwin City, KS
Personal Secretary for Michael J. Green
• Composed and prepared correspondence
• Handled accounts receivable
• Performed receptionist and general secretarial duties

Summer
1997

SPEEDO INC.
Baldwin City, KS
Secretary
• Performed data entry on PC
• Maintained mailing list database
• Purchased office supplies

Summers
1995 - 1996

EXECUTIVE SUNN CENTERS
Baldwin City, KS
Receptionist

ADDITIONAL
INFORMATION

I am familiar with these computer programs: Microsoft Windows 98, Microsoft Office 2000, and WordPerfect.
I can type 81 words per minute.

REFERENCES

Available upon request.

Jackson Garvey
1134 N.E. 14th
El Dorado, Kansas 67402
(316) 555-3086

Career Goal

My short-term objective is to obtain a position as a warehouseman. For the long-term, my goal is to complete college training in engineering and manufacturing.

Education

El Dorado High School, McCullom Road, El Dorado

> Courses studied: metal shop, computer applications, three years of wood-working, and three-dimensional design.

Work Experience

Warehouse Worker for Gates Tire Company, El Dorado, Kansas, June to August 2000
> Assisted with receiving shipments, stocking, and sending shipments. Drove forklift and operated loading dock.

Landscape Maintenance for private individuals. June to August 1999
> Planted and removed plants and provided lawn maintenance for a variety of personal clients.

Field Worker for Townsend Farms, Inc., June to August 1998
> Planting and harvesting for several crops for small family farm operation.

Skills

Able to operate the following: lathe, table saw, drill press, sander, bench grinder, arc welder, Hyster 2450 forklift.

Activities

Junior varsity and varsity baseball and soccer. Member of Greater El Dorado Soccer Club.

References

Available on request.

• JANINE HARTLEY •
168 N.E. Clarkston
Battle Creek, Michigan 49017
Telephone: 616-555-3420
E-Mail: JHart@xxx.com

• <u>JOB SOUGHT</u>   Position in retail sales for hardware or electronic products.

• <u>EDUCATION</u>   1994-1998
Battle Creek Central High School, Battle Creek, Michigan
Specialized coursework:
Marketing I
Spanish IV
Accounting II
Electronics
Woodworking Shop

• <u>WORK EXPERIENCE</u>   **11/96 - present**
Battle Creek Auto Parts
Duties: serving customers, maintaining warehouse supply, stocking and shelving parts, receiving shipments. (Left when store closed).

2/95 - 10/96
Wendy's Store #1023
Duties: fast food preparation, order processing, clean-up and operation of kitchen machinery.

• <u>ACTIVITIES</u>   Outdoor school counselor, one year of basketball.

• <u>REFERENCES</u>   Available on request.

JUAN AGUILAR

158 Halladay S.W. • Benton Harbor, Michigan 49028 • Telephone: 616-555-7379

Job Desired

Printer's apprentice in newspaper printing department

Education

1996-present
Benton Harbor High School; Expected graduation date: June 2000.

Pertinent courses: graphic arts, journalism, photography, computer science

Skills & Experience

Ability to operate the following: Graphic printing press, screen printer, camera, copy machine, Compugraphic 2824 typesetter, Macintosh computer (Quark Xpress, Page-Maker, Adobe Photoshop, Aldus Freehand).

Work Experience

Production chief for Harbor High Herald. 1998-present.
Duties include set-up and layout of boards for printing preparation. Successfully completed transfer from traditional typesetting and layout to electronic pre-press with ability to scan photographs into system, then crop and size electronically to fit layout of text and other graphics.

Printing assistant for Michigan Printing. Summer 1999.
Assisted with preparing camera-ready mechanicals for film, making photo negatives for printing plates, positioning plates on press, checking press runs, operating cutter and folder. Worked with stripping department on cutting masks and windows in film.

House painting for private residence, interior and exterior. Summers of 1997 and 1998.

References

Available on request.

CRISTINA GONZALES
98 Freedom Blvd.
Seattle, WA 98122
(206) 555-4691

**POSITION
DESIRED:** A salaried community service position
enabling me to work with and help others.

EDUCATION: Seattle High School, 2000
GPA 3.50/4.00, four-year member of honor society.

I plan to attend a four-year university to obtain a
degree in psychology.

**SCHOOL
ACTIVITIES:** Sophomore class president
A.S.B. member
Commissioner of Hospitality
Soccer team member
Softball team member

**OUTSIDE
INTERESTS:** Writing
Soccer
Softball
Reading
Swimming

SKILLS: Able to speak fluent Spanish.
Type 40 words per minute.

**WORK
EXPERIENCE:** **Wal-Mart**, Seattle, WA
Merchandise cashier
5-98 to 9-00

REFERENCES: Available upon request.

IRIS FAN

239 Three Lakes Drive
Sheboygan, WI 53084
(414) 555-1293

BUSINESS EXPERIENCE

Summer 2000—*Financial Analyst*, United Airlines, Chicago, IL

- Analyzed profitability and future revenue opportunities of frequent flyer program.
- Developed strategies that are anticipated to result in savings of $15 million.

1995 to 1999—*Account Executive*, Thompson Advertisers, New York, NY

- Formulated and implemented advertising programs for a major consumer products company.
- Managed a budget of $20 million and supervised a staff of four.
- Developed business-building concept for an established product line resulting in a 10 percent increase in market share.

Summer 1994—*Brand Assistant*, Procter & Gamble, Cincinnati, OH

- Conducted competitive analysis for new product introduction.
- Tested new product concept and evaluated launch plan.
- Analyzed brand performance and developed sales conference presentation.

EDUCATION

Sloan School of Management
M.B.A., Finance and Marketing
June 2001

University of Ohio
B.S., Finance
1995

GARY LUPAS

809 N. Washington Street
Bismarck, North Dakota 58501
Telephone: 555-3994

OBJECTIVE

Position in agribusiness utilizing my supervisory and organizational skills.

EDUCATION

Central Senior High School, 1000 East Century Avenue, Bismarck
Diploma awarded 2000

Courses completed: business series courses in agriculture, law, and marketing; special project course in which I devised and prepared a marketing and development plan for a new agricultural support services business.

RELEVANT EXPERIENCE

Hay Bailer/Field Boss, Klair & Klock Larson Farm. Summers 1997-1999
Worked each summer in berry fields, earning at the top 10 percent of all field hands (paid by ton bailed). In 1999, I was hired as a field boss and was responsible for supervising workers, paying fees, and checking for quality.

Swim Instructor/Life Guard. Bismarck Community Pool. 9/98-6/99
Supervised swim activities at indoor pool facility. Taught swimming lessons to 4th, 5th, and 6th grade children. Hold current life-saving certificate.

SKILLS & ACTIVITIES

Experienced with wide range of farm implements and machinery. Valid driver's license. Swim team member (first place in state competition).

REFERENCES

Available on request.

ELIZABETH M. LEIGH-WOOD

387 Sunny Hills Drive
Madison, WI 53711
(608) 555-1524

OBJECTIVE   *A position as a lifeguard. I am certified in Standard First Aid and CPR and have passed a lifeguard training course.*

EDUCATION
- Madison High School, 2000
  GPA 3.80/4.00
- General education/Honors classes
- Next year I will be attending Cardinal Stritch University in Milwaukee, WI, on a track scholarship.

SCHOOL ACTIVITIES
- Four-year Member of Associated Student Body Council
- Four-year Member of Wisconsin Scholarship Federation
- Four-year Member of Varsity Track Team
- Two-year Member of Varsity Swim Team

ACTIVITIES
- 1999 - 2000: Hospital Volunteer
- 1998 - 2000: American Cancer Society Volunteer Christmas Gift Wrapper

SKILLS
- Fluent in French
- Hardworking and outgoing

WORK EXPERIENCE
- Whalers' Car Wash, 5/99 - 10/99
- Lifeguard, Sunny Hills Neighborhood Club, 5/98 - 8/98
- Baby-sitting, weekends

REFERENCES Upon request.

STEPHANIE TIRRELL

889 Copley Road
Akron, Ohio 44308
Telephone: (216) 555-1941

OBJECTIVE

Because of my love for children and my interest in their development, I am seeking a position as a caregiver in a quality preschool or day care environment.

EDUCATION

Central Hower High School, Akron, Ohio
  Expected graduation date: 2001
  Specialized courses: Child Development, Early Childhood Education

Mt. Union College, Akron, Ohio
  Summer of 2000 open enrollment program.
  Courses: Child Development, Beginning Psychology

RELATED EXPERIENCE

Childcare: I have been providing competent childcare since 1995. I provide care consistently for four children in two different families.

Counseling:. In October 1998 and April 1999, 1 worked as a counselor at the Trout Creek Outdoor School, supervising sixth grade students and teaching basic plant identification and plant ecology. Also presented lessons on plants at several grade schools.

Volunteer: Since June 1998 I have offered tours at the Akron Park Zoo, educating children about zoo animals, natural habitat, and endangered species. During October 1999 I participated in the "Zoo Boo" Train. I dressed in costume and entertained train riders along the route.

REFERENCES

Available on request.

Brian Schlosser

243 Pleasant Avenue
Providence, Rhode Island 02903
401/555-2335

Objective

To obtain part-time employment as a stage hand for theatrical productions in a small theatrical company.

Education

Hope High School. Will graduate in June 2001. Current GPA: 3.3

Shea High School, Pawtucket, Rhode Island. Attended 1998-1999.

Relevant Experience

- Worked as stage manager for three school productions
- Operated lights and sound for musical production of "Oklahoma"
- Assisted with set design and building for three plays
- Experienced with all aspects of theatrical production
- Worked as stage hand for a production at Brown University
- Played the lead in "Brigadoon"
- Sang in the chorus in "Godspell"

Work History

Cashier and line cook for Taco Time, Providence. 4/97-present.

Paper distributor for the Pawtucket Evening News. 3/97-3/99.

Activities

Member of Thespian Society. Participated in various aspects of student theatrical productions at Hope High School.

Madrigal Singers and Concert Choir, Shea High School.

References

Available on request.

Sherria Gonzalez

235 Gramercy Avenue • Ogden, Utah 84404 • 801-555-1409

Objective

Obtain a summer internship with a local business so that I may utilize my clerical skills and learn more about personnel issues. My long-term goal is a career in personnel management.

Education

Lamond High School, Ogden   Class of 2000

Courses pertinent to job objective: business and economics, computer applications, typing, career education. GPA: 3.28. Currently serving as a counseling office assistant, where I answer telephones, type file, and schedule appointments.

Work Experience

Wimpy's Burgers, Phoenix Drive, Ogden   1997 to present
Responsibilities: serve customers, prepare food, operate cash register, handle money, close store.

Jazzercise, Burns, Ogden   1997 to present
Responsibilities: provide quality care for children of parents participating in Jazzercise exercise programs.

Skills

I am experienced with Macintosh and IBM computers, and I have good typing (70 wpm), filing, and telephone communications skills. I am also a quick learner and strive to be accurate in everything I do. Fluent Spanish speaker.

References

Available on request.

MICHAEL SUTHERLAND
2757 Dolphin Dr. • Arnold, MD 21012 • (301) 555-5390

Education   **UCLA School of Theater, Film, and TV,** Fall 1999
• Comprehensive Major: Directing and Theater Management

Arnold High School, June 1999
• Forensics Competitive Speech Team (4 years)
• Drama and Musical Productions (3 years)

Awards   • Bank of Maryland Fine Arts Award -
   2nd place Region Finals Scholarship, 1999
• Veterans of Foreign Wars Speech Award, 1998 and 1999
• Student of the Year - Arnold High School, 1998
• Boys' State Delegate, 1998
• 21st place in State Forensics for Thematic Interpretation
   (Pieces included: *Torch Song Trilogy, Into the Woods,*
   Brighton Beach Memoirs, Measure for Measure), 1998
• Rotary Speech Award, 1996 and 1997
• Walter Johnson Musical Comedy Award
   at Anne Arundel Community Stage, 1996

Performance Theater Experience

• Director, Collaborator, and Performer, *AIDS Teen Theater*, 1999
• "Billy Crocker" in *Anything Goes*, 1998
• "Vincentio" in *Taming of the Shrew*, 1998
• "Albert" in *Bye-Bye Birdie*, 1997
• "Frank Butler" in *Annie Get Your Gun*, 1996
• "Charlie" in *Charlie and the Chocolate Factory*, 1996
• "Ed" in *You Can't Take It with You*, 1996
• Writer and Performer, *AIDS Teen Theater*, 1995 and 1996

Technical and Managing Theater Experience

Anne Arundel Community Stage
• Production Assistant - *Fiddler on the Roof*, 1999
• Assistant Stage Manager - *Into the Woods*, 1997
• Assistant Stage Manager - *Camelot*, 1996
• Chorus and Stagehand - *Evita*, 1995
• Stagehand - *My Fair Lady*, 1995

Peace Child
• Assistant Stage Manager, Props Assistant, 1997
• Assistant Technical Director USA/USSR Production, 1996

References   Available upon request

John S. Kelsey

Current Address:
865 Olympic Drive, #10F
Los Angeles, CA 90089

Permanent Address:
4689 Beach Street
La Jolla, CA 92093

Cellular Phone: (310) 555-4579

EDUCATION:

University of Southern California
Los Angeles, CA
B.A., Economics/History anticipated Winter 2001

VARSITY ATHLETICS

Cross Country, 2001 Captain
Track and Field, Qualified for 2001 Pac 10
Conference Championships in 10,000 meters

EXPERIENCE:

Summer 2001: California Mortgage Insurance Company
Los Angeles, CA
Loan Administrator: Answered customer demands for information and other assistance. Processed loans and organized loan files. Served as liaison between home office and field office.

Summer 2000 and Fall 2001: Merrill Lynch
Los Angeles, CA
Analyst: Researched stocks and mutual funds. Performed hypothetical analyses on computer. Assisted brokers with their daily operations.

Summer 1999: The Highland Group
Los Angeles, CA
Intern: Screened and developed government proposals for management consulting client. Participated in the development of a strategic plan for The Highland Group.

RELEVANT SKILLS:

Network Technician: expertise in Microsoft Systems Management Server 2.0, NT 4.0, NT workstation and NT servers.
Fluent in American Sign Language.

Kendra Wallen

1137 N.E. 189th • Provo, UT 84606 • (801) 555-2740

• • •

• Objective

To obtain a position as a summer-school assistant teacher in an arts-related program.

• Education

Timpview High School, Class of 1999
Courses include: childhood education, Art (two years), advanced studio painting, and computer applications in art.

• Experience

Since June of 1994, I have worked as a child care provider to children of various ages, responsible for preparing food, feeding, diapering, and general care. Each summer I worked full-time and offered innovative children's art projects that were designed for specific ages and abilities.

In June of 1996 and 1997 I taught art during vacation Bible school program for elementary school children on the Navajo Reservation.

• Special Skills

Ability to operate a variety of computer software and hardware programs, specifically programs providing graphic arts and page layout capabilities. Hold valid CPR card.

References and portfolio of children's projects are available on request.

JONATHAN DEAN COURIER
8638 Walter Drive • Evanston, IL 60204 • (708) 555-4825

CAREER OBJECTIVE

An engineering position involving civil/structural analysis and design.

EDUCATION

Northwestern University
Master of Science degree in Civil Engineering
Credits completed toward degree: 21/33

Bachelor of Science degree in Civil Engineering, 1998
Major: Structural Engineering
Minors: Geotechnical Engineering and Construction

Engineer in Training, Illinois

WORK EXPERIENCE

Summer 1999   **Elijah's Architects & Engineers, Inc., Chicago, IL**
Engineering Intern
Worked in the structural division, dealing with the design of
criminal justice and educational facilities.

1998 - 1999   **School of Civil Engineering, Northwestern University**
Teaching Assistant
Helped with Architectural Engineering, Structural Steel Design,
and Senior Design classes; tasks included instruction and grading
of students.

Summer 1998   **Civil Engineering Buildings, Northwestern University**
Building Receiving Technician
Handled various assignments during the final construction phases
of new additions.

ACTIVITIES AND HONORS

Distinguished Student, Fall 1997
Student Member, American Society of Civil Engineers
Theta Chi Honorary: Marshal, Spring 1997, and President, Fall 1997

REFERENCES AVAILABLE UPON REQUEST

15 Church Street
Rutland, Virginia 05701
(802) 555-1939

Aki Mioshi

Job Sought

Department store security staff position, working evenings or weekends.

Education

Rutland High School
   67 Library Avenue, Rutland
   Class of 2001
   Current GPA: 3.7

State Police Explorer Program
   Attended: Summer 1997

Accomplishments

- Started RADD, Rutlanders Against Drugs and Drinking
- Elected Vice-President of Junior Class, Rutland High School
- Lettered in track and field, volleyball, and softball
- Listed on Honor Roll every semester since Freshman year
- Fluent in spoken Japanese

Work History

Waitress
The Pines Restaurant, Rutland
10/99 - present
Duties: greet and serve customers, communicate orders to kitchen staff, direct preparation of salads and deserts. Responsible for quality of service provided to customers. Earned bonus for excellence and courtesy, December 1999.

References are available on request.

JOSEPHINE ELIZABETH CROCKER
P.O. Box 317A
Trenton, NJ 08625
(609) 555-4832

OBJECTIVE: To gain an entry-level position in the environmental field with a firm offering advanced training.

EDUCATION AND TRAINING
• B.S. Environmental Health Science, Trenton State College, Trenton, NJ
1996 - 2000. 3.2 GPA in major, 2.8 GPA overall.

COURSES
Principles and Practices of Environmental Health
Accident and Disaster Control
Technical Seminar in Environmental Health
Public Health Administration
Microbiology
Epidemiology
Health Biostatistics
Public Health Education
Administrative Seminar
Practicum in Environmental Health
Organic Chemistry
Applied Microbiology

• Internship, Oneida County Health Department, Environmental Division.
May - August 1998.
• Internship, Vilas County Health Department, Environmental Division.
May - August 1997.

AWARDS AND HONORS
• Inter-sorority Council Outstanding Greek Woman, 1999.
• Who's Who Among Students in American Universities and Colleges, 1999.
• Order of Chi Omega Greek Honorary, 1998.
• Inter-sorority Council Most Outstanding Spring President, 1998.
• Inter-sorority Council Most Outstanding Chapter Member, 1997.
• Society of Distinguished Collegiate Americans, 1997.

ACTIVITIES
• Chi Omega, President.
• Inter-sorority Council, Chief Justice of Judicial Board.
• UCP Telethon, Phone Bank Coordinator.

REFERENCES: Will be provided on request.

V i n   Q u a m   P h o n g

1321 Longview Drive • Woodbridge, Virginia 22192
703-555-4958

O b j e c t i v e

Entry-level graphic arts or production position

E x p e r i e n c e

Garfield News
Production Chief, 1997-1998
Graphic Artist, 1996-1997
Created layout for student newspaper. Designed advertisements. Prepared paste-up boards for printing. Sized and cropped photographs for reproduction. Specified type sizes and styles for typesetters. Selected and designed art images to enhance visual design of newspaper. Worked with editorial staff to determine placement of news articles and photographs.

Freelance Artist
1996-present
Designed and prepared mechanicals for logo for my father's restaurant supply business. Drew portraits at State Fair. Worked for several student groups to design banners, signs, and logos for school-related activities.

E d u c a t i o n

Garfield High School. Anticipated date of graduation: 1999.

My elective coursework has focused on art and design, often involving extracurricular projects because I had completed the class assignments and sought additional opportunities to challenge my skills. Art and Design GPA: 4.0.

R e f e r e n c e s

Available on request

Darryl J. Richmond

356 N. Alameda
Santa Rosa, California 95406
(707) 555-3964

Objective

Summer carpenter crew position with home construction company.

Experience

Tiara Construction Company
Sebastapol, California
Summer 1996 and 1997
Supervisor: George Linde, (707) 555-5015

Worked with carpentry crew; famed and roofed houses; sheetrocked interiors; installed insulation in walls and rafters.

Growers Outlet, Stocker
Santa Rosa, California
September 1996 to present
Supervisor: Janet Brendler, (707) 555-2000

Work with grocery supervisor to stock shelves, receive and direct shipments of produce, maintain quality presentation in produce department.

Education

Santa Rosa High School
Santa Rosa, California
Expected graduation date: 2002

Pertinent courses: wood and metal shop, building construction, mechanical drawing, architecture.

References

Available on request.

BRIAN KANEKO

PERMANENT ADDRESS:

57 Rochester Way
Marietta, GA 30060
(404) 555-5445

PRESENT ADDRESS:

P.O. Box 4855
Stanford, CA 94309
(650) 555-1007

OBJECTIVE: An entry-level position in construction management using my technical, organizational, and interpersonal skills to assist with project control tasks.

EDUCATION:

Stanford University, Stanford, CA
Department of Civil Engineering
Master of Science Degree Candidate, May 2000
GPA: 3.2/4.0
Harvey Mudd College, Claremont, CA
School of Civil Environmental Engineering
Bachelor of Science Degree, May 1998
GPA: 3.9/4.0

COURSE WORK:

Civil Engineering Materials, Construction Project Organization and Control, Risk Analysis and Management, Construction Management, Heavy Construction and Earthwork, Legal Aspects of the Construction Process, Decision Analysis in Construction.

EXPERIENCE:

Research Assistant   June 1999 - Present
California Transportation Institution, Stockton, CA. Research several design and construction-related areas of bituminous materials as part of the Strategic Highway Research Program, sponsored by the Federal Highway Administration.
Staff Engineer   Summers 1997 - 1998
Thompson Engineers, Marietta, GA. Assisted in the preparation of a complete operation and maintenance manual for a leachate treatment plant and provided support in the compilation and review of all operation- and maintenance-related submittals from the general contractor and all subcontractors.

ACHIEVEMENTS:

Engineer-in-Training (EIT) Certification
Dean's List, College of Engineering, Stanford University
Dean's List, College of Engineering, Harvey Mudd College
Graduate Assistantship, Harvey Mudd College

SKILLS: Computer Languages: C/C++, Visual Basic
Computer Applications: Lotus 1-2-3, Excel, SAS, AutoCAD
Fluent in Japanese

REFERENCES: Available upon request.

Janice Anne Richland

10205 Catlin Avenue • Brookline, Massachusetts 02146 • (617) 555-0116

Objective

Retail sales position with music store

Skills

Good knowledge of both contemporary and classical music. Work well with people. Able to operate cash registers and most office equipment.

Work Experience

Cashier

Wendy's Hamburger Restaurant
Thayer Road, Brookline
Supervisor: Raejean Matthews (617) 555-9444
June 2000 to present
Duties: Greet customers, take orders, communicate orders to line cooks, operate cash register, handle cash, close and balance register receipts at shift's end.

Clerical Assistant

Brookline High School
Main Office
Supervisor: Annette Jameson (617) 555-7800
Summer 1999
Duties: Answered telephones, routed calls through six-line switchboard, typed letters, filed, greeted visitors, assisted teachers and students as needed.

Education

Brookline High School, Brookline, Massachusetts
Expected graduation date: June 2001
Pertinent Courses: Wind ensemble, orchestra, jazz band, choir, music theory, business.

Achievements

First place league solo 2001; four Outstanding Solo Jazz awards 2000-2001; MAME Youth Series O.S.O. 2000; All-State Band 2000; Honor Roll student.

References Available

LaToya Cook   **512 Lynn Road, Excelsior Springs, MO 64024**
                     816/555-3225 or E-Mail:
                     lacook@xxx.com

Goal: *A position involving writing and editing.*

Experience: **Editor,** *The Easterly Breeze* **(student newspaper)**
                     • Wrote series on racial integration programs in Missouri high
                       schools that won a state Junior Journalist award in 1996 from the
                       Missouri Association of Newspaper Journalists. One article from
                       the series was published in the MANJ newsletter.
                     • Write monthly column about student life and issues at East High
                       School.
                     • Interview teachers and students for personality profile articles for
                       publication in the student newspaper.
                     • Edit stories written by other students for spelling, grammar, and
                       AP news style.

                     Reporter, *Encounters* **(student yearbook)**
                     • Wrote articles on sports for publication in yearbook.
                     • Wrote captions for photographs.
                     • Assisted staff photographers with taking group photographs.

Education: East High School
                     101 Richmond Street
                     Excelsior Springs, MO 64024
                     9/95-6/98
                     Current GPA: 3.75
                     Pertinent Courses: Journalism, Photography, Honors
                     English (three years), Intro. to Law, American Government

References: *Available on request*

Lynn Simmons

2620 Harrison Avenue
Cheyenne, Wyoming 82001
Telephone: 307-555-2883

Job Sought:	Summer firefighting crew.
Education:	Central Senior High School 5500 Education Drive, Cheyenne, Wyoming 82001 Graduation date: June 2001
Training:	Hold valid CPR/Lifesaving Certificate Trained in firefighting and prevention by Cheyenne County Fire Department
Experience:	U.S. Forest Service Summer 2000 Spent two weeks with fire crew in Yellowstone National Park on fire damage control. Dug fire trenches, cleared brush, and opened clogged stream beds. U.S. Forest Service Summer 1999 Worked as camp cook's assistant on fire crew on site in Yellowstone National Park. Maintained food provisions for firefighters, assisted with first aid treatment of minor burns, served meals, worked at camp canteen.
References:	Available at your request.

BEVERLY M. LEBLANC
P.O. Box 8175
Creighton University
Omaha, NE 68178
(402) 555-3686

OBJECTIVE

Environmental engineer position involved with the design of wastewater/water treatment systems, groundwater quality, remediation, groundwater modeling, and hazardous wastes site investigation.

EDUCATION

Creighton University - Omaha, NE
Master of Science in Engineering - 2000
Major: Environmental Engineering
Overall GPA: 3.64/4.00   Major GPA: 3.84/4.00
University of Minnesota - Minneapolis, MN
Bachelor of Science Engineering - 1998
Major: Mechanical Engineering

TECHNICAL SKILLS

- **Major Advanced Courses:**
  Water Quality Analysis, Water Treatment Plant Design, Land Treatment of Wastes, Wastewater Treatment Plant Design, Industrial Wastes Treatment, and Sanitary Engineering.
- **Computer Languages:**   Visual Basic, COBOL MVS
- **Operating Systems:**   MS DOS/MVS; Windows 95, 98, and NT; OS/390
- **Hardware:**   AS 400, OS/390
- **Software:**   Word, SAS, Oracle Database

EXPERIENCE

Fall 1998 - present   **Graduate Research Assistant**
Environmental Engineering Department
Creighton University
Monitoring the operating and treatment efficiency of rotating biological contractors.

Summer 1997   **Programmer**
Environmental Engineering Department
University of Minnesota

Summer 1996   **Operator**
Minneapolis-St. Paul Wastewater Treatment Plant
Minneapolis, MN
Monitored routine operation of facility.

Summer 1995   **Laboratory Analyst**
Science Department
University of Minnesota

ACTIVITIES

- Member of Civil Engineering Honor Society
- Student member of ASCE, WPCF, NSPE

REFERENCES   Will be provided on request.

David Jakes

2390 N. Harvey, No. 1
Baltimore, Maryland 21225

(503) 555-6870

OBJECTIVE

Obtain an entry-level position in a business where my organizational and leadership skills can help make a positive difference.

EDUCATION

Douglas High School Expected graduation date: June 2001

RELATED COURSEWORK

Personal Finance, Career Education, Marketing, Computer Keyboarding. Current G.P.A.: 3.28

EXPERIENCE & SKILLS DEVELOPMENT

- Promote sales of martial arts merchandise and karate lessons.
- Assist with office operations, answer telephones, schedule lesson times, assist students and clients.
- Teach Kenpo Karate, Thai Boxing, and Freestyle Sparring to children and adults, in both private and group class situations.
- Distribute flyers to individuals on college campuses and in mall parking lots.
- Abilities include sales, telephone communications, computer keyboarding, organization, and customer service.

WORK HISTORY

Baltimore Kenpo Karate School, 1999-present

REFERENCES

Available on request

Estrella Angelino

2240 W. Yucca Street
Santa Fe, New Mexico 87538
(505) 555-5121

Objective

Finding a challenging part-time job in sales and customer service with opportunity for future advancement.

Relevant Coursework

Typing I & II	Office Systems and Procedures
English I, II, & III	Computer Applications I & II
Finance and Accounting I & II	Computer Accounting

Education

Capitol High School, Santa Fe
Diploma Awarded June 1998

Work Experience

Square Pan Pizza
Paseo del Sol, Santa Fe
(Hired April 1997; store closed December 1997)
My responsibilities included greeting customers, taking orders, handling cash, operating the register, answering telephones, cooking, cleaning, and assisting with closing.

The Bite of Santa Fe
(Volunteer in 1996-1998)
Served as volunteer for the city's annual weekend celebration of food and music in downtown Santa Fe. Duties included working with the public, taking orders, handling cash, and serving ice cream and soft drinks.

St. Vincent de Paul, Santa Fe
(Volunteer since 1997)
Worked as a volunteer helping serve food and distribute clothing and supplies to people in need.

REFERENCES AVAILABLE